The Photographer
FAR FROM THE TRUTH

1984 TOUR

BROOKLYN ACADEMY OF MUSIC

EINSTEIN ON THE BEACH

PINA BAUSCH
WUPPERTALER TANZTHEATER

SHOWBILL

BAM
BROOKLYN ACADEMY OF MUSIC

The Waverly Consort

THE CHRISTMAS STORY

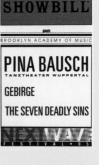

SHOWBILL

BAM
BROOKLYN ACADEMY OF MUSIC

PINA BAUSCH
TANZTHEATER WUPPERTAL

GEBIRGE

THE SEVEN DEADLY SINS

NEXT WAVE
FESTIVAL • 85

BROOKLYN ACADEMY OF MUSIC

BROOKLYN ACADEMY OF MUSIC

BAM
BROOKLYN ACADEMY OF MUSIC

THE HAMBURG BALLET   PROGRAM III, IV, V

BAMBILL
BROOKLYN ACADEMY OF MUSIC

SPOLETO
COMES TO
BAM

BAMBILL
BROOKLYN ACADEMY OF MUSIC

THE
GERSHWIN
CELEBRATION

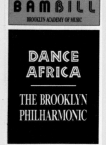

BAMBILL
BROOKLYN ACADEMY OF MUSIC

DANCE
AFRICA

THE BROOKLYN
PHILHARMONIC

BROOKLYN ACADEMY OF MUSIC PRESENTS THE 11TH ANNUAL

DANCEAFRICA

The Second Decade

Brooklyn Academy of Music presents

The Cherry Orchard

THE FIRST
NEW YORK
INTERNATIONAL
FESTIVAL
OF THE ARTS
JUNE 11–JULY 11
1988

THE CELEBRATION OF THE CENTURY!

BROOKLYN

SALUTES

ISRAEL

ארבעים

40th

Anniversary

1989 NEXT WAVE FESTIVAL
GALA BENEFIT
CELEBRATING THE 10TH ANNIVERSARY
OF
NEW MUSIC AMERICA

NEW

BROOKLYN ACADEMY OF MUSIC
NOVEMBER 8, 1989

BROOKLYN HURRICANE
RELIEF CONCERT

MONDAY, OCTOBER 23, 1989

BROOKLYN ACADEMY OF MUSIC

Welsh National
OPERA

Wolfgang Amadeus Mozart
La Finta Giardiniera

Brooklyn Academy of Music

Falstaff

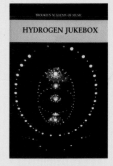

Brooklyn Academy of Music

The Wizard of Oz
The Jungle Book

PERFORMING
ARTS
PROGRAM
FOR
YOUNG
PEOPLE
FAMILY FUN SERIES

BROOKLYN ACADEMY OF MUSIC

HYDROGEN JUKEBOX

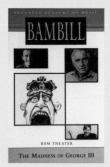

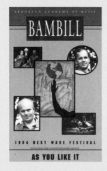

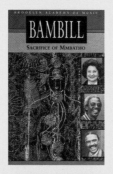

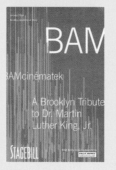
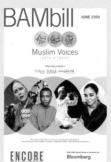

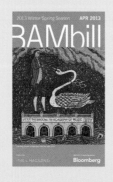
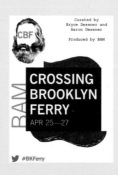

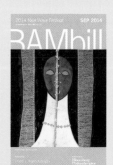

BAM

...AND THEN IT HIT ME

BAM

...AND THEN IT HIT ME

A MEMOIR
KAREN BROOKS HOPKINS

Heather —
Keep focused!
work hard —
Art Forever
All Best
KBH

powerHouse Books Brooklyn, NY

Dedicated with profound love to Matt Hopkins and Ron Feiner.

TABLE OF CONTENTS

Opposite:
Known around BAM as "signy," these iconic letters rotate at the intersection of Flatbush and Lafayette Avenues, and are a Brooklyn landmark, 2014.

Previous spreads, from page two:
Audience during a performance in the Howard Gilman Opera House, 2013.

Scene from the Trisha Brown Dance Company piece *Set and Reset*, Next Wave Festival, 1983.

Ballet Folklórico Cutumba, DanceAfrica Festival, spring 2011.

Richard Fallon, Georges Corraface, and Jeffery Kissoon in *The Mahabharata*, Next Wave Festival, 1987.

Scene from the Malpaso Dance Company production *Dreaming of Lions*, spring 2017.

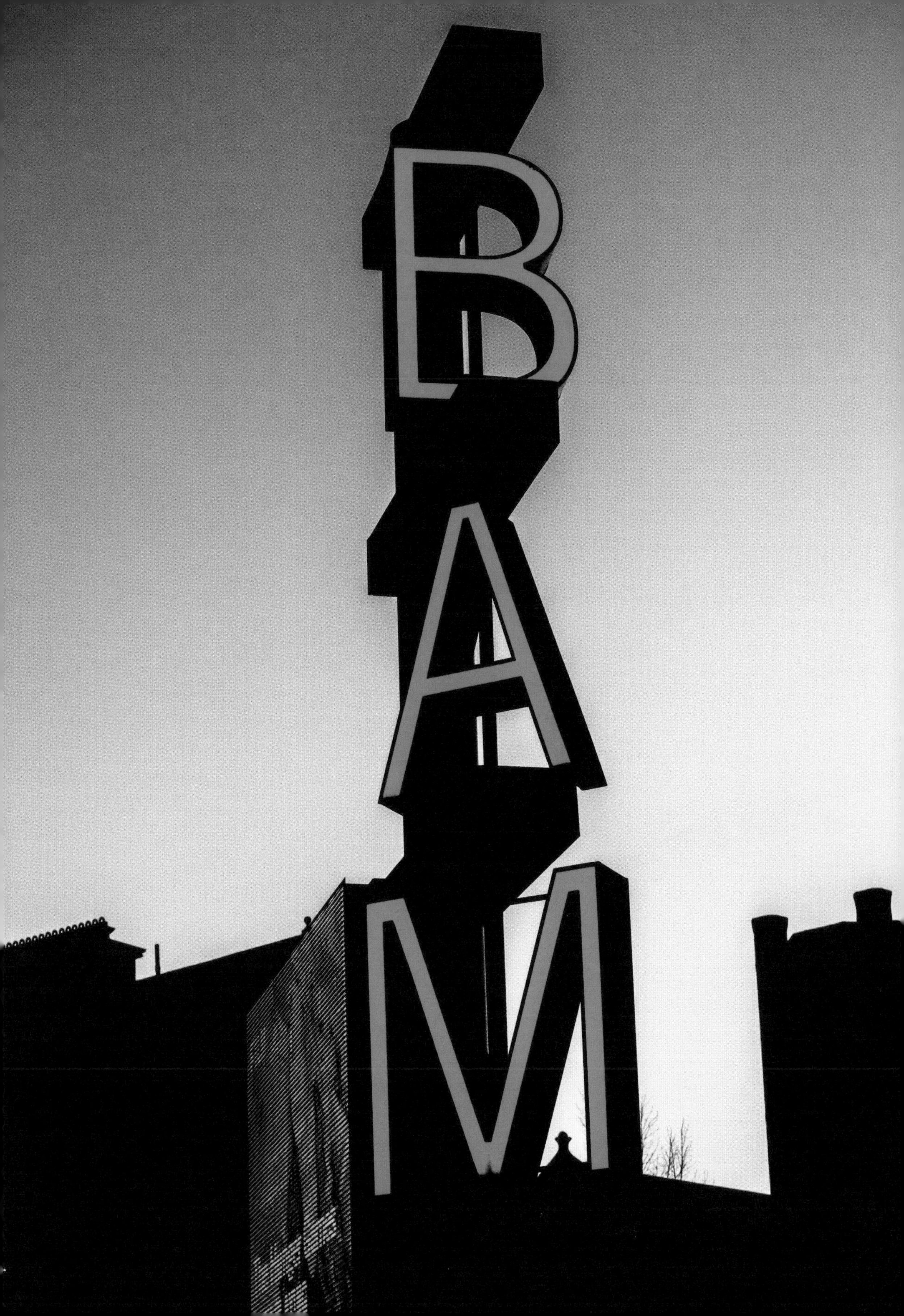
BAM

am a person of singular focus and resolve. For much of my adult life, I achieved what I call "the rule of one"—one son, one job, one boss, one home, one brother, one ex-husband, and one twenty-two-year relationship. My professional life has always been all consuming, and so I have tried, out of necessity, to keep everything else as simple and as streamlined as possible. For thirty-six years (1979 to 2015), almost without fail, I woke up every morning at six a.m. and rode five miles on my exercise bike. While riding, I read a handful of newspapers and magazines, scanning the stories for leads and inspiration, making notations in the margins, which came out wavy and incoherent because of the bike, necessitating translation by one of my loyal assistants.[1] After the workout, I showered, got dressed, and went to work, moving methodically through my day of countless meetings and events, which stretched late into the night, never losing sight of the overall objective: at BAM, we were on a path to glory, and no one was going to stop us. As I declared on many occasions during my thirty-six-year run to our board, staff, artists, audience, and anyone else who crossed my path, BAM was not a job, but a crusade![2]

Though sensitive to the challenges faced by others, I am not someone you will hear kvetching about hardships or tribulations. However, I am highly impatient about things that interfere with my plans, such as weather and traffic. My feeling is that our time on this planet is too short to be spent complaining, if we can actually solve the problem. We have to work with what we've been given. There is much to be done in this life, and we must not succumb to negativity or cynicism but rather press on with the task at hand. At least, that is what I try to do each day, even when things look bleak and when faced with unexpected setbacks and loss. I got back up on my bike each morning and kept riding.

My story can be summed up as follows. At the age of twenty-nine, I interviewed for a position in the development office of the Brooklyn Academy of Music (BAM). I was hired and worked there tirelessly for nearly four decades, eventually ascending to the presidency, helping to raise hundreds of millions of dollars for the institution while it became one of

1 This process of untangling the notes became widely known to my staff as "KBH as a second language." I believe BAM's human resources department gave my potential assistants a test to see if they could read my scrawl. This was a qualification for getting the job. Even in today's sophisticated technological world, I prefer pen and paper. I was finally forced to adopt email when it simply became impossible to communicate without it. I hired a "tech coach," locked my office, and swore that neither he nor I could leave until I was reasonably proficient. The BAM staff hovered outside my door that day waiting to see if I had the ability to actually be part of the twenty-first-century process of communicating. Luckily, I succeeded, but let's not go crazy. My skills on the "information superhighway" are essentially relegated to the parking lot.

2 While my opinions about using this term have evolved over the years, and it's not the right word for everyone, it was my mantra at the time. I adhered to the definition of a crusade as "an energetic and organized campaign concerning a social, political, or religious issue." For me, BAM was all three.

the most significant cultural centers in the world. BAM was and still remains the epicenter for contemporary experimental performance in all disciplines. During my time there, we revolutionized the nonprofit arts model, built an enduring institution, and elevated Brooklyn's place on the cultural map. All those years, I never looked back, not once. I had neither the time nor inclination to pause and ask: What does this mean? What can be gleaned from all that we have accomplished and what else must be done? A little reflection might have been a good thing, but at the time, it was not in my playbook.

In the years that have passed since I stepped down from my position as president of BAM, I have finally been given the gift of time to ponder and process the wild and amazing ride that characterized my thirty-six years there. This book will feature personal stories and raw reflections, tales of glamour and of grit, as I look back—with wonder, pride, and occasional regret—upon my career and reflect upon the near misses, the twists of fate, the total failures, the great triumphs, and the personal sacrifices I made along the way. In the following pages, including what I hope will be a series of "entertaining and illuminating" footnotes, I will recount some of the greatest moments in BAM's history, including unforgettable stories featuring artists and celebrities—such as Laurie Anderson, Ingmar Bergman, Peter Brook, Chuck Davis, Paul Simon, Rufus Wainwright, and Princess Diana—with whom I worked over the years. I also will explore the challenges I faced as a female executive, and will offer constructive approaches and advice for people at all stages of their careers, regardless of whether they work in the for-profit or nonprofit sectors. Though I will enumerate key strategies for institutional success, this is not a business textbook or a nonprofit manual—and neither is it a comprehensive history of BAM or its groundbreaking work. At its core, this is a very personal story about life, leadership, and fundraising at one of the most daring cultural institutions in the world, and a testament to the role the arts play in urban transformation and the survival and growth of cities, neighborhoods, communities, and individuals, and what it takes to build world-class institutions and authentic, diverse communities.

A *New York* magazine cover story! With Harvey, Joe, and Doug Allen (then VP of marketing), discussing plans for the Next Wave Festival, 1987.

Stereo-viewer card of
the original Brooklyn
Academy of Music
on Montague Street,
ca. 1861.

17

CHAPTER ONE:

I'm Your Gal

’m a person of strong preferences. Once I'm into something or someone, I become hooked, usually for life. That's how I've always been about the theater. I was born in Baltimore, Maryland, on September 24, 1951. My parents, Howard (a furniture salesman) and Paula (a housewife turned Jewish Community Center program director), supported my love of drama from the time I was eight years old and first got involved in acting and directing plays at summer camp. From this early age, I knew I would end up in New York City, my spiritual and artistic home.

In college, I majored in drama and later earned a bachelor's degree in theater from the University of Maryland in 1973. After graduating, I planned to pursue my lifelong commitment to the arts. At twenty-three, however, I had to find a job, so I joined the group sales staff at a new theater in the L'Enfant Plaza in Washington, DC. A few weeks into the job, the Yom Kippur War broke out and there was an appeal from various Jewish organizations for volunteers to work on the Israeli communal farms (called "kibbutzim") throughout the country, as they were shorthanded now that most young adults were serving in the army. While I wasn't religious in any way, I had visited Israel briefly once before and was moved by the place and felt motivated to return. My pal Tina Silverman and I went to the local Jewish Community Center, filled in forms, and signed up as volunteers. We were told what to pack and to be ready anytime. The call came three days later and we departed for New York.

When we arrived at JFK airport, we were met by an unforgettable scene. Hundreds of kids our age—playing guitars, hanging out, and making friends—were waiting in the terminal for instructions regarding our departure for Tel Aviv. An air of hippiedom prevailed, as it was the early seventies. We were told, since we were flying into a war zone, not to tell anyone our specific destination. This added a heightened sense of importance to our mission.

After many hours of waiting, we finally boarded planes for the thirteen-hour flight. By now Tina had hooked up with a cute guy we had met in the terminal, while I connected with some crazy Zionists from Chicago. It was a different world then and supporting the Israeli cause seemed to be a much simpler affair than it is today, especially for a Jewish girl from Baltimore. It was a powerful moment for me, halfway across the world, when we approached the airfield at Ben Gurion and saw the yellow stars of David on the ground as the sun came up. The El Al sound system played "Hatikvah," the Israeli national anthem, as we landed, and every young volunteer on that plane had tears in their eyes.

The kibbutz year and a half was a total adventure. Tina and I both met our future first husbands there and Tina would go on to live in Israel for the next twenty-two years. My future husband, Tony, was a gentle bird watcher from Gloucestershire who had, like many Brits, come to Israel for the sun and free housing, which was offered on the kibbutz in exchange for work. While Tony was involved with the kibbutz's fishing industry, working outside in the ponds, I secured a nice job in the laundry, where it was warm and cozy. The

Even as a toddler with my bubbie in the background, I was working the phones.

laundry also served as the central gathering place for all the women dropping off dirty clothes. Needless to say, this was ground zero for community chat. I actually learned quite a bit of Hebrew there, because I didn't want to miss out on any of the kibbutz gossip! Tony was not Jewish, and when he had arrived at the kibbutz months earlier, the last thing he had expected was to end up surrounded by war. However, the kibbutzniks needed help, so he stayed, and we became a couple.

The kibbutz experience—living in a rural environment while a war was raging and simultaneously experiencing my first serious personal relationship—had a profound impact on my young life, broadening my horizons intellectually and emotionally.

When I returned to the States, I landed a job working for a fledgling theater program run out of the Jewish Community Center of Washington, DC. But after two years of producing plays like *Happy Hanukkah, Charlie Brown*, and tours of the *Chelm Players*—a series of Sholem Aleichem stories we adapted into plays—I grew restless and started plotting my path to New York.

Some friends from the University of Maryland—Ken Bloom and Harry Bagdasian—had started a company in downtown DC called the New Playwrights' Theatre, which developed and presented new works by young playwrights. They had somehow acquired a building for their work. I approached them and said, rather desperately, "I've gotta get out of the JCC. Tell me what you need, and I'll do it." To which they responded, "We need someone to raise money." So, without hesitating, I agreed to do just that. As I embarked on becoming an arts administrator, I simultaneously enrolled in a master's program at George Washington University, earning an MFA in directing. The dual tracks of my experience, pursuing both the creative and the business sides of the arts, would prove to add both depth and knowledge to my future career.

As it turned out, when it came to raising money, I was a natural. I had what I like to call "the fundraising gene." I'd never done it before, but somehow I knew just what to do. The week I started working for New Playwrights, the *Washington Post* published a list of the fifty largest companies in DC. I spotted it in the paper and thought, aha, I'm going to go and ask all of these companies for money. And that's pretty much what I did. In a few months' time, I managed to increase the New Playwrights' Theatre's revenue and began to sense that I had found my calling.

During that first year, I applied to a service organization called the Foundation for the Extension and Development of the American Professional Theatre (FEDAPT), which offered workshops for arts administrators at the Eugene O'Neill Theater Center in Waterford, Connecticut. They had advertised a weeklong retreat on fundraising, and I was selected as an alternate. Much to my delight, someone dropped out and I was invited to attend. That single week in Connecticut fundamentally changed my life and the trajectory of my professional goals. It was there that all of my ideas about fundraising coalesced into a singular vision, one that has shaped and fueled my career ever since.

The workshop was held near the childhood home of Eugene O'Neill in New London, Connecticut, one of our nation's greatest playwrights. It felt like a sacred space from the moment I stepped onto the grounds. Nearly twenty young arts administrators from small

Clockwise from top left: As a preteen Harold Hill in the all-girl Camp Wohelo version of *The Music Man*— definitely big trouble in River City!

And in keeping with playing the boys' parts, here I am as Bert, the chimney sweep in the camp's production of *Mary Poppins*.

Around age twenty, channeling Janis Joplin.

Maternal grandparents Mamie and Hyman Friedman—"Mom-Mom and Pop-Pop Friedman." A childhood loaded up with family events, Jewish holidays and Baltimore delicacies: steamed crabs, coddies, and Mom-Mom's cheese strudel.

Five generations of the Brooks family. On the bottom right is Great-Grandmom Wilf holding my son, Matt. Behind her is my mother, Paula; then me; my father, Howard; and in front, his mother, Mom-Mom Brooks.

My pal, Tina, and I entertained the kibbutzniks on Shabbat by singing songs we made up combining the few Hebrew words we knew with English. Here we are signing our rendition of "Tea for Two" performed as "Tay for Shnay."

On the road in Europe with my British boyfriend (later husband), Tony Hopkins.

theater companies had been selected to take part in this workshop. Over the week, we met with some of the top regional theater people in America, including the head of FEDAPT, Fred Vogel, and Bill Stewart, then managing director of Hartford Stage, who led the workshop and talked to us about many things, including how to raise money.

For me, the highlight of the week, and perhaps the most significant moment of my early career, was meeting Polly Brown, then head of development for the Guthrie Theater in Minneapolis. As Polly and I walked the well-trodden grounds of the O'Neill Center together, I got to ask her questions, and while listening to her describe the Guthrie's complex, layered, long-range approach to engaging donors, I had what can only be described as an epiphany. I suddenly understood the entire system and could see it clearly from every angle. I realized that, fundamentally, fundraising is like a military operation. The odds are always against you. It's going to be 90 percent rejection, with many "casualties" along the way, and you must constantly shift your strategy to find new ways forward. If you can't handle the uncertainty, then this isn't the career for you. In order to achieve victory, you need a battle plan for each potential donor. You must always be working, tirelessly, on multiple fronts, based on a comprehensive strategic plan with clear and achievable goals. Rejection isn't personal. As Michael Corleone, played by Al Pacino, says in *The Godfather*, "It's not personal. It's strictly business." You have to be strong and resilient to do this work. You have to grow a thick skin.

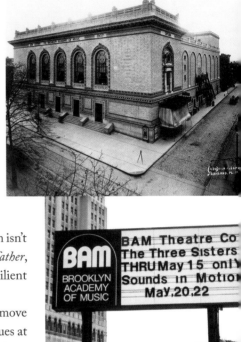

Coming out of that week in Connecticut, I knew that my next move would be to New York. In spite of some early success and great colleagues at the New Playwrights' Theatre, I lasted just one year before packing my bags and heading north. Like every aspiring theater professional, I had written to Joseph Papp, the founder of the Public Theater, and said, "I'm a young administrator, why don't you hire me?" Of course, I never heard back, but I always kept my eyes on the prize—a career at a great New York City arts organization. The same people at FEDAPT who had selected me for the workshop at the O'Neill Center let me know about a possible opening at the Brooklyn Academy of Music, which was trying to establish a repertory theater company. When I expressed my great enthusiasm and interest in the job, they[1] helped me get an interview, and I traveled to Brooklyn with all the idealistic energy of a hungry young professional, ready to do whatever it would take to build a lasting career in the theater.

On the fateful afternoon in summer 1979 when I first met with the impresario Harvey Lichtenstein about working at BAM, determined to get the job, I was still pretty green. BAM, too, was still finding its way. Though it had begun to establish itself as a serious home for cutting-edge choreographers and directors—such as Trisha Brown, Merce

Above, from top:
Brooklyn Academy of Music Opera House, 1910.
BAM marquee, 1977.

Opposite:
Junior's Restaurant—forever a Brooklyn icon, ca. 1970.

[1] Essentially one superstar individual, Joseph Melillo, was the program director of FEDAPT and, though I didn't know it at the time, he was someone who would play a major role in my life at BAM for over thirty years.

Cunningham, Meredith Monk, Robert Wilson, Jerzy Grotowski, and Peter Brook—it hadn't yet achieved financial stability or fully discovered its voice.

Harvey Lichtenstein—a forceful, charismatic visionary and BAM's president and executive producer—was a trained dancer who had studied at Bennington and Black Mountain College, performed for some reasonably well-known New York companies during his youth, and then reemerged in his thirties as a formidable producer and a tireless champion of experimental theater, dance, and opera. Driven by intuition, moxie, and sheer strength of character, he was one of the least practical and most contradictory people I have ever known, and he was always willing to bet the ranch on an idea or an artist in which he believed. It's what made him great, and it was also one of the principal challenges of working for him over the course of twenty tumultuous years.

During our first meeting, in the dark, decaying opera house that housed his office at 30 Lafayette Avenue, he shared his expansive vision for BAM, recounting how far the institution had come since he had taken over in 1967 and reflecting on what it could one day be. As I sat across from him in his wood-paneled office, listening to him talk, he fixed his penetrating, owl-like eyes on my face, silently trying to determine if I had what it took to join the team. Then, he leaned forward in his chair and said in his distinct and gravelly voice, "Look, Karen, I need someone who can work like hell."

Without missing a beat, I leaned forward and replied, "I get it. I'm your gal."

"You're hired," he forcefully responded. We stood and shook hands. This was the moment everything converged. BAM became my home, my universe: everything.

After the interview, Harvey sent me down the street to Junior's[2] on Flatbush Avenue Extension, world famous for its cheesecake, to meet with the board finance committee

chair, Stanley Kriegel, a man who was pure Brooklyn— he lived in the same house his in-laws had lived in a generation earlier and was married to his equally Brooklyn wife, Charlotte, for decades—and was hell bent on making the borough shine despite the deprecating Brooklyn jokes, the economic decline, and the sense of hopelessness felt by many at the time. He was a BAM board member for over thirty-five years.

Stanley always said I was his protégé. I, in turn, always told him he "wasn't just the oldest board member at BAM, he was the oldest board member on earth!" He adored Harvey and appreciated the challenge of resurrecting the "old academy," a venerated Brooklyn institution that, in its earlier heyday, had been a stomping

2 A couple years later, Junior's caught on fire. I happened to pass by on the night of the blaze and observed a large group of hard-core Brooklynites standing on the median on Flatbush Avenue Extension as the building burned. They were chanting "Save the cheesecake!" Brooklyn won my heart at that moment. The Rosen family, who had owned Junior's since its inception in 1950, rebuilt the place on the same spot, maintaining their exact orange-and-white color scheme, right down to the napkins and logo.

ground for Mark Twain, Booker T. Washington, Isadora Duncan, Sarah Bernhardt, Paul Robeson, and even Franklin D. Roosevelt.[3]

In 1903, the original BAM building[4] burned, and the new academy, built with monies contributed by a committee of one hundred of the foremost citizens of Brooklyn, was relocated in 1908 to the border of the Brooklyn business district, in Fort Greene, where it still stands today. During the early to mid-twentieth century,

the academy hosted performances by Ruth St. Denis, Martha Graham, Marian Anderson; speeches by President William Howard Taft, William Butler Yeats, and Thomas Mann; and concerts by Gustav Mahler, Arturo Toscanini, Sergei Rachmaninoff, Duke Ellington, Benny Goodman, Count Basie, and Louis Armstrong. After World War II, the institution fell on hard times when audiences and sponsorship began to wane as the economics of the surrounding neighborhoods and communities changed.

In 1967, Harvey Lichtenstein was appointed president, catalyzing the rebirth of the academy as a cultural force in New York City. Harvey soon established the institution as one of the country's leading dance centers and gave artists and companies such as Merce Cunningham, the American Ballet Theatre, Alvin Ailey, and Twyla Tharp an artistic home. At the same time, he created residencies and spaces for some of the world's most daring theater companies and artists, such as The Living Theatre, led by Judith Malina and Julian Beck;[5] the Polish Laboratory Theatre, led by Jerzy Grotowski; the Royal Shakespeare Company (RSC); Robert Wilson; and the International Centre for Theatre Research, led by Peter Brook. Harvey also presided over the recovery of the place after a massively damaging water main break in 1977 flooded the opera house, which required support from both the city and the private sector to restore it to its historic grandeur.

3 See page 287 for a brief history of BAM and information on each BAM venue.

4 The original building opened in 1861 in Brooklyn Heights. That building was the site of many historic events, including the Brooklyn and Long Island Sanitary Fair in 1864. The fair, which ran for a week, was, in essence, a large-scale fundraiser with booths and events taking place every day. The proceeds helped pay for bandages and other supplies for Union soldiers fighting in the Civil War. Remarkably, the Brooklyn Sanitary Fair raised four hundred thousand dollars, an astonishing sum at the time. Because of this phenomenal success, I used to declare that the mantle of fundraising was on us for well over a hundred years.

5 Harvey always told the story about our maintenance staff asking him why there was always so much discarded underwear on the floor of the opera house following performances by The Living Theatre. The Living Theatre actors were known for disrobing down to their birthday suits at most performances. It was a kind of celebration of the human body in keeping with the vibe of the era.

Above and following spread: Scene from The Living Theatre production of *Paradise Now*, 1968–69.

Opposite: Interior view of flood damage to BAM after a water main break on Ashland Place, 1977.

This radical reimagining of BAM and its core aesthetic, and his leadership following the flood, established Harvey as a cultural impresario of the highest order that ushered in a new era of expansion and reinvention for the institution, and cemented the academy's reputation as an international center for experimental performance. In addition, because of the flood, Harvey strengthened his relationships with key city officials, paving the way for millions of dollars in government investment to renovate and upgrade BAM's buildings. "Harvey likes you," Kriegel coyly said after we sat down. "We're going to hire you—on trial. In a year, we will decide if we'll keep you on permanently." In that moment, I was hired as a development officer, making a starting salary of eighteen thousand dollars. And for the next thirty years, at nearly every BAM event, Stanley would introduce me with a wink by saying that I was "doing okay" but "was still on trial."

What Harvey didn't tell me during the interview, and what I soon learned on the job, in a sort of baptism by fire, was that the BAM Theater Company, one of his pet projects, had been bleeding money from the moment it opened in 1977 with its first production, *The New York Idea* by Langdon Mitchell. Harvey was a dreamer, and his dream was this totally ambitious, insane, enormous thing that had never been established in America before, a great repertory theater company, like the RSC, which would feature some of our best actors and directors presenting classics alongside groundbreaking productions of new fresh works. It was a beautiful vision. It was also one of the first and hardest lessons that I was to learn as a young development officer.

If you are going to do something bold and visionary, something that's never been done before, it's important to raise a lot of money in advance. You need at least three years' worth of funds in the bank, which will allow you to make mistakes and to occasionally fall on your face. With all bold ideas, such as the BAM Theater Company, there's the possibility that things aren't going to work out the way you had hoped they would as unforeseen obstacles arise, and therefore it's critical that you build enough cushion so that you can afford to be wrong.

Harvey, of course, didn't work that way. As he designed a second iteration of the BAM Theater Company after splitting with Frank Dunlop, the first artistic director, he still was trying to make it on a shoestring. For the new venture, he had raised virtually nothing beyond the first year, and even that was light. When I joined the BAM development staff, the company was set to relaunch during the next season under the direction of the legendary RSC veteran David Jones, and I don't think we had three months of money, let alone three years, in the coffers. I was thrilled by the challenge and the opportunity to build a great theater company from the bottom up. I believed we were going to do something historic with David Jones, who had a formidable reputation from his time at the RSC. That said, I don't think Jones was prepared—without more money, time, and a legion of loyal allies—to take on the massive work of a repertory company. I certainly wasn't prepared for the sheer amount of money we would lose—millions of dollars—in an incredibly short period of time.

The rebooted BAM Theater Company wasn't just a fiscal disaster, it was a critical train wreck. Everything about it was ambitious, but very little of it made practical sense, including the pairing of relatively obscure classical texts, such as Shakespeare's *The Winter's Tale*, which was intended to mark David Jones's debut as artistic director, with less-than-well-known actors. The critic Walter Kerr reportedly fell asleep during *The Winter's Tale* and then wrote a lackluster review, summing up the production as "a very long night. . . . The people grow thinner as a difficult play stretches out." The reviews that resulted from some of the other BAM Theater Company shows were even more damning, bearing the kinds of headlines and zingers that sink artistic reputations forever. In 1981, the *New York Times* critic Mel Gussow wrote in his review of Arthur Penn's failed production of Ibsen's *The Wild Duck*, "Mr. Penn, who has had such notable success with contemporary drama, has taken a perverse approach in his first attempt at a classic, and has managed to drown 'The Wild Duck.'" As I recall, the headline in one of the papers read "Dead Duck in Brooklyn." And, in his review of Emily Mann's production of Sophocles's *Oedipus the King*, Frank Rich delivered the final and fatal blow: "Given this production's additional misfortunes . . . it would be hard to argue that much remains of 'Oedipus' in Brooklyn. But there is a tragedy. Just last year, in its first season, the BAM Theater Company promised to make a major contribution to this city's cultural life. Only a Sophocles could have imagined that this troupe's proud ascent would lead to so swift and sorrowing a fall."

Harvey always believed that the critics, no matter how much they disliked individual productions, would never purposefully denigrate or undermine the BAM Theater Company itself, especially in its earliest stages of development. So when the all-powerful Frank Rich (known by many in the field as "The Butcher of Broadway") equated the company's abrupt rise and fall to a Greek tragedy, Harvey took it all very personally. Regarding the company, Harvey could be a pretty volatile guy if you crossed him. I mean, this was a man who, when you were driving with him, would yell at red lights. He was pissed off that they slowed him down.

Helen Hayes, a longtime friend of BAM, led the appeal to raise $300,000 after the 1977 flood.

Unfortunately, by that point, there was little that could be done to keep the company alive.[6] The other thing that Harvey hadn't anticipated was that in order for the company to be successful and sustainable, its productions would need to attract large audiences over a long season. This meant running the shows for real stretches of time

6 Harvey pulled out all the stops to try and save the company but, finally, it simply could not be saved. One of his best ideas was to ask the great actress and "first lady of the American theater," Helen Hayes, to shoot a television commercial promoting the season. One of the plays, a lesser known work by her late husband, Charles MacArthur, titled *Johnny on a Spot*, was in the repertory and she was very supportive of both the production and the repertory concept. On the day of the shoot, I was given the opportunity to ride in the limousine to her home in Nyack, New York, to pick her up and accompany her on the trip back to Brooklyn. She was so kind and generous with her time, even showing me around her home, which was filled with memorabilia from her remarkable career. She asked if I wanted to hold her Oscar, which she won in 1932 for the film *The Sin of Madelon Claudet*. I was humbled and thrilled. It was a big moment for a young arts administrator who idolized Helen Hayes and her generation of leading ladies.

STAGE VIEW
WALTER KERR

Ibsen, Alas, Is a Dead Duck

Tenney Walsh,
Frank Maraden
and Joan Pape in
Ibsen's "The
Wild Duck"—
"gratuitous
violations"

Talk about a bad
review! The BAM
Theater Company
production of *The Wild
Duck* by Henrik Ibsen,
panned by the *New
York Times* in 1981.

Theater

ere's a tin ear at work in Brooklyn these nights, where Ibsen's "The Wild Duck" has just been added to the seasonal repertory at the Academy of Music, though precisely whose ear is responsible for the most flagrant damage isn't easy to say. Cer- y Thomas Babe, who has adapted the text from a trans- by Erik J. Friis, will not soon be forgiven his more ob- and more labored updatings: one's nerve-ends do from each casual "what the hell" or each self-con- s "horny" that falls from the lips of frock-coated, frog- ed 19th-century gentlemen. And director Arthur Penn, g his hand at Ibsen after a distinguished career dealing contemporary stage and screen materials, has at the least been guilty of letting so many leaden out-of-kilter ets stand. He's even let stand some of Mr. Babe's more ul flippancies. After all the tail that's gone on about ounded duck kept on a pile of straw in the Ekdal fami- attic, a doctor strolls in to ask cheerfully what every- s chattering about now: "More duck dropping?" he

Some things should be taken out and buried on the before rehearsals begin.

But words and phrases aren't the issue. What's truly in- itive, crashingly crude, are the gratuitous violations of matic tone. By the end of Scene Four, for instance, a few s of shattering importance have aken place. The com- est, well-meaning but eternally meddling idealist gers Werle has persuaded the daydreaming Hjalmar al that he is indeed mired in illusion, including the illu- that he is a happily married man with a loyal wife and g daughter. A stormy family session has followed. In lyn it is very stormy, with Hjalmar (Frank Maraden) adeagling himself against the walls in crucified pos- s when he isn't creeping up on his poor wife completely en beneath his black photographer's hood. The confron- n has produced some truths, more than Hjalmar is pre- d to assimilate. His wife (Joan Tate) has admitted to an rced liaison with Gregers's father; furthermore, there possibility that little Hedvig is not Hjalmar's child at all. the disabused husband goes, slamming the door behind even more forceably than Nora once did. At which t, just before the lights go down on the sequence, the has a rueful line — all anger spent — that's meant to marize the situation thus far. Onestandard translation, lf Fjelde, puts it this way:

"Ah, me . . . That's the way it goes when these crazy le come around, summoning up their ideals."

Another, by James Walter McFarlane, tries it this way:

"Ah yes . . . This is what happens when you get these d idiots coming round with their fancy demands."

But Mr. Babe has an urge to liven it up:

"It's when these fine men come in with their ideals — s when you have to lock up your daughters!"

As I listen to the line, I think I heard myself praying for ngth. What, I asked myself and the universe, can Mr. be up to? Surely he is aware that the phrase "lock up daughters" commonly refers to an imminent promise duction and/or sexual assault. It certainly does in the century musical version of Henry Fielding's "Lock Up Daughters," which was widely and successfully re- d in the late 1950's and early 60's. Even if one has never d of the Fielding piece, the injunction is really self-ex- story. But, in Mr. Babe's mind, to whom does the ituously added phrase refer? To Hjalmar's wife, who betrayed so very long ago and — in the play — is no daughter? To Hedvig, who is a mere child? It is true Hedvig is now in some personal danger from Werle's odery, but it is not the sexual danger that the words so ishly threaten. Neither is it in any way comic, as the is inevitably are. Baffled, we are at least given a scene- ge to think matters through. Why, in addition to every- g else, has Mr. Babe felt the need of adding a laugh ch is not really forthcoming) to a line that all other ver- treat straightforwardly?

Perhaps we're getting closer, now, to difficulties that inherent in Ibsen's play and that are somehow enor- ly magnified in the BAM production. The play is a

tricky, two-faced affair, tonally speaking. That is one of the things many critics have admired about it, on paper at least: the fact that exceedingly upsetting — if somewhat less than tragic — events are taking place while the princi- pal movers and shakers of these events are being quite openly lampooned. On the one hand, a family is being torn apart, and little Hedvig is reaching for a gun she will use fa- tally. On the other, the important men of the piece — Hjal- mar and Gregers — are increasingly seen as fools: not pre- cisely comic-strip fools, but laughably obtuse "thinkers" nonetheless.

Hjalmar fancies that he will someday rescue himself and his family from poverty and oblivion by inventing some- thing. The "something" is extremely vague, and not really thought of yet. "I do get tired thinking," he confides ear- nestly to anyone who will listen. Gregers, more philosophi- cally inclined, fancies that he can solve the problems of other people — in this case, the unlucky Ekdal's — by ex- posing what is sham in their lives. Kill the sham, and all will be well. Unfortunately, killing the sham sometimes kills the people, as Eugene O'Neill would so often, and sometime later, point out.

Keeping the bumbling comedy of the two men's small moral enthusiasms in some sort of balance with the catas- trophe that is growing out of them does represent a thorny staging and acting problem, as Ibsen himself realized from the beginning. In particular, the author warned the play's original producers that the part of Hjalmar was not to be "parodied." He wanted a fusion of satirical and more sober- ing values, not a vaudeville turn directly followed by a tear- jerker. Direct current, not alternating.

Whether or not his intention is perfectly realized in the text, or perfectly realizable on stage, I can't personally say; I've never seen a production that brought it off People whose judgment I respect tell me, however, that they've had the good fortune to catch one or another performance that managed the miracle, and so I shall continue to keep my eyes open. Have faith, will travel. But alas and in any event, this ultimate revelation isn't on view at BAM.

As the initially stodgy, then increasingly ludicrous, eve- ning moves forward in Brooklyn, a broad and uneasy onrush of farce usurps the whole of the dramatic terrain, brushing aside any and all contrasting moods. What is an audience to do, confronted with the physical spectacle of Hjalmar show- ing it exactly what happened to a noble-minded peacemaker when that noble-minded peacemaker attempted to stop a duel? The simple statement that the old man, stepping be- tween the duelists, was shot in the head from both sides, is funny before any attempt is made to act it out. But when the energetic Mr. Maraden takes a bravura stance near center stage and points two barrel-like fingers at his curly headed temples, the effect is approximately as elevating as some- thing done in a film musical starring The Ritz Brothers. Of course the audience laughs. But the laugh is a guilty one: you can see that those who have laughed looking at their neighbors in embarrassment, as though wondering if they should have first asked permission.

Still, they have laughed, and you can sense that a con- clusion is being reached. The web of seriousness has been torn, the pact of belief between author and audience dis- solved. The rupture is now final, and cannot be mended dur-

Continued on Page 18

in order to build up a subscription base,[7] but it also required advertising dollars, which we simply did not have. In those days, before the Internet, advertising for the theater, to keep the "rep" continually in the news, was almost exclusively done in magazines and newspapers. The subscription base for the BAM Theater Company, in its two-year run under David Jones, from 1979 to 1981, averaged 60 percent at its peak. Had the company lived to see another couple of seasons, who knows what might have been possible. But without consistently good reviews or time to build up subscribers, the project was basically doomed. In spite of a four-hundred-thousand-dollar grant from the Ford Foundation, we lost a lot of money in a matter of months. This was the situation into which I had unknowingly walked, headfirst, as a young development officer, when I accepted the job at BAM.

To his dying day, the untimely demise of the BAM Theater Company was one of Harvey's greatest regrets. After his retirement, he still spoke regularly about his unfulfilled wish to establish a true repertory theater in New York, housed in Brooklyn. The traumatic memory of the BAM Theater Company still lingers in the halls of the institution, so much so that at the time of my departure, the leadership and staff would still joke that, because of the BAM Theater Company, the words "Thou shall not produce" were forever engraved upon the walls of the executive offices. Of course, a lot of producing has taken place since those days, but always with great caution and substantial fundraising and planning in place early on.

Working for Harvey was never dull. Even though he retired in 1999, BAM remained an intense work environment, from the day I walked through the doors in 1979 until the day I left in 2015. Harvey was the most determined person in the world. He knew about every medium and art form, which is something one rarely sees, and he always put the artists and their visions first. If he didn't have the money to realize their dreams, we'd be charged with finding it. In spite of his zeal and his habit of taking big risks, he was also a master at running the business of BAM, and he could handle everything, from cultivating artists and donors to the most minute details of daily operations. No matter how bad it got, he lived to fight another day, so he was a remarkable person to learn from and be mentored by, even if he was never easy.

When I first showed up for work, an eager twenty-nine-year-old fundraiser with ambition and drive to spare, I quickly discovered that the development office, crammed into an out-of-the-way attic space above the opera house, was the land that time forgot. It was the dawn of the computing age, and we had this floor-to-ceiling thing called the System Six, about eight feet tall and five feet wide, which we all thought very impressive, even though its only function was word processing. Nevertheless, "the Six" was revered. However, the majority of our work still took place on handwritten file cards. BAM was nearly bankrupt, and in order to begin digging us out of the crater left by the first season of the BAM Theater Company, I was tasked, as my first job, with organizing the spring gala.

7 Subscribers who purchased tickets to multiple shows are the bread-and-butter customers for theaters with multiple offerings. Subscription purchases provide advance cash and assure that bodies will fill seats way before the show reaches the stage. During the seventies and eighties, subscribers were the mainstay of theaters all over the world.

During his first decade as the leader of BAM, Harvey had collected an eccentric and motley group of supporters for the board of directors, including a few Brooklyn residents who seemed like they hailed from the beginning of time. One of the more colorful members of the board, who also served as gala chair that season, was the vice president of the International Longshoremen's Association, Anthony Scotto. An allegedly powerful member of the Gambino crime family, which ruled the Brooklyn waterfront for decades, he had recently been indicted on thirty-three federal bribing and racketeering charges.[8] Nevertheless, I was determined to work with him to ensure the gala's success.

I remember calling the International Longshoremen's Association and asking if I could come over to meet with Mr. Scotto and help him develop his invitation lists. As I enthusiastically blabbed on about mailings, invitation copy, and the dinner menu, the man who had answered the phone responded formally, with a thick Brooklyn accent. He eventually cut me off and said, "Young lady, Mr. Scotto will sell the gala tickets his own way." I may have been young and wet behind the ears, but I knew enough at that moment to back off and let Mr. Scotto do it in his own way.

It turned out, when Mr. Scotto told people to show up, they showed up, they sat through the gala, and they paid. The gala was, for the most part, a success, with the exception of a seating fiasco that cast a shadow over the event and served as a lesson for galas to come. Out of necessity, we had to seat some of Mr. Scotto's guests in the front mezzanine of the opera house, which offended many of them greatly—and these were not the types of people you wanted to offend. "Don't make us sit there. We want to be in the orchestra, in the front," some of Mr. Scotto's associates forcefully said, pointing toward the front row. Lesson: gala seating is not about watching a play; it's about status.

When I think back to my first months on the job, I was doing twenty different things: running galas, writing grants, calling prospects, and meeting with foundations. I was the original multitasker. At the time, I was working for a man named Philip Jessup, a BAM vice president who was in charge of the development office. Jessup, as it turned out, was not suited for fundraising. He was a decent person, but he had neither the tenacity nor the passion for the job. He had come from the William Donner Foundation, where he had grown accustomed to giving money away rather than raising it. Ultimately, Jessup didn't last very long under Harvey's relentless style of leadership. At the end of my first year, he left BAM and moved to Canada, where I heard he got involved with an environmental organization working to combat acid rain, while I embraced Brooklyn and the daily joys and struggles of Lichtenstein.

Right before Jessup left, my son, Matt, was born, and I took a three-month maternity leave. When I came back to work, I decided to go for Jessup's job. I had been fairly successful in raising funds, even in my first year, and Harvey had gotten to know me over that time. He knew I was an effective, tireless worker and he knew he could hire me really cheaply. I think he paid me twenty-nine thousand dollars, but since I had started a year earlier at eighteen thousand, going up to twenty-nine was a big step. Also, I was given the title of

---

8 Naturally, because that's the way things sometimes roll, his indictment was announced just a few days after we had secured his agreement to chair our annual gala, but even with all of his other problems, Mr. Scotto remained committed to the job.

vice president, the youngest in BAM's history. Harvey figured I was self-starting, he could work me to death, and would not have to pay me very much, a perfect trifecta for hiring a BAM senior executive. So, that's how I got the job.

Needless to say, it was a crazy time. I had a small baby at home and a husband who was from Gloucester, a town in the English countryside. Tony was more suited to hiking and camping than the hardball daily life of the city, making things even more complicated as I settled into the new job. BAM was bleeding money, the BAM Theater Company was imploding, and things were getting so bad that a few times, we had to postpone payroll just to stay above water from week to week. Under my leadership, the development office began moving rapidly in a new direction. I was working day and night to find new donors, managing the galas, and handling foundations, while my colleague David Bither, who soon departed for a life's work in the record business (as he definitely preferred listening to records than writing proposals), cultivated and maintained relationships with corporations, and other colleagues wrote various grant applications. There weren't many of us working in the office, and we were inventing our approach on our feet and improvising as things blew up all around us.

Right around the time that the BAM Theater Company started falling apart, Harvey announced a fundraising event at the fashionable River Café on the Brooklyn waterfront looking out on the Manhattan skyline, which never took place. This was one of many setbacks to our solvency. Ultimately, the project was doomed and the theater company had to be shuttered. By this point, BAM had racked up an enormous deficit, close to 2.5 million dollars, which threatened to bury the entire institution, whose total budget at the time was probably a little over three million dollars. Desperate times called for desperate measures, and, at Harvey's instruction, I was part of an effort (along with then–chief financial officer Sharon Rupert) to keep BAM afloat by orchestrating a five-bank bailout.

Buildings in the BAM neighborhood were in various states of collapse. These brownstones were located on Lafayette Avenue, on the site that is now Betty Carter Park, ca. 1970.

A man named Ed McDougal at Bankers Trust was the key banker who helped us pull the five financial institutions together, mostly from banks that don't exist anymore,[9] to loan us the money that we hoped would give us enough leeway to recover from the deficit. Of course, when we finalized the loan, it felt like we had just enough rope to hang ourselves. It kept us from closing our doors, but didn't do much beyond that. Each bank put in a certain amount, totaling around three hundred thousand dollars, so that no one bank was on the hook for too much, and each received a donor credit for agreeing to the loan. It all felt a bit surreal. There I was, in my second year working at BAM, and I was negotiating bank loans to keep us solvent for another three to six months.

In those tumultuous first few years of my tenure in the development office, things were anything but boring. Every other week, it seemed, we were dealing with yet another crisis. One of the most memorable ones erupted out of BAM's box office, when we discovered that some of the box office staff members were stealing. Lenny Natman, a loyal employee who served as assistant house manager at the time, and who later died of AIDS at a very young age, knew there was collusion between the house manager, a guy named John Miller, and the box office. Miller was this truly eccentric fellow who always wore a coke spoon around his neck on a silver chain. He was a total trip.

The box office was staffed with unionized workers, which presented a challenge when we tried to fire them all at once. This was their scheme: It was the era of the hard ticket, before computers, and, as people walked up to the box office to buy tickets right before a show, otherwise known as "rush tickets," they would typically receive a discount. The box office staff, however, had been selling these tickets at full price, stamping the stubs as rush, and then pocketing the difference. Once suspicion was aroused through Lenny's revelation, a trusted employee was stationed at the opera house entrance to ask customers what they had paid for their tickets, and the full fraud was revealed. Various members of the box office staff were involved, along with the house manager, and since Lenny Natman was an honorable person, the scheme, as he revealed it, was told to Judith Daykin, who was then executive vice president, and Harvey.

When the box office staff showed up for work the following week, BAM's lawyer, Ron Feiner (who would turn out to be my future life partner for twenty-two years),[10] was waiting for them with the stamped "rush ticket" stubs that had been sold at full price, hard evidence of their scheme. Many of the box office staff were fired in one fell swoop along with John Miller, who then moved to California and died a year later. Given the optics and how the story might affect fundraising, we decided not to go public, but we reported the incident to the union, which managed to find jobs for some of the guilty individuals at Broadway theaters or Madison Square Garden by Friday. That was how seriously they took

---

9 In spite of the mess that we caused, BAM was not the reason for their demise!

10 And just in case you are wondering . . . Ron had been BAM's lawyer since the late seventies. And yes, we knew each other for years, working together on all of BAM's various problems. Ron was a flirt, and he was as smart as he was charming and funny. So it seemed like good karma that we found ourselves in a significant personal relationship, which launched in 1993 after we were both divorced. Of course, we followed the appropriate conflict of interest protocols as our status became public. More about this personal narrative can be found in chapter 14.

the problem. Still to this day, I run into these guys behind ticket windows at Broadway theaters and whenever I see them we awkwardly exchange hellos, while a flood of memories come back to me about how, on top of not having any money and struggling to stay open week to week, our own box office staff was caught stealing from us. Things had gone from bad to worse.

There were so many crazy disasters taking place during those first few years that some days I hardly knew which way to look. When the BAM Theater Company closed, Harvey was simply devastated. He would have done anything to save it. At the same time, as Harvey licked his wounds, staff morale began to plummet. We had to pare back the number of employees and those who remained were stretched and underpaid. Fort Greene, the neighborhood that surrounds BAM, was economically depressed and intimidating to some Manhattan patrons, who were then very sought after as donors and audience members. During the early eighties and Ronald Reagan's trickle-down economy, which had forsaken underserved urban communities, Manhattan theatergoers, even the adventurous ones, were increasingly reluctant to cross the East River and come to Brooklyn, so much so that BAM became the butt of many a joke, the most famous of which went like this:
Manhattanite 1: "There's this terrific production I just saw."
Manhattanite 2: "Oh, yeah? Where's it playing?"
Manhattanite 1: "Well, it's at the Brooklyn Academy of Music, then it'll be in London."
Manhattanite 2: "Great. I'll see it in London."

The way many people regarded the divide between Brooklyn and Manhattan at the time was like the barrier between North and South Korea.

Oddly though, mirroring the old adage about turning lemons into lemonade, all of the adversity of the late seventies and early eighties is really what laid the foundation for BAM's ultimate success. These circumstances and our Brooklyn location, out of the spotlight, gave us the freedom to do whatever we wanted if—and that was a big if—we could figure out how to pay for it. It forced us to do a lot of soul searching, to refine our mission, and to get better at articulating what made the institution unique. Because we had no money, we had to be very strategic about our spending. Instead of presenting a lot of small productions and events spread out over the year, we decided to go big with a handful of ambitious, highly visible projects, ones that people couldn't see anywhere else. This left our theaters dark for many nights that year, which was an unfortunate but necessary step as we retreated, regrouped, and reevaluated, therefore earning our chance to live another day. This proved to be one of the key ingredients to BAM discovering and owning its true identity and to the unprecedented comeback on the horizon.

By doubling down on the edgy, idiosyncratic work of visionary artists whom Harvey knew and loved, and offering bold new productions and concerts that one could only see in Brooklyn, we began to refine BAM's identity and carve out a space for it in the New York City cultural scene. A few years earlier, Harvey had fortuitously hired a new vice president of marketing, Charlie Ziff, who was an extremely talented professional. Charlie came up with a number of very successful marketing concepts, such as "Shakespeare on Flatbush" and the "Anti-Nutcracker" (a production for *Nutcracker* haters), and, most critically, he was the marketing executive who officially rebranded the Brooklyn Academy of Music as

BAM. Though Charlie, who left BAM for the Ford Foundation and later died of AIDS,[11] didn't stay on the job long enough to see BAM's full transformation, he made invaluable contributions to what can only be described as a moment of convergence, when everything came together: BAM's name, its irreverent marketing strategies, its brand and look, and the advent of a new festival that would come to define the institution, with a focus on hybrid, experimental, cutting-edge work across all performance disciplines. After surviving the demise of the theater company, BAM had finally found its calling and its true identity. It didn't make sense, given our Brooklyn location and our budget, to try and be a second-rate Lincoln Center. We decided it was better to be a first-rate BAM.

FILM

Karen Brooks Hopkins
NOW PLAYING

"Signy," the digital marquee, featured "KAREN" on the day of my gala, 2015.

11 Sadly, the AIDS crisis, which was a full-on epidemic at that time, prematurely ended the lives of many great artists and arts administrators just at the peak of their careers, such as the brilliant choreographer Arnie Zane; fashion designer and major BAM supporter Willi Smith; staff members Donald Krintzman and Bob Applegarth; my close friend and advisor Stephen Reichard; and so many more. It was crushing to attend so many funerals during that period. The loss of these treasured colleagues and friends left a gaping hole in our vibrant New York artistic community.

CHAPTER TWO:

The Next Wave

In the early 1980s, faced with imminent financial demise due to the losses inflicted by the BAM Theater Company debacle, Harvey, in his "no guts no glory" style of nonprofit arts management, again bet big on what he knew and loved. This time, his wager was on new work by contemporary creators like composers Philip Glass and Steve Reich, minimalism, things that nobody else was touching, things that were really in his DNA. It was a time of great productivity, and there was this incredible creative flow at BAM in those days. From a fundraising and institutional standpoint, the stakes couldn't have been higher. We knew we had to act boldly if we were going to turn things around, and so we began to develop an approach to working with funders that would treat them as integral partners in the conception and delivery of our programs, marketing strategies, and various projects from the very beginning.

In addition to producing and presenting new works, Harvey was interested in commissioning visual artists to collaborate with performing artists on interdisciplinary projects. He had a vision of touring some of our more successful productions to the heartland of America, an idea that would later turn out to flop—the rest of the country wasn't yet ready for Harvey. He sought, among other things, to publish a serious magazine, featuring pieces by established critics and writers about the work on our stages.[1]

In the first year of what we ended up calling Next Wave, which started as a series, we presented Philip Glass's minimalist operatic masterpiece *Satyagraha*, and the corporate giant Philip Morris came on as a sponsor with a twenty-five-thousand-dollar grant, which would be the first of many donations from the company to come. *Satyagraha*, which took its title from Mahatma Gandhi's concept of nonviolent resistance to injustice and featured a libretto adapted from the ancient Hindu poem the "Bhagavad Gita," is arguably Glass's greatest work, one that redefined opera in the twentieth century. *Satyagraha* received effusive reviews and sold out its run. Around the same time, we produced seminal works by three major dance companies: Laura Dean, Trisha Brown, and Lucinda Childs, which drew new audiences for BAM from all over the city—and the region. One of the pieces by Trisha Brown, *Set and Reset*, featured unforgettable scenery by Robert Rauschenberg and a virtuosic score by Laurie Anderson and went on to become critically recognized as one of the most important works in the history of postmodern dance. Another piece, called *Dance*, choreographed by Lucinda Childs with music by Philip Glass and set design by Sol LeWitt, created a huge controversy, which of course brought out the press and sold out

Opposite:
Great visual artists created iconic posters and program covers for the BAM Next Wave Festival right from the beginning. This one is by Francesco Clemente, 1984.

1 One iteration of the magazine was called *Wa* – short for *Wave* – featuring a graphic style of cutoff letters and words that looked cool but were often indecipherable. This graphic style, conceived and designed by the brilliant Michael Bierut of Pentagram in tandem with then–marketing vice president Tambra Dillon, became BAM's calling card and visual identity for years to come despite the fact that the missing letters often made the material, while entertaining to read, challenging to understand (much like many of the shows)!

the house for the run. *Dance* was pure minimalism and you either embraced it as hypnotic and mesmerizing or it drove you totally nuts. At the end of the show some people literally pelted the stage with tomatoes while others stood and cheered. I stood at the back of the house as usual, watching this display, and thought to myself, This is great. Everyone is so passionate. I knew that New York was just right for me.

The unprecedented success of the Next Wave Series, the consolidation of our programming, and our focus on what BAM did best catalyzed radical change within the institution, as well as within the borough of Brooklyn. BAM was becoming a destination for intrepid, adventurous, hip audiences in search of experiences they simply could not have in the more traditional cultural spaces of Manhattan. The second year of the Next Wave Series, 1982, featured new work by the minimalist composer Steve Reich, the Flying Karamazov Brothers, Laurie Anderson, and the Bill T. Jones/Arnie Zane Company, further cementing BAM's burgeoning reputation for bold, risk-taking programming and laying the foundation for what would soon become the Next Wave Festival.

The impetus and energy for what evolved into the Next Wave Festival did not come directly from the theater world but rather originated in the art world. Harvey had gone to lunch with RoseLee Goldberg, the art historian who would later found Performa, the renowned multidisciplinary performing arts program, and he came back with the kernel of an idea: "We're going to merge the whole thing into a festival," he said—one that would explore the interconnections between disciplines and would establish BAM as the global epicenter of experimental performance. As it turned out, we would work closely with people from the art world to develop the concept.

We hired the consultants Anne Livet and Steve Reichard (of Livet Reichard), who were well known in the visual arts community, to formulate a marketing and fundraising strategy to attract audience members from the contemporary art scene who would be more adventurous and receptive to new work. We wanted to engage artists, collectors, curators, critics, influencers, and thought leaders to drive other audiences to follow in their footsteps and come to BAM. We knew that if the contemporary art world bought into BAM and what it represented, the rest of the New York cultural scene would too. To this end, Livet and Reichard helped us establish a Producers Council—a new fundraising stream generated by thousand-dollar contributions from individuals through annual dues, and we were able to land the famous pop artist Roy Lichtenstein and his wife, Dorothy, as our first council chairs. This was a major catch and Roy Lichtenstein's early buy-in went a long way toward establishing BAM's legitimacy within art circles as it attracted other high-profile artists to get involved.

My goal, from the very outset, was to help BAM raise enough money to launch the festival, while giving it more cushion than the BAM Theater Company had enjoyed, so that we could afford to stumble and make mistakes in the early stages of its development. The first person we approached for support was Howard Klein, who headed the arts program at the Rockefeller Foundation. Howard was a big fan of Harvey, and his boss, a woman named Alberta Arthurs, who ran the entire arts and humanities division, agreed to become an early funder and to host other potential supporters at a meeting, including attendees from Rockefeller, the Ford Foundation, Warner Communications, AT&T, and Philip Morris, as well as others, to discuss building a base of contributions for our still

Clockwise from top left: Glenn Branca came to BAM in 1982. His music was so loud that it somehow made the lights blink on and off in the old Carey Playhouse.

Poster created by Roy Lichtenstein for the first Next Wave Festival, 1983.

Poster for the Next Wave Festival, 1984.

Poster for *Einstein on the Beach*, Next Wave Festival, 1984.

Poster by Frank Stella for the Next Wave Festival, 1985.

Subway poster for the Next Wave Series, spring 1983.

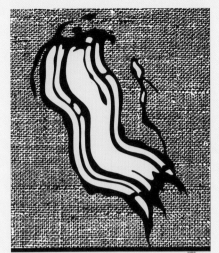

NEXT WAVE FESTIVAL

4 October–4 December 1983

BROOKLYN ACADEMY OF MUSIC

REMY CHARLIP
Choreography by
Remy Charlip
October 17 – 21

TIM MILLER
Performance Artist
DEMOCRACY IN AMERICA
October 24 – 28

MARK MORRIS
DANCE GROUP
Choreography by
Mark Morris
Nov. 28 – Dec. 2

**3 Premiere Events
October 17–December 2**

For ticket information call
Chargit (212) 944-9300

BROOKLYN ACADEMY OF MUSIC
B A M 30 Lafayette Avenue, Brooklyn, NY 11217

STEVE REICH + MUSICIANS   GLENN BRANCA

LAURIE ANDERSON   DANA REITZ + DANCERS

NEXT WAVE: NEW MASTERS AT THE
BROOKLYN ACADEMY OF MUSIC   ROBERT WILSON + JESSYE NORMAN   BILL T. JONES
MAX ROACH/ANNIE ZARF   BAM

NEXT WAVE FESTIVAL BROOKLYN ACADEMY OF MUSIC
OCTOBER TO DECEMBER 1985

EINSTEIN ON THE BEACH
An Opera in Four Acts by

ROBERT WILSON — PHILIP GLASS

Choreography by
Lucinda Childs

DECEMBER 11–23, 1984
FOR TICKET INFORMATION CALL CHARGIT (212) 944-9300
BAM
BROOKLYN ACADEMY OF MUSIC
30 Lafayette Avenue, Brooklyn, New York 11217

nascent idea. Howard was a slim, well-dressed man of medium height with a trim gray beard and a twinkle in his eye. He loved his job and his look reflected the stature of the foundation. To this day, I always say that the funding for the Next Wave Festival was born in the boardroom of the Rockefeller Foundation.

We also had the good fortune of landing a major challenge grant from the National Endowment for the Arts, which was led during the Reagan years by Frank Hodsoll, a former lawyer and Foreign Service officer who was arguably one of the greatest and most pioneering NEA chairpersons, after Nancy Hanks and Roger Stevens. The idea of a vibrant festival of new work amid Brooklyn's struggling economy appealed to the Reagan administration, which needed a clear win to show it wasn't biased against Democratic-dominated big cities while it was cutting government programs left and right. Those were the days when the arts in America were respected as part of citizenship and the agency received bipartisan support showing none of the rancor and divisiveness that was yet to come.

Between all of the funders who stepped up to the table after the fateful Rockefeller meeting, we were able to raise several hundred thousand dollars in multiyear grants, which was what we needed to get the multidisciplinary, multicultural, multinational festival off the ground. The overarching concept was to give artists like Robert Wilson, Laurie Anderson, Steve Reich, and Philip Glass, whose more ambitious works were primarily presented in Europe, a stage in America for their large-scale productions, while providing up-and-coming artists a developmental platform, in essence an opportunity to move from the loft to the proscenium stage, where their work could be showcased alongside that of the more-established contemporary artists. Ultimately, it was the mixing of well-known artists with fresh new experimenters, all producing hybrid, boundary-dissolving, genre-bending work, which interrupted the established definitions of dance, theater, and music, that coalesced into the Next Wave Festival's signature vision and would go on to define BAM as an institution. As a programming strategy for each festival came together, our method evolved with a goal of anchoring the entire enterprise with blockbusters (the BAM version of a contemporary name performer like Robert Wilson or Pina Bausch) and discoveries—combined with a mix of local Brooklyn and New York artists positioned next to their global counterparts, a deep commitment to racial diversity, and a variety of arts forms, some of which were just beginning to gel.[2]

In October 1983, we launched the Next Wave Festival with a mixed-media work called *The Photographer/Far from the Truth*, directed by JoAnne Akalaitis with music by Philip

2 The final "pièce de résistance" and essential piece of the puzzle was controlling the inventory—i.e., deciding how many individual performances of each show to offer the audience. By keeping it tight, we were able to increase demand, creating the illusion (or perhaps the reality) of a "hard to get" desirable ticket for shows featuring artists that essentially no one had ever heard of. This proved to be a magical solution to selling tickets for unknown work.

Above:
Steve Reich, 1984.

Opposite, from top:
Scene from act 1 of the Philip Glass and Robert Wilson production *Einstein on the Beach*, Next Wave Festival, 1984.

Valda Setterfield in *The Photographer/Far from the Truth*, Next Wave Festival, 1983.

Glass, who had both defined their careers with the famed experimental theater company Mabou Mines, and choreographed by David Gordon, also a downtown dance luminary. It was an eighty-minute performance that blurred the lines between dance, music, and theater, all the while questioning our assumptions about the verisimilitude of photography. Although it was by no means a critical knockout, the piece firmly signaled the Next Wave Festival's ambition to upend and challenge traditional conceptions of visual and performing arts genres, while forging new connections and forms. It also served as a beacon for people from the downtown/Soho art world to make the trek across the East River to BAM to see our three primary performance spaces: the 2,100-seat opera house, the one-thousand-seat Carey Playhouse, and the modular, three-hundred-plus-seat Lepercq Space. Also, by now we had hired my old FEDAPT friend, Joseph Melillo, as the first director of the Next Wave Festival. His first day on the job, Harvey handed him a single piece of paper listing shows he wanted Joe to investigate with the idea of presenting them at the inaugural festival scheduled to open a few months later. Somehow, despite the limited lead time, Joe got the job done, starting with *The Photographer/Far from the Truth*.

The night of the opening, I stood in the back of the opera house, scanning the crowd with amazement, taking in all of the new faces. Anne Livet and Steve Reichard had clearly done their part, going so far as to bring people from Manhattan art galleries to BAM, by bus or by car, whatever it took in order to get to get the hippest audience in the room. Kids with pink hair and tattoos, piercings, combat boots, and leather jackets were pouring through our doors. Judith Daykin, who was then BAM's executive vice president, walked over to me, leaned in close, and said, "I've never seen a more unattractive group of people attend a theatrical event in my life." A few minutes later, Steve Reichard walked up and ecstatically exclaimed, "Oh my God, have you ever seen a more fabulous-looking group of people attend a performance event?" And I thought, as the saying goes, beauty is truly in the eye of the beholder. Also, it occurred to me that BAM, housed in a neglected neighborhood of a forgotten borough and long considered the errant stepsibling of New York's larger cultural venues, was starting to make its mark. At another performance a few years later, I remember looking out into the crowd and thinking that we'd hit a bull's-eye by attracting this eclectic audience, which that night included both Jacqueline Kennedy Onassis and Claus von Bülow, the British socialite who had famously been put on trial for attempting to murder his wife. Wow. The full range of luminaries, high and low, are here tonight, I thought. We have arrived.

In 1982, leading up to the festival, we also presented multimedia performance artist Laurie Anderson's *United States: Parts I-IV*. It was her masterpiece and a risky production because it had to be seen over two nights since it ran a full eight hours. When it sold out immediately, we knew it would be a success, as another audience barrier had been broken. In 1983, the year we launched the festival, we also produced *The Gospel at Colonus*, a musical adaptation of Sophocles's *Oedipus at Colonus*, featuring a full gospel choir, the actor Morgan Freeman, and the singing group the Blind Boys of Alabama, conceived by the director Lee Breuer, also from the avant-garde theater company Mabou Mines, and

the composer Bob Telson. The production received rave reviews, sold out its run, and would become the kind of popular and critical hit that the Next Wave Festival needed, earning a Pulitzer Prize nomination for its score, an Obie Award, and, years later, enjoying a brief Broadway run.

The impact and importance of fundraising at that critical moment in BAM's evolution cannot be minimized. We all played our part, and mine was a significant role.[3] I came up with what I call a "scorched earth" strategy for building our base of support. The goal was to create a team of funders who would all be in it with us together, and layer the money that we raised in such a way that no one critical flop or setback could deter our progress. During this time of unprecedented growth, our supporters would be as critical to our success as the artists. The institution could only take big risks because these foundations, corporations, and high-net-worth individuals were willing to risk with us. Howard Klein and Alberta Arthurs of the Rockefeller Foundation had

taken a big chance supporting the Next Wave Festival and bringing together a coalition of funders in their Manhattan offices. Their willingness to support us paid dividends for BAM, because we harnessed their funding and used it to embolden artists to do things they'd never done before.

In an odd way, there is a kind of nobility in fundraising. Most people in Europe feel a sense of ownership of their cultural institutions, which are subsidized by government funds. But here in America, that subsidy doesn't exist. Instead, we have this unbelievably vital and connected relationship to our funders and our audiences, precisely because we need their

3 It was gratifying that during the early years of the festival we received major press coverage not only for the groundbreaking concept and specific productions, but even the fundraising achieved some notoriety. The *New York Times Magazine*, in November 1986, ran a lengthy piece headlined "The Avant-Garde Courts Corporations" and subtitled "The Brooklyn Academy of Music Raises Millions for its Performance-Arts Festival" (see page 126). The donors were thrilled! Years later, the venerable *New Yorker* magazine published a cartoon about fundraising at BAM (see page 194). This was particularly satisfying since raising money is not the type of content that generates much humorous commentary.

money. Therefore, we have to engage with our audiences in a very personal and profound way. The necessity of fundraising engenders a special connection with community and audience that otherwise would not exist. Everything about this is challenging, and you often wish you didn't have to do it, but fundraising forces institutions to understand and bond with audiences in a different way. And therein lies the power of the system, a version of benevolent American capitalism at its best.

One of the fundamental tenets of my scorched earth approach to fundraising is to follow every lead, no matter how insignificant it may at first seem. One of the greatest leads of my early career came from a now "ancient text." It was a reverse telephone directory, and it was our bible for prospect research in the days before computers and databases. With it, you could look up an address and then find out who was currently living there. My team and I had identified 1 Pierrepont Street as a prominent address in Brooklyn Heights and had discovered that a man named Hamish Maxwell lived there. It turned out that Maxwell had been the head of the Australian branch of the cigarette company Philip Morris and had recently returned to New York to run Philip Morris International.

We originally wrote him a solicitation letter because he lived at 1 Pierrepont, and he sent us a check for fifty dollars. Then we figured out exactly who he was professionally and, through a series of Brooklyn connections and another BAM supporter named Sydney Lewis, who hailed from the tobacco state of Virginia, where Philip Morris grew their crop,[4] we found a way to meet him. We stayed in touch over the years, and continued to cultivate him as a donor, bringing him into the BAM family as he rose through the corporate ranks. Philip Morris was under a lot of fire in those days, but they were huge arts supporters and BAM's Next Wave aligned with their messaging of individuals following their own path and ultimately going against the grain. Dealing with the tobacco issue was complex and we each have to find our own way with this type of fundraising. I handled it by determining that this company manufactured a legal product that generated enormous wealth for its shareholders and significant salaries for its senior employees. I decided that it was better that a portion of this largesse go to BAM and other charities rather than just enhance the company's profits. It's controversial, I know, but we couldn't have survived without them and they proved, over the many years we worked together, to be a creative and generous partner who, led by VP for Corporate Contributions and Cultural Programs Stephanie French, and later by Jennifer Goodale, VP for Corporate Contributions, were an integral part of making the festival a global cultural phenomenon. Eventually, Maxwell became the CEO of Philip Morris, and by then he was deeply committed to BAM and our mission, so that fifty-dollar donation eventually became a $450,000 donation, and Philip Morris, later the Altria Group, became a major sponsor of the Next Wave Festival for decades to come, ultimately generating more than eleven million dollars on behalf of BAM.

4 Lewis was quite a character in his own right—leading a major retail company in the south and who, with his wife Francis, collected an amazing range of avant-garde visual artworks.

Above:
Stephanie French and Bill T. Jones.

Opposite:
Our generous donor Howard Gilman hosted a party for all the artists on the occasion of the Next Wave Festival's fifteenth anniversary in 1997. **Front row, L–R:** Jene Highstein (artist), Kristin Jones (artist), Merce Cunningham (choreographer), Mark Morris (choreographer), Harvey Lichtenstein (BAM president/ executive producer). **Back row, L–R:** Andrew Ginzel (artist), Susan Marshall (choreographer), Joanne Akalaitis (director), Bill T. Jones (choreographer), Lou Reed (musician), Bob Telson (composer), Ping Chong (artist), Howard Gilman (benefactor), Pina Bausch (choreographer), John Kelly (artist), Joseph V. Melillo (BAM producing director).

Like the leader of a military-style campaign, I continued to move my team out on multiple fronts, hitting the ground as hard as we could, working every flank, leaving no stone unturned, in order to build a serious, multilayered base of support for the institution. We were gaining ground attracting new corporations to the table, and through our Producers Council, led by Roy and Dorothy Lichtenstein, we were creating a pipeline of high-net-worth individuals for the board. We made and maintained contact with our youngest audience members from the moment they walked through our doors, developed midlevel professionals to join the ranks of our greatest supporters, and even began a process of encouraging some donors to leave legacy gifts to BAM after they died. It was our intent to create a cradle-to-grave approach to building a community of supporters who were as committed as we were to BAM's success and who would stay with us forever. And at the same time that we started to successfully assemble this food chain of support, BAM found its niche and hit its stride with the Next Wave Festival. Of course, it was all interrelated. All of these pieces: the programming, the marketing, the graphic design, the artists, the audiences, and the fundraising were inextricably linked. It was a magical moment, as all of these things unfolded simultaneously, and BAM, and the many communities of which it was composed, began to speak with one unified voice.

CHAPTER THREE:

The Mahabharata

Harvey Lichtenstein was anything but predictable. As a leader, he often displayed a crazy and at times contradictory combination of traits. On the one hand, he was not afraid to surround himself with talented, opinionated people. He had no interest in yes-men. On the other hand, ten people could advise him to do something one way and if he believed it should be done another way, he would follow his instincts. Harvey trusted his own judgment, which inevitably led him to devote himself fully to his favorite artists and their needs and desires. We used to say "There is one god. His name is Harvey," and these artists were the people he loved the most, and he was their greatest champion. There were the special ones, such as the choreographers Pina Bausch and Twyla Tharp, for whom he would do anything, no matter the cost. If the director Peter Brook wanted to do something big, Harvey would immediately commit to making it happen, in the purest, most uncompromised form, even if he had no idea where we would find the resources. So naturally he and I argued a lot, especially about money.

There were many times when I tried to dissuade him from pursuing certain projects, or when I tried to convince him to produce them with fewer dollars, but when it came to this core group of visionaries, nothing I said could penetrate his stubbornness or sway his opinion. He was resolute and unwavering in his commitment, and it was, for lack of a better word, maddening. Some days I would walk around BAM, boiling over with anger, completely infuriated with him, but then I always rolled up my sleeves and worked harder than before to realize his vision. I can't exactly explain why I never dug in my heels or walked away. There was something about the single-mindedness of his conviction, even when I thought he had lost his mind, that caused me to stay in his "club" and do whatever I could to find the money.

Over the years, there were many colossal projects at BAM, which—against all odds—Harvey willed into existence. *The Mahabharata*, produced in 1987, was the wildest, most paradigm shifting of them all. It was, hands down, the most important piece of theater we ever put onstage, resulting from three things: Harvey believed in it, Peter Brook was working at his creative peak when he conceived of and directed it, and the piece took no prisoners. For most audiences, it was an absurd proposition, a nine-hour theatrical adaptation of an ancient Hindu epic. And yet there had never been anything like it and, some might argue, there hasn't been since.

Harvey's devotion to Peter knew no end. He had befriended him in 1971, when Peter brought his legendary RSC production of *A Midsummer Night's Dream* to Broadway. It was one of the most influential stagings of a Shakespearean play in the twentieth century—stripped bare, set in a simple white box, and imbued with the palpable magic of circus tricks, acrobatics, and actors performing at the height of their abilities. "Brook's *Dream*," as it was known in the theater world, deviated from the pervasive Victorian-era style of most Shakespearean productions of the time, breaking through "the crust" of conventions

Sotigui Kouyaté, Ciarán Hinds, Georges Corraface, and Hélène Patarot in the Peter Brook/Jean-Claude Carrière production of *The Mahabharata*, Next Wave Festival, 1987.

and habit, as Peter would say, to get to the essential truth of the play. Harvey somehow persuaded the producer David Merrick to allow the production to come to Brooklyn for a two-week run after the show closed on Broadway, a proposition that captured Peter's interest because Harvey promised to set aside a large number of affordable tickets for each show, something that hadn't been possible on the Great White Way. After presenting Brook's *Dream* in Brooklyn, Harvey and Peter became good friends, and two years later, Harvey brought Peter back with *A Conference of the Birds*. In addition to his power as a storyteller and theater maker, there was something even more profound in Peter's work, the way he connected to life through the theater.

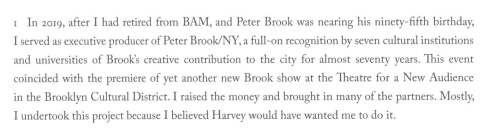

Peter's productions weren't simply entertainment. They were spiritual journeys that demanded as much of audiences as they did of actors. At the center of his plays resided the transformational power of human imagination and theatrical representation. His plays were spare by design, in order to leave room for the audience to join the worlds that his company created. I had known and been obsessed with his work since my college days, when I had seen his production *The Ik* at George Washington University. The play told the true and unsettling story of a Ugandan tribe of hunters driven from their homeland and dehumanized by starvation. The play explored the thin thread that holds our humanity together. The work was so powerful that I returned night after night to see it. If you were a theater person, and you got to experience Peter's work in this era, you were locked in, because it was completely experimental and yet totally clear. There was nothing pretentious or arty about it. It was direct, profound, and it made sense. It was spare, and yet it was rich and full. Everything about Peter was compelling, from his penetrating blue eyes to his artistic clarity. I had worshiped him as a student and had come to BAM explicitly with the hope of one day working with him.[1]

After Harvey experienced *The Mahabharata* at Peter's gloriously decrepit theater in Paris, the Bouffes du Nord, he resolved to bring it to BAM. He came back buzzing about it. He knew the production was major and was fiercely determined to present it in Brooklyn. Harvey invited Peter

1   In 2019, after I had retired from BAM, and Peter Brook was nearing his ninety-fifth birthday, I served as executive producer of Peter Brook/NY, a full-on recognition by seven cultural institutions and universities of Brook's creative contribution to the city for almost seventy years. This event coincided with the premiere of yet another new Brook show at the Theatre for a New Audience in the Brooklyn Cultural District. I raised the money and brought in many of the partners. Mostly, I undertook this project because I believed Harvey would have wanted me to do it.

to come look at the BAM opera house as a potential venue, but when Peter saw it and all of its opulent Beaux-Arts decor, he immediately said, "No, it's too nice. It's too formal. We can't do it here." Rather than accepting no for an answer, Harvey, in his usual never-say-die quest for victory, set out to find a space that would work. He intuited that this would be the most important work of his lifetime and, because of this, he never gave up. This was Harvey's genius, even though it was insane on nearly every practical level.

There are different, conflicting accounts of how they found the space. Legend has it that while walking down Fulton Street, one block from our main building, Harvey and Peter stumbled across the old, boarded-up, dilapidated Majestic Theater—a former 1904 vaudeville and movie house. They broke a window, climbed in, and upon seeing the decaying grandeur of the space, immediately declared, "This is it." Harvey called the city and got a very sympathetic response from Diane Coffey, who was the dynamic and formidable chief of staff to Mayor Ed Koch and was supervising the city's Department of Cultural Affairs at the time. Diane somehow managed to appropriate four million dollars to recreate the Majestic in the state-of-the-art-ruin style of the Bouffes, where the past and present, the spectator and the performer, all share the space.

We had a theater. We had a nine-hour play. But we had no money to present it. So I spent a day listening to Peter talk about the inception of the work when he was at BAM, and afterward I said to Harvey, "This is the greatest fundraising story of all time. We're going to get a group of donors. We're going to go to France. We're going to watch the play over three nights. And we're going to have Peter tell his story to the donors. They will become enraptured with the piece, as we are, and then the money will flow." And, just as Harvey had set out to build a theater, and Peter to create an epic play, I set out to forge a direct connection between Peter and a group of donors. My aim was to generate a committed army of supporters who felt they were part of it—connected to the creation of the theater and the play—from day one. Harvey said, "Okay. Let's do it."

So that's what we set out to do, except that shortly before we departed for Paris with nine of our most important donors, the 1986 Libyan crisis occurred, after a discotheque in West Berlin was bombed and the United States retaliated against the presumed culprit, Libya, with air strikes on Tripoli and Benghazi, resulting in the closing of the borders around France and nearly everywhere else in Europe. There was chaos and fear, and, despite it all, we were still trying to move ahead with a week of events planned in Paris, including tours of the Centre Pompidou and Musée national Picasso-Paris, lunch with the ambassador, a meeting with the mayor, and fine meals in restaurants such as the Jules Verne on the second story of the Eiffel Tower. All of these activities were designed to supplement the experience of seeing *The Mahabharata* at the Bouffes du Nord each night in French, culminating with a meeting with the creators to talk about the production. Steve Reichard, one of the art world consultants who had been instrumental in launching the Next Wave Festival, organized the museum visits, while I was responsible for the meals—and in Paris, no matter what is happening in the world, every meal is an event.

The Libyan crisis had emptied the city of tourists, which worked in our favor, because the French, who often scorn American visitors, simply could not do enough for us now that we were the only tourists in town. I remember one night when phones were ringing, events were unfolding, and there were a variety of details to which I had to attend. I called

VISIT THE
PARAMOUNT &
OX THEATRES

CLOSED FOR ALTERATIONS
ALWAYS A GOOD SHOW AT
THE PARAMOUNT & FOX THEATRES

THE BEST IN ENTERTAINMENT
PARAMOUNT and FOX THEATRES

527 CIVIL

WAL ISNE
FAN
"VALLEY
STARS FR

MAJESTIC

ALAN LADD HITLER BEAST of BERLIN
G RATOFF IN KING OF THE CIRCUS
PLUS 3 STOOGES COMEDY

ALAN LADD
BERLIN KING OF
CIRCUS 3 STOOGES

ALAN LADD in
HITLER BEAST of BERLIN

KING of
CIRCUS

HITLER

56

the ambassador's residence to make sure everything was in motion for lunch the next day (with only my high school French as backup). The person on the other end of the line kept repeating, "*Ne quittez pas. Ne quittez pas. Ne quittez pas!*" I hung up and called the concierge and said, "What does '*Ne quittez pas*' mean?" And he said, "Don't hang up." And I sighed, "Ah!" and began frantically dialing the ambassador's residence again. Managing the trip proved incredibly complex. There were many moving parts, and of course I wanted everything to be perfect and according to plan, or we risked losing the financial support that we were working so hard to build. The donors had been enchanted by the idea of the production and all of them decided to attend despite the problems in France—so I wanted to make the experience as smooth and as compelling as it could be, but it remained unclear whether they would commit the money to bring the production to BAM.

Toward the end of the trip, I booked a room at this place called the Grand Hotel, for a lunch with Peter Brook and his collaborators, Jean-Claude Carrière, with whom he had created *The Mahabharata*, and Chloé Obolensky, who designed the costumes for the show (there were well over a hundred costume changes), made out of all white muslin, which gave the entire production a look of holiness and purity. The idea was to give the group some time to talk with the artists and to engage with them about the production. In spite of our best efforts, I hadn't been able to reserve a meeting space at our price point in any of the nicer hotels, and, much to our dismay, when we arrived at the Grand Hotel, we discovered a truly depressing room. We had been staying at the Meurice Hotel, a former nineteenth-century palace, which was elegant and impeccable. In France, decor is everything, and the decor of the room I had booked at the Grand left much to be desired. It was anything but grand. But over lunch, as Peter, Jean-Claude, and Chloé began telling the story of how *The Mahabharata* first came to them as a work, the drab walls of that room completely disappeared.

The gist of the story was that Peter and Jean-Claude had been working on a show about the Vietnam War that profoundly affected a member of the audience, as Brook productions tend to do. This individual ventured backstage after the performance and handed Peter a piece of paper that said something to the effect of "This is the essence of everything you need to know about the world." Peter tracked down the ancient poem the man referred to in his note and discovered a story of a great battle, in which the future of mankind would be decided. On the day of the battle, the two opposing armies assembled and looked across the terrain at each other. Just before the fighting began, some of the warriors recognized each other as family members and said, "We're cousins," and then questioned why they were fighting. Peter was moved by the artistic and spiritual depth of the work, which turned out to be a version of the "Bhagavad Gita," a seven-hundred-verse Hindu poem dating back to fifth century BC. He and Jean-Claude investigated it further and learned that it was a small part of a larger work, a Sanskrit epic called *The Mahabharata*, the longest single poem in the world. So they found a remarkable scholar in Paris, Philippe Lavastine, who knew the entire epic by heart, and proceeded, over time, to participate in long storytelling sessions with him, as well as embarking on a series of journeys to India to uncover the layers of meaning and character embedded in the work. They began going, week after week, to have the story told to them. And through this painstaking process, they learned *The Mahabharata* in the most ancient way, as people had learned it around campfires for millennia. And then, being the great men of the theater they were, they (along with the equally brilliant Marie-Hélène Estienne, Peter's professional partner) created a nine-hour piece of theater based on what they had learned.

The story of how *The Mahabharata* came to exist as a theatrical work was fundraising gold, and Peter was the best storyteller of them all. When he spoke, the listener was acutely aware that they were listening to a master. The tale of how they discovered *The Mahabharata* was like an ancient epic, and their recounting of the way they delved into the work continued for the rest of the afternoon, as the donors hung on every word. Finally, after the sun had set, and the creators brought the whole saga to its conclusion,

Joe turned to me in his inimitable way and said with a smile, "In a word, historic," gesturing toward what had just transpired. And that was how we launched our fundraising plan for this production. We knew at that very moment it was going to be something transformative; that it would be a major work of art, and that anyone who sat through it would cherish the experience forever.[2]

When we returned to Brooklyn, we immediately began to go down the donor list to secure their commitments to back the production. Then, I suggested to Harvey that Peter should come back to New York and that for a week we would organize different groups of prospects to which he could tell this story. And that was exactly what we did. We hosted a luncheon at *Forbes Magazine* (Bob Forbes was a member of our board) and invited the other BAM trustees to hear Peter talk about his work. We convinced the philanthropist Martin Segal to host a dinner for Peter with various potential funders. We also met with foundation heads and corporate leaders and hosted lunches with potential donors. We did many different things to create buy-in for the fundraising around the work. In every case, the idea was to build a relationship between the donor and Peter Brook.

We raised the money in a relatively short period of time. And then came the actual building of the theater. Because the old Majestic was being remodeled in the style of Peter's Bouffes in Paris, for the express purpose of housing *The Mahabharata*, we had scenic painters laying in faux marble next to real marble. And the back wall of the theater, which was painted, layer upon peeling layer, to capture the decomposing beauty of the space,

2 While in Paris at the show, at approximately hour four of *The Mahabharata*, one of our group members got up and crossed in front of the stage, directly in front of the full cast, and exited the theater, presumably to answer the call of nature. Intermission was definitely hours away and sometimes these situations cannot be avoided. Joe Melillo peered at me over his program, raised one finger, and said in a faint but disturbing whisper, "There it is, one massive faux pas by one bad apple, and now we have an international incident. BAM may never recover." And it was, in fact, an international incident. Brook's manager cursed us for "generations to come," and it was only when Harvey actually delivered the new Majestic Theater as a remarkable New York venue to house the production, that she agreed to lift the curse. All this from one unplanned trip to the ladies' room!

became the back wall of the theater for all time. Art, life, and construction all came together in the building of the space. Under Peter's direction and the supervision of his designer Jean-Guy Lecat, the aesthetic demanded that history and artistry and audience share the space, and that nobody should be too comfortable (the spartan bench-type seats ended up causing a great deal of trouble in the years to come).

Anyone who sat through *The Mahabharata* wore it like a badge of honor. We presented the play many different ways—in three parts, all night, all day. I saw it at least ten times, and at every sitting the play kept revealing level upon level of subtlety and meaning. The company was spectacular, and we were all particularly in love with the handsome Italian actor, Vittorio Mezzogiorno, who played the protagonist, Arjuna, "the Archer." In fact, after first meeting him in France, when he came with the show to Brooklyn months later, I ventured to say hello and compliment his performance. "I remember you," he said with a charming, thick Italian accent. I melted. It was just another part of the magic of being connected to this great work. The piece was pure gold, and yet the *New York Times* critic Frank Rich completely missed it. He did not give it a great review. Fortunately, it was critic-proof by this point, but it deserved the greatest review in the world. It's something that people still talk about today, regardless of whether they were there. It was just one of those pieces.

The *Mahabharata* gala posed a number of unique challenges. We needed to celebrate this unique production and continue to raise money for it at the same time. Since the show was nine hours long, we couldn't simply invite people to watch it and then serve dinner afterward and, alternatively, we couldn't serve before the show since we had to start the performance early due to its length. After a protracted negotiation with Peter, we persuaded him to stage a one-hour excerpt from the production, followed by a gala dinner in the BAM opera house lobby. This solution proved highly successful, as many people wanted to experience the show but not everyone within our donor circle would commit to seeing the full production. To our great delight, Bianca Jagger agreed to chair the gala. Her celebrity and style assured a lot of press coverage and glamour. Everything lined up, almost magically, for what promised to be an unforgettable evening.

On the big night, one of our high-profile guests, the rapper LL Cool J, wasn't having any of the spinach *soufflé en croûte* and Chilean sea bass that Bianca had selected for the menu. At a certain point, when he had reached his limit of high-end cuisine, the rapper, whose 1987 album *Bigger and Deffer* had recently spent eleven weeks in the number one spot of Billboard's R&B albums chart, simply called the local Chinese delivery place and had them bring shrimp fried rice and egg foo young right to his table. The look on the deliveryman's face was priceless when he entered the lobby and saw a thousand people dressed to the nines all eating and drinking. LL Cool J's tablemates, it should be noted, were thrilled with his dinner selection, too.

Above:
Rehearsal for *The Mahabharata*, Next Wave Festival, 1987.

Opposite:
LL Cool J, rap singer, icon, and BAM gala guest, was a hit with the neighborhood kids, 1987.

What people didn't know at the time of the production was that Harvey, in addition to spending the money that we had raised for *The Mahabharata*, and all of the money from the ticket sales, took the entire BAM cash reserve and spent that, too. We received an appropriation of four million dollars from the city to create the theater. We had raised hundreds of thousands more for the show. And, simultaneously, there was an effort, led by Neil Chrisman, our board chair at the time, underway to build a cash reserve, wherein he and I had painstakingly raised several hundred thousand dollars from the National Endowment for the Arts in the form of a challenge grant. Without my knowing, Harvey spent every cent of that too. By the time I understood what had happened, the money was gone, and I then had to explain it to Neil and the board.

Harvey did what he did for a reason, but it created many financial problems over the long haul. At the end of the day, was it worth it? Oh, yeah. It was definitely worth it. But, by the end of the run, financially speaking, we were back to where we had started after the failure of the BAM Theater Company. We had reinvented BAM, produced this magnificent play, and now had this new theater, which Harvey didn't know how we would program or support in the years ahead. After *The Mahabharata*, we brought Peter back to direct *The Cherry Orchard* (which, thank God, Frank Rich adored) and then the theater was used sporadically for several years. Harvey's modus operandi was always ready, fire, aim. Nevertheless, producing the play was the greatest decision we ever made. After *The Mahabharata*, running a new theater was a piece of cake.

The story of *The Mahabharata* and how we generated support for it became deeply interconnected. There was drama on both sides. Raising money for BAM was indistinguishable from programming. As I've said many times before, this was part of our special sauce: the programming, the marketing, the fundraising, Brooklyn; it was all entwined. It all felt the same. BAM defined itself with productions that would never have been seen anywhere else, singular works like *The Mahabharata*. And through these landmark pieces we were able to create this sense that if you wanted to see a unique production, you had to see it during the short window it appeared at BAM. Every big piece became an event. This crystalized the relationship between artistic creation and our core business strategies, codifying the BAM brand and establishing Fort Greene, Brooklyn, as an international destination—destination BAM.

Opposite:
The Majestic Theater
pre-renovation, 1987.

Above:
The Majestic Theater
post-renovation, 1987.

Following spread:
LL Cool J at the gala
with former board chair
Asher Edelman and his
wife at the time, Maria
Regina Leal Costa
Mayall Edelman, 1987.

As Patron of Welsh National Opera, I am delighted that they are making their first appearance in the United States at America's oldest arts centre, the Brooklyn Academy of Music. My congratulations also to the Academy on the inauguration of "BAM Opera" with this production of Verdi's Falstaff.

Through its imaginative productions and extensive touring programme, Welsh National Opera has become one of Britain's leading opera companies and a source of pride to us all. The Company is an innovator in the world of opera and will feel very much at home at the Brooklyn Academy of Music, which is widely recognised as a focus for innovation in the performing arts.

I am very pleased to be able to join you this evening and I look forward to a marvellous performance.

Diana

January, 1989

CHAPTER FOUR:

Princess Diana in Brooklyn

I n the late 1980s, in the spirit of the bold, large-scale programming choices we had been making since the founding of the Next Wave Festival, we decided—perhaps without fully understanding the demands of the form—to branch out into opera. Since the beginning of Harvey's tenure as the leader of BAM, we had produced or presented several of the most groundbreaking minimalist operas of the time, including Philip Glass's *Satyagraha* and *Einstein on the Beach* and John Adams's *Nixon in China*. These were costly, large-scale productions, which drained resources but also paid cultural dividends in terms of the audiences they attracted to the BAM opera house and our growing reputation as a place where big, bold work could be seen that was not available elsewhere.

As we surveyed the field, there appeared to be an opening in the New York opera scene. The New York City Opera was perennially broke and lacked a clearly defined mission at the time, while the Metropolitan Opera, then a well-funded pillar of the music world, remained heavily entrenched in the traditions of the nineteenth century (i.e., the performers stand in front of expensive scenery and sing). To be sure, the divas at the Met sang brilliantly and beautifully, but they often seemed disconnected from the action onstage, and perhaps that was part of what was turning younger audiences off to opera. We believed that if we scrubbed off the crust of the operatic form, which had calcified, to some extent, at institutions like the Met, that opera could resonate—in a more direct and sincere way—with young people, and they could take in and feel the power of the form. Harvey's goal was threefold: (1) to identify productions with real theatricality that would connect to a broad audience; (2) to resuscitate musical forms that had been largely dismissed by most opera companies, such as, the Baroque, that were experiencing exciting new interpretations and (3) to present productions created by new and different artists such as choreographers and pop and avant-garde composers who were dabbling in the genre. We had a vision for making opera less grandiose and presenting unique productions from around the world that, because of cost, size, and general aggravation, were generally unheard of; a perfect recipe for BAM to jump in and make opera more relevant for a new generation of audience members.

When Harvey decided to move BAM into opera, he hired a bon vivant opera aficionado named Matthew Epstein, who had worked for Columbia Artists Management, which managed a lot of singers and musicians from the Met. Epstein, who served as BAM Opera's artistic director, had this grand aesthetic vision for how we would produce opera on a massive scale. Of course, we didn't have the money to fulfill his vision. We barely had enough funds to mount operas on a modest scale! The whole idea was ridiculous and foolhardy, and Epstein eventually resigned when the economic limitations became apparent. (For example, he hired limousines to bring important people from the world of Manhattan opera to meet Harvey. It made sense, given the stature of these luminaries, but limos were not an option. Even paying for Family Car Service on Fourth Avenue in Brooklyn, our local go-to, quick pickup, was somewhat challenging in terms of cost.) Nevertheless, we persevered, as we always did, believing that we might be able to put together enough money to launch a season of opera and then would try to keep it going, in spite of the odds.[1]

In his search for operas that could serve BAM's mission, Harvey had seen William Christie's production of *Atys* in Versailles and deemed it a masterpiece. Christie, a conductor and musicologist, was born in Buffalo, New York, and had studied at Harvard and Yale before moving to France in 1971 and founding the company Les Arts Florissants, dedicated to breathing new life into rarely staged baroque operas from the seventeenth and eighteenth centuries. *Atys* was an obscure type of early French opera by Jean-Baptiste Lully with a libretto by Philippe Quinault based on Ovid's *Fasti*, a Latin poem that was published in 8 AD. The opera was not favored by Parisians of the seventeenth century; however, it was a favorite of King Louis XIV, for whom it was performed several times, earning the title "the king's opera."[2] Somehow, in producing it, Christie had found a way to make the baroque instrumentation and music sound as contemporary, urgent, and driving as punk rock, or any other music being produced today. The French went wild for it, and even invested money in an international tour. When it came to BAM in 1989, *Atys* blew the doors off the hinges, introducing a baroque form to young, diverse audiences with such vitality and force that it expanded the very idea of what an opera could be. That's what BAM did best, challenge the very notion of genre itself, and *Atys* did just that. Harvey cited the opera as one of the greatest highlights of his career, and we brought *Atys* back to BAM two more times in the decades to come. The wigs alone were a spectacular visual achievement. There were dozens of them, each made with meticulous care and requiring a team of twelve wig masters to handle the "hair" changes. It was like the rest of the production, breathtakingly beautiful.

Over the years Christie became a regular at BAM, bringing nineteen productions,[3] which were all well received and did in fact help resuscitate the entire genre of baroque opera for a new generation of audiences. One memorable moment came when the Province of Normandy gave us the funding to bring a production of *Médée* to BAM as part of a celebration acknowledging the fiftieth anniversary of the famous World War II battle

1 Harvey was less enthusiastic about classical music presentations at BAM, even though he was a fan. There were many others better suited to handle that expensive art form. He did try at one point to take over the struggling Brooklyn Philharmonic, but he never really wanted to run an orchestra nor did he want to add BAM's precious resources or real money to their coffers. Eventually, after fifty-eight years and a prestigious history, they went out of business in 2013.

2 The death of Lully: I may have invented a few of the facts here, but I'm told that in those days of the baroque, conductors led the orchestra with a long pole instead of the "smaller" baton we are familiar with today. In any case, it is said that Lully became so entranced during a performance that he jabbed himself with the pole, contracted gangrene, and died. This tale of "death by opera" was a sign, warning us of the travails we would face working in this genre.

3 A new Christie production brought devoted fans from all over the country to BAM. On occasion, even Justice Ruth Bader Ginsburg managed to recuse herself from the Supreme Court to experience the Maestro's magic.

that had taken place there. Many veterans came to the performance and dinner as our guests. I recall the moving and emotional speech, given by a senior government official who was sent from Normandy to commemorate the occasion. She said, "Many people have commented on the strained relationship over the years between the Americans and the French, but it is not so in our province. In Normandy, your sons are sleeping beneath our apple trees." It was another instance of art and life coming together.

Another visionary whom Harvey greatly admired was the German director Peter Stein. Peter had been hired by the Welsh National Opera to direct Verdi's *Falstaff*, and we immediately decided that it would make an excellent addition to BAM Opera's first season. The production was large, technically complicated, and incredibly expensive. The only way it would make it to our stage was if we first found money, a lot of money. So we started to work on an ambitious plan to raise the funds to support the production right away. I contacted Brian McMaster, who served as the general director of the Welsh National Opera, and told him that we wanted to throw a gala and that we needed a patron to anchor the event who was a major supporter of his institution. Half-jokingly, I asked, "Could you maybe get the queen to do it?" And he replied, "No, but I can do better. Let's try for Princess Diana. After all, she's the royal patron of the Welsh National Opera." My jaw hit the floor and, without hesitating, I said, "Do it."[4]

4   Royalty had come to BAM before but not on the level of Princess Diana. In February 1986, Princess Margaret was a guest of honor at a gala sponsored by Abraham & Straus (A&S), the leading Brooklyn-based department store of its day, featuring Sadler's Wells Royal Ballet's *The Sleeping Beauty*. At the end of the night, after the dancers had performed, a three-course dinner and dessert served, and all speeches delivered, Her Royal Highness and her entourage rose to leave. We escorted them to the elevator and breathed a sigh of relief, but just as we were exhaling, the elevator door reopened and Her Royal Highness's lady in waiting appeared, followed by Princess Margaret herself, at our checkout table where the gift bags were being distributed to the guests as they left. Princess Margaret looked at our staff, who were standing there in disbelief because of her hasty return, and exclaimed (loudly), "I'm not leaving without my A&S bag!" Following this remark, the lady in waiting, standing straight and tall with elbows crooked, fists clenched, and a stern expression,

Princess Margaret greets guests and performers at the Sadler's Wells Royal Ballet gala, spring 1986.

accepted two gift bags from our staff. Then, in their royal fashion, she and Princess Margaret (for the second time) made their grand exit into the New York night. If only we could have had a video of the moment, A&S might have doubled their sponsorship for all future royal BAM events!

On another occasion, Princess Caroline and Prince Albert of Monaco came to BAM for the opening of Les Ballets de Monte-Carlo production of *Cinderella*. The receiving line for the Princess got too crowded and one man (he was balding, middle age and somewhat nondescript) kept coming back to the line pushing his way in. Finally, I became irritated and asked him why he was so rude and what did he think he was doing. "Excuse me, Madam President," he replied, "I am Prince Albert, aren't I supposed to greet the guests?" I was horrified. *Quel désastre*! Another royal faux pas!

McMaster made it his mission to visit the Court of Saint James's and get this incredible thing, which seemed like a total fantasy to us at the time, to happen. We didn't have high hopes, but we knew that if we were somehow able to pull it off, it would be phenomenal for BAM. A few weeks later, the phone rang in the office. It was one of those gray mid-March mornings in New York when you're positive spring will never come and no one interesting will call. My assistant informed me that Brian was on the line with important news. A ray of sunlight shot across the Brooklyn skyline. Perhaps this would be the morning, I thought. This could be the call. McMaster spoke with his perfect Oxford accent, in a hushed but enthusiastic tone. "The answer is yes," he said. "The Princess of Wales will come to BAM."

Needless to say, we were beyond excited. The whole thing was amazing. This would be perhaps the most important fundraising event for BAM for all time, and the most serious undertaking of my career to date. In May, nine months prior to the event, I was on vacation with my family in Vermont at a remote country inn. Harvey called the front desk. (Remember, no cell phones then.) It took about ten minutes for the innkeeper to pronounce "Lichtenstein" clearly enough for me to understand it was Harvey. He told me that I had been invited to England for an audience with Anne Beckwith Smith, Her Royal Highness's lady in waiting and personal secretary. I would travel there in August, along with Brian McMaster; Beth Rudin DeWoody, co-chair of the gala and BAM trustee; and Denis Azaro, a senior member of BAM's development staff, and, if all went according to plan, we would confirm "the royal visit" and begin making arrangements.

On the way to London, much to my dismay, British Airways lost my luggage, and I was forced to go on a significant shopping spree in Cardiff for clothes that would be presentable at the royal palace. It was annoying for sure, but a shopping spree for clothes to wear to the Palace was not exactly without its pleasures! Later that afternoon, when I called the small London hotel near Covent Garden that Brian McMaster had booked, to see if Beth, who had served on the BAM board for many years, had arrived, the man who answered the phone said, "I'm afraid Ms. DeWoody checked out, but she has left you a note. Shall I open it?" After I said yes, the man proceeded to read the note in the most rigid of accents, as if he were looking down his nose at every word: "Dear Karen, this place is a fucking dump. I'm going to the Berkeley." The man was clearly incensed, but, in fact, the place was a dump, one of those cheap hotels where you stepped out of bed and your foot landed in the shower. This created a minor setback, but Beth, a resilient New York social leader and art collector with an immense joie de vivre, found lodging that suited her better and we survived.

The next day, after we finished our planning work in Wales, we met Beth at the Court of Saint James's, where we had our first session with Anne Beckwith Smith, who instructed us on precisely how everything would be executed, from the Scotland Yard security team reconnaissance mission to BAM, to every last detail of the dinner, including the "flower moment," when the designated eight-year-old flower girl would present Princess Diana with dozens of red roses. The whole extremely complex enterprise—with its thousand moving parts—was designed to create and perpetuate the fantasy of "Her Highness." I now believe the building of the Great Wall of China must have been a simpler affair than preparing for the visit of a princess. But, in the end, it was fantastic, a fundraiser's dream.

When we returned from England, everyone at BAM was totally charged up. There were lots of meetings with the whole staff—except Harvey, that is, who had no interest in the arrangements for the princess until the night of the event, when she captured his full attention. (He was actually focused on the opera, a component of the operation most of us had forgotten about.) Two months later, the princess's royal security detail flew over for a walk through of the venues, and it was then that we knew it was real. We started marketing the event through all of our various channels. One of the first things we did was secure permission from Buckingham Palace for *People* magazine to become the main sponsor of the gala. Diana was the most photographed woman in the publication's history. Her image had graced the cover of twenty *People* magazines, and so they naturally wanted to get involved, and, hands down, *People* magazine became the biggest gala sponsor in the history of BAM.

From that point forward, it was all systems go. We were fundraising our brains out. Everything was clicking. The British consulate got involved in the planning. We raised funds from the tourism side. We raised funds from the government side. It was like a well-oiled machine. We had layer after layer of supporters lining up to participate—individuals, corporations, foundations. It was pure money magic, and it was all because of Her Royal Highness, Princess Diana. Although she had made unofficial visits to New York City in the past, Diana had never conducted an official visit. So the BAM Opera gala became the pretext for this to happen, and it turned out to be a very big deal, bigger than we understood at the time. As the date approached, it became clear that everyone who was anyone wanted to attend, and pretty soon we had sold more than twelve hundred gala tickets.

The plan was for gala attendees to see Peter Stein's *Falstaff* at the BAM opera house before being transported to the Winter Garden, a grand venue in Battery Park with views of the Hudson River, which had just opened that year. The Winter Garden could handle a party for our twelve hundred people, which was good because at the time, such a large number of people couldn't be accommodated in Brooklyn. In 1989, there wasn't even one suitable hotel in the entire borough. Her Royal Highness's motorcade would wait right outside of BAM to take her back to Manhattan after the opera, with the full crowd following. I was assigned the nearly impossible task of introducing the princess during intermission at several simultaneous receptions to all of the patrons and VIPs who wanted to meet her. There would be champagne for the entire audience before the opera, and countless photos with gala chairs, not to mention an additional reception for the designers of the princess's wedding gown (on display from the Palace), which Princess Diana would also have to attend. Finally, New York City's mayor, Ed Koch, was scheduled to show up and welcome everyone before the performance.

Two days before the gala, Dan Rather decided to run a segment on the *CBS Evening News* about Princess Diana coming to New York. Some of us went out and bought a little TV so we could watch the segment at BAM, where we were busily working on seating strategies and other preparations. We all called our parents and told them to tune in at 6:00 p.m. It was going to be the first major piece about BAM on national television, and we were excited. That night, we all gathered with great anticipation in BAM's executive offices to watch CBS's advance coverage. The news began, and at the top of the story they ran a photo of Princess Diana. Rather stated that the princess was coming to New York on her first official visit to the city. "But," the anchor then asked in a slightly sardonic tone, "where is she going?" The image cut from Her Royal Highness to a pile of garbage and photos of people sitting on street corners. "She's going to Brooklyn," he continued grimly, while gritty imagines of dilapidated buildings and broken sewers flashed across the screen. "And why is she going there?" he asked, barely masking his judgment and disdain, before going on to trash BAM and Brooklyn. Needless to say, we were devastated, and we immediately called CBS and told them, "Dan Rather is no longer welcome here." CBS had actually bought a table for the gala, and with revenge in our hearts we got out the floor plan and started moving their seats to the very back of the space. CBS was dead to us.

The night of the gala, four security forces descended upon BAM: the FBI, Scotland Yard, Her Royal Highness's own private detail, and the NYPD. They all did a massive security sweep, with bomb-sniffing dogs, and we were required to set up metal detectors, through which anyone entering our buildings would have to pass. As part of the festive decor, there were close to five hundred balloons scattered throughout the lobby, and when the security forces came through on their sweep, the balloons kept popping loudly, sending the police, agents, and security guards scurrying each time. Finally, her detail told us the balloons had to go. So, a few minutes later, five hundred balloons made their exit.

Then we learned that activists were planning a protest across the street. As the protesters gathered out front and began shouting about the Troubles in Northern Ireland and calling for people to boycott BAM and Princess Diana, limos started lining up in front of the building, filled with VIPs, public figures, politicians, and wealthy donors. Even Donald Trump rolled up in a limo that night, though he was the last person to actually send in payment for his ticket (oh, the irony). Obviously, he had no interest in the opera, but he couldn't be excluded. He had to be part of this "HUGE" historic event.

Inside, there was a box in the opera house where Her Royal Highness would sit, dressed to the nines, decorated with greenery and bejeweled, for all to see. As the curtain opened, the orchestra was to play the "Star Spangled Banner" and then "God Save the Queen," and as they played the latter, Princess Diana would enter her box. Now, this was New York in the 1980s, so, of course, everyone was wearing black. The women were dressed in black gowns. The men all wore black tie. And so when the princess entered her box—young, tall, and gorgeous—dressed completely in white, an audible gasp went up from the crowd as people took in her radiance. Everyone stood. She smiled and gestured gracefully toward the audience, welcoming us all to the event. It was thrilling. She sat down. The rest of the audience followed her lead. And the opera began. But as I have often said, "Who can remember the opera, when the real show was in the audience that night?"

At intermission, we all breathed a sigh of relief because we had made it through the first act, but the evening had only just begun. I had been trained by the princess's handlers to call her either "Mum or Her Highness." You weren't allowed to say "Diana" or anything else, for that matter. So, as it was my job to introduce her to people, I would say, "Your Highness, I would like to present so-and-so," and patrons would come up and have their thirty seconds with her, for which they had paid twenty-five hundred dollars a ticket. People were lining up at the various receptions, drinking champagne, and I was trying to move them through quickly, without being rude to patrons or to the princess. But, naturally, many tried to overstay their time and hog the show, and so I really had to assert myself a few times, letting people know when their time was up.

This was the donor-relations challenge of the century, giving people their time with the princess but moving them through in a matter of seconds. Of course, Her Royal Highness could not have been warmer or friendlier throughout. She really played her part beautifully. We even came up with a system for moving people in and out of the box seats during the performance, so patrons who had paid more got a chance to sit with her. Lou Rudin, the father of our gala chair, had a royal decoration (the CBE, or, Commander of the Order of the British Empire) and so he got to sit with Her Royal Highness for the first act. Then, Amber Lightfoot Walker, the other co-chair of the gala, got to sit with her for the second. While the action onstage was dynamic, it paled in comparison to the performance we were staging in the audience, as we rotated patrons into proximity of the princess. Every second of every minute was choreographed the entire night. Confidentially, it is a fact that when you are a real princess, you must have your own bathroom in order to maintain a fully private space—away from other mortals—for fulfilling basic needs. For the gala, the princess was given her own dressing room, fully equipped with both toilet and shower, and the day after the big event, it was discovered that someone had absconded with the royal toilet seat. For years, we tried to find the culprit, but the toilet seat never showed up on eBay.

"Her Royal Highness," I often reminded my staff, "is not a person, but an industry," and the Princess Diana gala proved this maxim time and time again. The princess gig is a full-on, universal fantasy, and her job is to make us believe, and believe we did. Every aspect of her visit to BAM, every detail, was designed to reinforce the idea of royalty, to create this magical aura around her that people would forever associate with the night they were graced by her presence. The night ran like clockwork, and everyone, from the Scotland Yard types to the FBI agents, came out of central casting (seriously, these were truly men of steel—with names like Wayne and Doug, which we spelled Wain and Dug), and they were ready to lay their lives down at a moment's notice. When the opera was over, the entire audience—more than two thousand people—leaped to their feet and delivered a thunderous standing ovation. Her Royal Highness was quickly whisked away to her limo, which was then led by the NYPD motorcade over the Manhattan Bridge to the World Financial Center, down in Battery Park. All of Flatbush Avenue was stopped for this.

As Princess Diana's limo pulled up at the World Financial Center, we raced to get everything in place for her grand entrance. The Winter Garden had this wide marble staircase leading down to the floor where the tables were arranged. When Her Royal Highness appeared at the top of the staircase, we had to be ready to cue a handful of young American girls who, at different stations on the marble steps, would come out, present Her Royal Highness with flowers, and then curtsy. Of course, the honor of having your child participate as a flower girl at this event wasn't assigned freely. We fundraised for that opportunity, too. *People* magazine paid for one of their executives' children to have a flower moment. Beth's daughter, Kyle, got a flower moment, too, since her mother was chairing the gala. We also invited some girls from our Brooklyn neighborhood to participate, as we wanted to keep the local Brooklyn spirit embodied in all aspects of BAM's "persona," but, truth be told, we took all of the fundraising opportunities we could. This type of thing is simply the nature of fundraising, and to pretend it isn't is delusional. Lesson: No one is giving you money to get lousy seats. People pay for access and special treatment. It's as simple as that.

Following spread: With Princess Diana and Harvey. Check me out in those glasses!

Harvey greeted Her Royal Highness at the top of the marble stairs and, arm in arm, they descended into the Winter Garden, stopping to receive the curtsying flower girls along the way. This was the money shot, Harvey and Princess Diana, the royal coronation of BAM. To capture it, we had photographers all penned together in a press section. The next morning, the *New York Post* ran an iconic photo of the Princess coming down the steps. Once the flowers had all been presented and the photographs had all been taken, the guests all went to their tables. And, since you weren't allowed to take photos of Her Royal Highness eating—it was strictly verboten—the photographers took a break during dinner.

Then came the faux pas of the year. Brooklyn borough president Howard Golden and his wife were seated at the Her Royal Highness's table, but they were tired after the opera and had decided to bag the dinner. They really didn't like the opera very much and felt they had spent enough time with Her Royal Highness, so they had resolved to go home. When we realized there were empty seats at the royal table, this nearly became a full-blown social disaster, but the ever-resourceful Beth Rudin DeWoody saved the day. David Dinkins, who was serving as Manhattan borough president at the time, happened to be a friend of hers and was seated at her father's table. Thinking on her feet, Beth deftly moved the Dinkins over to the princess's table, filling the glaring holes left by the Goldens. (This faux pas just barely eclipsed one from earlier in the evening, when Ed Koch had delivered his curtain speech in a cheap suit instead of the gala's formal black-tie dress code. Apparently, he'd been on the way to a Democratic Party fundraiser at the Waldorf. What can you do? New York is New York.)

The whole evening was one for the history books. We raised a million dollars that night. To be clear, that was a million dollars in February of 1989. The socialite and philanthropist Amber Lightfoot Walker joined the BAM board. *People* magazine came on as a major sponsor, and we made countless new friends, cultivating prospects and donors for years to come. It was an extremely long night but exhilarating. When it was finally over, I remember all of the BAM staff, all of the British consulate staff, all of the security details, and members of the BAM family, threw a great party to celebrate pulling it off, which lasted until the wee hours of the morning. Of course, you're never going to please everyone. Inevitably, some people are going to be upset about the placement of their seats,[5] or the fact that they didn't get a chance to speak with the princess. But it was still the greatest gala in BAM's history. Nothing could take that away from us.

The next morning, the event was covered prominently in the press. Both the *New York Post* and the *Daily News* ran front-page stories, alongside extensive coverage in the *Guardian*, the *New York Times*, and an array of other newspapers. It was fundraising gold, and it elevated BAM's prestige in New York City and throughout the world. I can still close my eyes and see those lines of limos pulling up on the streets of Fort Greene, Brooklyn. Take that, Dan Rather.

---

5 And . . . no matter what you do or how many pre-event tastings you plan, someone is always complaining about the food. In New York, it's a fact that food is an obsession. Seriously, someone could spend two hundred dollars on an opera ticket, hate the show, and you never hear from them. But . . . if they don't like their appetizer at a gala, you receive a death threat via email.

FOUNDED IN 1801 BY ALEXANDER HAMILTON

NEW YORK POST

LATE CITY FINAL

FRIDAY, FEBRUARY 3, 1989 / Rain, windy, low 40s today; cloudy, mid 30s tonight / Details, Page 2   40¢ in New York City 50¢ elsewhere

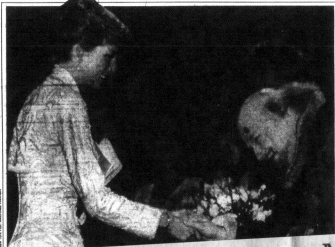

DI'S NIGHT AT THE OPERA

Princess Diana congratulates Donald Maxwell, who sings the title role of Falstaff, after glittering opening night of the Welsh Opera's production at the Brooklyn Academy of Music. The Verdi opera was the climax of a day in which Di took the city by storm — dazzling homeless children at a Lower East Side day-care center and visiting the FAO Schwarz toy store.

MORE ON THE ROYAL VISIT: PAGES 4 & 5

New York Post / MICHAEL NORCIA

For the Princess of Wales, a Night at the O

By GEORGIA DULLEA

The Princess of Wales went to the opera last night in the County of Kings, popularly known as Brooklyn.

A charity gala in her honor drew a black-tie crowd of 860 guests, among them scores of notable New Yorkers, to the Brooklyn Academy of Music where the Welsh National Opera performed Verdi's "Falstaff." At times, their attention was divided between the action on stage and the action in the royal box, bedecked with swags of purple and red satin and greenery.

Between acts of the opera, the guests in the two-tiered royal box played musical chairs. Five took turns sitting next to the Princess while nine others rotated around the box.

When the Princess first appeared in the box, the audience stood and the orchestra played "God Save the Queen." The Princess wore a long dress of white satin with a beaded bolero and carried a bouquet of white roses.

'Out of Dress Code'

From the stage, Mayor Edward I. Koch apologized to the Princess for welcoming her in a business suit. "Your Royal Highness," he said, "I'm out of dress code because of a town hall meeting in the Bronx."

The $1,000-a-ticket gala, which benefited the Brooklyn Academy, drew luminaries from society, business, publishing and politics. Sir Antony Acland, British Ambassador to the United States, was there along with Gordon Jewkes, the British Consul General. Among New York political figures were Borough President Howard Golden of Brooklyn and State Comptroller Edward V. Regan.

Part of the crowd
a photograph, of

'She's left the smell of perfume on my hand.'

home."

The performance and dinner that followed at the World Financial Center was the splashiest part of the Princess's three-day visit, which offered glimpses of both extremes on the city's social spectrum — from ... with to grinding poverty.

Coll
nea

M
wife
tlen
dro
cro
and

Star staircase almost steals Diana's show

Eyewitness

Martin Walker

NEW YORK is the city of grandiose designer parties, but the formal banquet they concocted for the Princess of Wales was pitched a bit high, even for the Big Apple. To get the idea, imagine a Busby-Berkely musical crossed with a Nuremberg rally.

It was the stairway that did it, sweeping flights of grey Italian marble. I was standing at the bottom of this Champs-Elysées of a staircase, among British embassy and palace officials.

Then the Princess appeared at the top of the

corporate guests of the various sponsors of the event.

Entire tables of showbiz types were guests of the Home Box Office Corps, and bankers invited by American Express. Our own Welsh Development Agency had invited 120 past and prospective investors in the principality, and People magazine had the biggest guest list of all. This was only fair, because they have put Princess Di on their cover 57 times, and each time she boosts circulation about 200,000. At a dollar a copy, she has earned $11 million for them in news-stand sales alone.

Thus, it was not exactly the glitterati and social elite of New York who watched the Welsh National Opera's Falstaff and dined with the Princess. It was more a case of build a factory in the Rhondda, and get an evening with Princess Di thrown in for free.

So what was billed as a charity gala in aid of the Brooklyn Academy of Music was just an item on a lot of corporate PR budgets. This showed in the oddest ways.

Endless free champagne was offered by Moët & Chan-

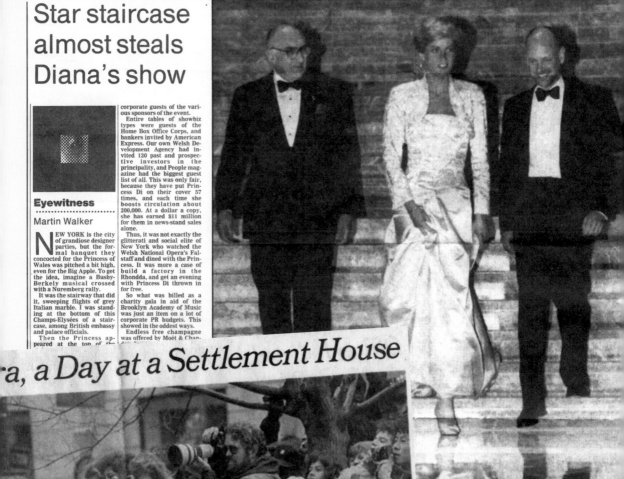

Academy, and Brian McMaster, of WNO   PHOTOGRAPH: DAVID

...ra, a Day at a Settlement House

The New York Times/William E. Sauro

...th Avenue from the F.A.O. Schwarz store yesterday waiting to catch a glimpse, and perhaps ... of the Princess of Wales, left.

...in a housing project ...ent. ...mo, the Governor's ...e Princess at the set-...where the royal visitor ... a day-care center, ...hat with preschoolers ...hild's shoelace. Princess spent more

stayed for lunch.

Compared with the Princess's other appearances yesterday, last night's gala afforded almost no chance for an unscheduled brush with royalty.

During the opera's intermissions, 200 corporate patrons were invited to one of two receptions and rewarded ...h a sip of champagne and a closer

donor, were among those sharing the best seat in the house. As the curtain rose, James R. Gaines, managing editor of People, was seated beside the Princess. He was supplanted several acts later by Elizabeth P. Valk, the publisher.

"We have written about her a great deal," said Ms. Valk of the Princess, who has reigned over People's pages since her marriage to Prince Charles,

Di's visit was big news.

Clockwise from top left:
New York Post, 1989

Harvey, Brian McMaster from the Welsh National Opera, and Princess Diana, the *Guardian*, 1989.

New York Times, 1989.

CHAPTER FIVE:

Great (and Low) Moments in Fundraising

The first thing you need to know about fundraising is that it's not brain surgery. It's harder than brain surgery. In surgery, the doctor opens up the body, goes in and identifies the problem, and—if there's a clear surgical solution—fixes it. When it comes to raising money, there is rarely a clear or linear solution. And there is no reliable map to guide you. You're constantly reinventing and redrawing the map that leads to the treasure. People and organizations sometimes approach me to ask, "How do we raise money?" as if there were a single, magical answer to this question.

Common sense and good manners are a big part of it. Without these basic tools, there is no possibility of sustainable success. And yet, surprisingly, these are often the first two qualities that seem to be lacking among various people I meet in the field. It's pretty straightforward: if people give you a grant, you say "thank you." You invite them to your events. You bring them into the fold. You encourage them to develop a sense of ownership in your organization in an ongoing, prolonged way, because getting a renewal is always easier than landing a commitment for the first time. You need to be extremely well organized and keep impeccable records, because some donors need only the smallest of excuses to drop their support. Sometimes if you miss a deadline by two days, you're done. It's over. There are a lot of good causes out there, a lot of dynamic individuals, and a lot of great institutions doing amazing work. So if you're going to cut through the clutter and make your way to the top of the pile, you need to be on your game. There is no room for error in fundraising.

The other thing that's needed to inspire donors is visionary thinking. Why is it that so many people and institutions seem to fear this the most? I suppose there is comfort in staying in a safe zone, but without visionary thinking, organizations end up falling into the trap of treading water and primarily working just to stay afloat. They raise money to keep their facilities clean, present basic programs, and pay salaries to their staff. The goal, in this case, is less to raise money than to minimize how much is spent. Visionary thinking is admittedly risky, but it also pays dividends. It's the best way for institutions to find the support they need to help them move beyond survival, so they can flourish and grow and bring their most dynamic and imaginative performances and exhibitions to the public. So I proclaim that the combination of good manners, trusting your intuition, and thinking outside the box—along with relentless planning and strategizing and discipline—are a recipe for success.

During my time at BAM, we pioneered systems that helped transform the more subjective elements of fundraising into clear business strategies. To achieve this, we came up with a large chart designed to project our full campaign plan and results. The projections bible, as we called it, featured a column for each source of funding: foundations, corporations, high-net-worth individuals, lower-level membership gifts, special events, and government agencies. Then, using this document and revising it as we moved forward with

Atys—the wigs alone were a masterpiece, 1989.

Opposite:
David Bowie and Philip
Glass at the fall gala,
1988.

Above:
Poster for the New
Music America series,
Next Wave Festival,
1989.

each solicitation, we meticulously tracked how much money we had raised from each type of donor, projecting the likelihood of renewals at somewhere between 75 and 90 percent, based on the strength of the relationship. We identified A-list prospects and projected them at anywhere between 30 to 50 percent likely to commit (see illustration on page 93), and took great pleasure in moving these prospects from "expected" status to "definite" when they pledged their support. This chart was the central map in our war room, and we revised it every couple of weeks, because the contours of the campaign were always shifting and changing. Someone you thought was a shoo-in suddenly said no, and—as soon as you crossed them off the list—somebody else arrived on the scene. We were constantly redrawing the lines of the map to reflect the reality, which was always fluctuating. But when all of the constituents were added together, and we began to have a sense of the projected and the expected revenue, the overall goal came into focus. We then placed this goal alongside the institutional budget to gauge how much harder we had to work to cover the existing programs, meet our expenses for the year, and generate new funding for ambitious initiatives. This was how we laid out and kept track of our progress. Creating accurate projections is the science behind the art of fundraising.

The trap that many organizations fall into is the routine of doing business as usual, one particular way, without regularly questioning their methods or outcomes. Just because a strategy worked once doesn't mean it will work again. Sometimes, the difference between failure and success is taking something old and replacing it with something new, or perhaps just repackaging it. That's where the creative work of the fundraiser comes into play.[1] The creative fundraiser is able to take a program and slice it twenty different ways for various prospects, appealing to their interests and values. Good fundraising is always done in layers, often repackaging the same programs in different ways and under different headings in order to raise the maximum amount possible. For example, at BAM, we raised money for the institution as a whole, then we raised it for each initiative, such as the Next Wave Festival or BAM Education. Then we raised funds for each show or for all international shows, or for just the opera house shows, or for commissioned works. Sometimes it was chronological, and we raised money for all events taking place in the month of March, for instance, and packaged them that way. Continuing down the food chain, we raised money for the opening night of each show, or for scenery, costumes, and whatever else was needed. Everything optimally would have a named sponsor, a person or family or company or foundation that would be attached and credited for each layer of the cake. Of course, we needed to raise money for general operating support, but generally it was more effective to

---

1   Here is an example of what I mean by *creative fundraising*. At one point, when planning an auction, I came up with the idea of asking Ron Feiner, BAM's lawyer, if one of his colleagues at his firm might donate a divorce. Ron's firm was unusual in that it included specialists in both entertainment and marital law. One of the divorce lawyers, Norman Sheresky, had handled celebrity cases and was well known in New York. I asked Ron if Norman would donate a divorce. I thought people would find it quirky and amusing and that, since it was a "unique" auction item, it would generate some press. What's more, I needed a divorce at the time, so I planned to bid on it, assuring that it would be "sold." Norman agreed, and I got a five-thousand-dollar divorce—one of the cheapest in history—from one of the most famous attorneys in New York.

FUNDRAISING PROJECTIONS CHART
Fiscal 2004 Fundraising Forecast
(numbers do not reflect actual fundraising and are meant to provide examples)

	Forecasted @12/15/03	Arrived		Definite		Expected		Prospect	
Private:									
Foundations	$ 4,419,603	$ 1,884,236	43%	$ 1,997,034	45%	$ 494,550	11%	$ 43,783	1%
Corporations	$ 2,028,899	$ 910,599	45%	$ 444,060	22%	$ 420,988	21%	$ 253,252	12%
Individuals	$ 3,101,340	$ 1,312,017	42%	$ 261,660	8%	$ 802,250	26%	$ 725,413	23%
Benefits	$ 856,503	$ 377,192	44%	$ 61,484	7%	$ 321,262	38%	$ 96,565	11%
In-Kind	$ 624,742	$ 83,825	13%	$ 195,917	31%	$ 72,610	12%	$ 272,390	44%
Underwriting	$ 455,000	$ 232,134	51%	$ 65,730	14%	$ 41,580	9%	$ 115,556	25%
BAMart	$ 313,517	$ 183,965	59%	$ 36,382	12%	$ 45,518	15%	$ 47,652	15%
Federal	$ 727,500	$ -	0%	$ 720,125	99%	$ -	0%	$ 7,375	1%
NEA	$ 57,500	$ -	0%	$ 55,000	96%	$ -	0%	$ 2,500	4%
NYSCA	$ 220,000	$ 205,100	93%	$ 5,000	2%	$ -	0%	$ 9,900	5%
State Line	$ 35,000	$ -	0%	$ -	0%	$ 26,252	75%	$ 8,748	25%
SUBTOTAL	$ 12,839,604	$ 5,189,068	40%	$ 3,842,392	30%	$ 2,225,010	17%	$ 1,583,134	12%
Public:									
DCA	$ 2,714,239	$ 1,281,922	47%	$ 1,418,317	52%	$ -	0%	$ 14,000	1%
PASNY	$ 441,209	$ -	0%	$ 441,209	100%	$ -	0%	$ -	0%
SUBTOTAL	$ 3,155,448	$ 1,281,922	41%	$ 1,859,526	59%	$ -	0%	$ 14,000	0%
GRAND TOTAL	$ 15,995,052	$ 6,470,990	40%	$ 5,701,918	36%	$ 2,225,010	14%	$ 1,597,134	10%

Historical Data (same period)

FY 2003	$ 16,440,791	$ 7,199,241	44%	$ 5,801,630	35%	$ 1,844,831	11%	$ 1,595,089	10%
FY 2002	$ 16,935,287	$ 7,614,331	45%	$ 5,888,169	35%	$ 1,887,762	11%	$ 1,545,025	9%
FY 2001	$ 15,427,603	$ 6,280,079	41%	$ 6,397,700	41%	$ 1,882,458	12%	$ 867,366	6%
FY 2000	$ 13,922,450	$ 5,165,361	37%	$ 6,137,594	44%	$ 1,743,407	13%	$ 876,088	6%

Above:
The projections "bible" is a crucial document that tracks the progress of a fundraising campaign, carefully delineating amounts raised or in process from each donor category.

Following spread:
An amazing array of cool artists and legends showed up for the New Music America gala! L–R: Allen Ginsberg, Moondog, Steve Reich, and Bob Weir with Felicity Seidel, 1989.

find ways of aligning donors to the specific aspect of our program or operations that most appealed to them. The art of fundraising lies in the fundraiser's ability to connect those with money and resources to the part of an organization's work that resonates for them at the deepest level. But even after you have done all of this, your work is far from over. Then comes the next piece, building long-term, enduring support. You must do everything you can to instill a sense of connection and pride in donors, so they will stay engaged and deepen their commitment and give again and again. Long term donor engagement is important. In fact, 80% of all contributions come from 20% of donors. Fundraising is a slog. As I often say, delayed gratification is the fundraiser's creed.

In this chapter I will describe a few of the greatest moments in fundraising from my time at BAM. My hope is that these stories will inspire readers to think more expansively and critically about both the art and the science of generating resources for the arts.

The first story is about a project called New Music America, which originated in 1979 at The Kitchen, an avant-garde venue in Chelsea, and soon grew into a nomadic festival showcasing the nation's most groundbreaking new composers and the work of pioneering composers and musicians, including artists like John Cage, Pauline Oliveros, Rhys Chatham, Laurie Anderson, and many other emerging talents. One of the goals of the festival, which brought it into near-perfect alignment with BAM, was to obliterate the boundaries between musical genres. For the festival's tenth anniversary, we decided to host New Music America's return to New York City, this time primarily based at BAM but also spread out to venues all over the city. We decided to present it as a citywide festival, housed within the Next Wave. Within that structure, we set out to present more than forty-five concerts in ten days in over twenty venues.

As we began developing our approach, we returned to fundamental questions. Was the scope of the project strong? Or by moving beyond the physical walls of BAM, were we

ALLEN GINSBERG   MOONDOG

STEVE REICH   BOB WEIR F. SEIDEL

95

spreading the institution too thin? Or was this perhaps an invaluable opportunity to grow the legend of BAM while creating a significant platform for new musical forms, allowing them to be heard by a much larger audience than ever before and expanding the borders of the musical landscape? Then we asked the most important question. How were we going to raise money for it?

As it turned out, my old friend, David Bither, who had worked with me during my earliest days at BAM, had gone on to Time Warner, and from there had become a senior executive at Elektra Records, which, at the time, was run by Bob Krasnow, one of the great men of rock and roll. Over his long career, Bob had worked with James Brown, Aretha Franklin, Ike and Tina Turner, the Pointer Sisters, Captain Beefheart, and many others, and had a formidable reputation as an innovator and an entrepreneur. I called David and said, "Dave, can you get Harvey, me, and Yale Evelev [who was leading the project for BAM] a meeting with Bob Krasnow? I have an idea for how we can create this thing together." And so David set up the meeting, which was no small feat. This was when the music business was still a business. At that time, making and selling records was a billion-dollar industry and Elektra Records was a big player in the world of great labels. At the meeting, I told Bob, "A lot of this music is not commercial. You could go as far as saying some of it is . . . well, strange. It's not rock and roll—in fact, it stands outside the landscape of mainstream music altogether. But we want to engage some of the biggest names in the music industry to help us produce this festival, because what we are trying to do is what great music producers do best—find new artists and bring their music to a wider audience." The idea, I told Bob, was to put together a recording industry council, which he would chair. Luckily, he completely got it and he agreed to take on this leadership role.

So when the Rock and Roll Hall of Fame came to New York that year, Bob—one of its cofounders—hosted a lunch for the head of every major music label, including competitors such as Warner, RCA, Sony, and others. These were the music titans of the day, and all of them were in attendance. We asked our friend, musician and performance artist Laurie Anderson, to perform at the lunch and, of course, she impressed everyone with one of her signature songs, "O Superman," and then she discussed the importance of the festival and of the new music scene in New York. Laurie had been associated with New Music America when she was first launching her career, so she was a perfect artist ambassador for the lunch. After Laurie wrapped up, Bob turned to the group and said, "Friends, I'm going to contribute twenty-five thousand dollars to this initiative. Is everyone in?" And sure enough, they were. Every record company made a pledge that very day. Some contributions were smaller and others larger, but everyone joined the club. That was phase one of the fundraising machine we built to support New Music America: the commitment of Bob Krasnow and Elektra Records, the power lunch, and the resulting buy-in across the entire record industry.

In phase two, we approached Tower Records, the biggest record store in New York at the time, and we asked them to do three things. The first was to dedicate window space to New Music America in the months leading up to the festival so that music audiences and record buyers could begin to visualize the ambitious scope of the project. We also asked them to publish a special New Music America edition of *Pulse!*, their monthly magazine, which featured the latest developments in the music industry. Finally, we asked them to produce a CD featuring new music with a specific track from each of the record companies that had come together to support the festival. Altogether, our approach to the New Music America fundraising had many layers. We had money coming in from the record companies, revenue generated from the CD sales, the in-kind donation of window space at Tower Records, and the special edition of *Pulse!*, through which we marketed and sold the CDs and promoted the festival. Of course, each of these layers generated multiple levels of further connection with the people who were donating.

Next, we approached Yamaha and said to them, "We want every artist in this festival to be playing on the most sophisticated equipment, with the best sound, right out of the box." And Yamaha signed on to provide free equipment and instruments to every venue in the festival, offering the most cutting-edge technology to support performances of the most cutting-edge music. With Yamaha in place as our equipment sponsor, we then set out to produce an opening night gala. With the help of the original members of the recording industry council, we sold tables to all of the major record companies and asked them to bring their artists and celebrity guests to the gala. So, in many ways, the fundraising not only amplified the programming, it enhanced it. Fundraising and programming for New Music America were inextricably tied together, working closely together every step of the way, and that's how we managed to rally the entire music community to back the idea and become part of it. As the final icing on the fundraising cake, Bob Krasnow joined the BAM board and served as a loyal donor and industry leader for many years to come.

This is what I meant when I stressed the importance of bold thinking in fundraising. It can't be overstated. At first blush, the idea of engaging some the world's top rock and roll producers to underwrite and support a sprawling, eclectic festival of avant-garde music seemed almost as challenging and as unlikely as BAM taking on the multivenue festival itself, but innovative programming demands forceful strategies. In the case of New Music America, everyone benefited. The record executives, who spent most of their time focused on how to turn out the next Top 40 hits, got to connect to something original and artistic in a way that was different for them, and this, in turn, enhanced their businesses by broadening their vision of new music around the world. We challenged these guys and said, "Look, we see that you're in both the culture and the entertainment business. You're at the cusp of what young people in America are connecting to each day. You generate a vibe that is all about innovation, but what are you actually doing to support it?" Instead of funding new initiatives or even arts-based businesses, the record industry mostly funded charity golf matches and called it "creative" because, of course, the money raised supported good causes. I have nothing against golf and I think this type of fundraising is fine, but real innovation requires smart, interested donors to step up, and all companies looking to define themselves as creative should want to associate themselves with projects that reflect excellence and originality.

In those early years of the Next Wave Festival, as BAM found its footing and started to take big strides, we discovered that many companies simply hadn't been asked to support the type of avant-garde performances that we championed on our stages. Many said no, but there were others who embraced it and were pleased to be invited to be a part of something daring, new, and different. And industry leaders like Bob Krasnow and some of the other executives we engaged, who made serious money in their forties and fifties,

Above:
Bob Krasnow, chair of the New Music America Recording Industry Council, 1989.

became prospects for our board. These individuals provided the kind of direct philanthropy that really moved the needle for BAM. The New Music America Festival was the first citywide partnership project we ever mounted paired with an expansive fundraising campaign that had lasting impact.

As a fundraiser, the hardest thing to do is to get someone with money and power to focus on your organization, especially when they have ninety thousand other things to deal with on any given day. But through personal connections and sheer determination, we got Bob Krasnow to focus on us, and that was the key to everything. Lesson: This is where the art of development resides, in envisioning the match and then making it. You must know your prospects as intimately as you know your projects, through research and attention to detail. Then, you can approach that donor and say, "You know, I could bring you seven hundred projects, but I'm not. I'm bringing you this one project, and here's why. It involves these artists, these topics, this history." And everything you mention in your approach, if it's to be a successful one, will tie directly to the interests, passions, and concerns of the donor, making the case that there simply could not be a better fit. By demonstrating that level of knowledge about the donors' interest, you are also showing them respect, and you end up raising the most money not by persuading some people to do something they don't want to do, but by persuading him or her to do something they may not yet know they want

to do. When you can demonstrate this depth of connection to the things that the donor cares about most, he becomes invested in the success of your project or organization. When it is really working, it's fun for all of the participants and everyone feels bonded by the work and invested in the outcome.

Another great fundraising story, which exemplifies many of the principles I described above, revolves around a single donor who ended up giving millions to the institution and cemented his own legacy through his contributions to the arts and to BAM. His name was Ronald B. Stanton, and I found him the way I discovered most prospects, by obsessively reading many different papers, reports, and documents related to finding money for BAM projects. For my entire career, the secret behind my approach was always reading. No matter how hard a day I might have had at the office, I tried to end each night reading everything I could get my hands on that revealed who was making money, who was losing money, who was connected, and who wasn't. I would come home, sometimes close to midnight, and, over a glass of Diet Peach Tea Snapple, pore over the same papers and magazines with which I started the day—the *New York Times*, the *Wall Street Journal*, *Forbes*, *Variety*, the *Chronicle of Philanthropy*, and others—searching for ideas.

This time, it was a story in the *Chronicle* about high-net-worth individuals who were under the radar that caught my eye. The piece profiled people and companies that made significant donations but whose names did not adorn a lot of buildings. One of the companies, Transammonia, a global firm that marketed, traded, and transported fertilizer and petroleum products, turned out to be the most successful privately owned company in New York at the time. As I scanned the story, what really jumped out and grabbed me was the name of the company's founder, Ronald B. Stanton. His name was familiar to me from the daily contribution lists of donors, which I read religiously. He had given three hundred dollars to BAM, and he was receiving patron tickets to an upcoming show. In the *Chronicle*, to my amazement, this same Ronald B. Stanton was recognized as a serious art collector who had given a hundred million dollars to Yeshiva University, the largest single gift at the time ever given in support of Jewish education in the United States.

I wrote Mr. Stanton a personal note, inviting him to a dance performance and preshow supper, and—miraculously—he came. At first I thought he wasn't going to show up at all, but he arrived late and, naturally, I made sure he was seated next to me. We started talking and I found him fascinating, a totally self-made man in every way. At dinner, he told me that in the 1980s, he had spent some time in Paris with his first wife, and a concierge who liked opera and baroque music had recommended an opera performance near his hotel. Fate intervened and he went to the wrong theater, and it was there, at the Opéra-Comique that Ron Stanton saw a production that changed his life. According to him, it was the most transformational, meaningful piece of music he'd ever heard. As he recounted the story of how he had stumbled upon this incredible performance and how much it moved him, it dawned on me that he was describing William Christie's production of *Atys*, the opera Harvey had seen in Versailles and had then brought to Brooklyn to launch the BAM opera program. Of course Ron loved it, the way Harvey loved it, passionately. The music, the setting, and the theatricality of the piece were all sensational. *Atys* was a masterpiece. I started to see how we might able to connect Ron with the very thing he valued and loved the most.

After that first evening, I invited him to lunch, where I learned more of his life story.[2] He was raised by a single mother in Germany. As Hitler rose to power, she fled with Ron to New York in 1937. His paternal grandparents remained in Wiesbaden and committed suicide along with a group of other Jews in order to avoid being sent to the concentration camps. As a young man, Ron served in the US Army and then landed a job at the International Ore and Fertilizer Corporation. He quickly ascended to become executive vice president for its fertilizer trading division, and then left to start his own fertilizer and petrochemical business, Transammonia, which made him a fortune. After divorcing his first wife, with whom he had a son, he married a woman he met in China named Mei Wu, and they had two children. Over his life, he had amassed an astonishing art collection, including works by Picasso, Renoir, and Matisse. Though he wasn't religious, he supported Yeshiva University because he cared about Jewish survival. Above all, he marched to the beat of his own drum. Ron liked what we were doing. He wasn't into the avant-garde, super-experimental stuff, but he believed in what we were trying to accomplish, and, at the end of our first lunch, he gave a substantial sum to BAM.

During that unforgettable meeting, Ron told me that he wanted to write a memoir so that his children and grandchildren would know his story. My friend Tina Silverman—the same one who had volunteered with me to go to Israel in 1973, and ended up staying for over twenty years—is an artist and writer who had recently returned to the United States

2   My idea of inviting donors to lunch was first, securing the meeting date; second, going to lunch wherever they wanted to go—restaurant choices are, for some reason, a big deal for many people; and third, raising money and getting the donor (whenever possible) to also pay for lunch.

and was looking for a job.[3] So I introduced Tina to Ron and they hit it off right away, and he hired her to ghostwrite his memoir. Tina quickly waded deep into Ron's life and over dinner a few weeks later she said to me, "You know, Ron keeps talking about that production of *Atys* he saw in Paris during the eighties. He speaks about it all the time. It's a shame it's not in repertory anymore, because he'd give anything to see it again." At this moment, a light turned on simultaneously in our heads, and we suddenly saw how we could match the prospect with the project, an electrifying connection that seemed almost too perfect to be possible. Could we bring *Atys* back to life after twenty years?

The next day, I dropped by executive producer Joe Melillo's office and said, "Tina and I have been talking, and we think there's a possibility that if we ask Ron Stanton, he might underwrite a revival of *Atys*. Why don't you check in with Bill Christie and see if he wants to do it again?" Joe immediately called Christie. Christie went wild. And then I called Ron Stanton and said, "Ron, we have an opportunity. A moment. You love *Atys*. We love *Atys*. We've been talking with Bill Christie, and he mentioned that he'd really love to do it again. And I think it would be just unbelievable. But it's all gone now. Nothing exists from the original production that you saw in Paris. They'd have to remake the whole thing. And so it would cost about, I don't know, around, say, three million dollars. Would you be interested?" And he said, "Yeah, I'd be interested." And I said, "Well, it's a lot of money, and it's just one production. But once it gets up and made, we can tour it to a few different places and get it back out into the world." Then, after a brief pause, I asked, "Do you want me to find other money for it or do you want to just do the whole thing yourself?" He took a second and then replied, "What do you think I should do?" I laughed and said, "What do you mean? You can't ask me that. I'm a fundraiser, so I'm going to say, 'Of course, do the whole thing yourself.' Why? Because you can afford it. We'll have a great time. And we can start right away. We won't have to wait two more years while I go running around trying to find the rest of the money. It will be, in essence, your gift to the world." Without hesitating, Ron said, "I'll do it." I ran straight to Joe and said, "He's going to pay for the whole thing." I was stunned and thrilled, a true miracle! And that was how, with one phone call and Tina's help, we brought William Christie's *Atys* back into existence.

The new production of *Atys* premiered in Versailles, underwritten by Ron Stanton, where it had originally been performed in 1682 and where Harvey had seen it when it was revived and performed both there and in Paris for the first time in 1986 before making its way to BAM in 1989. As part of the Stanton-funded second revival in 2011, we took a group of donors to Paris to see it, and Ron hosted a dinner for them. Then, like in the eighties, it was seen in Paris at the Opéra-Comique, and also in Basse-Normandie, the second home for William Christie's company, Les Arts Florissants. Finally, it came to BAM, where it made giant waves once again. Ron was so proud of what we had accomplished that he came to every performance, and his contribution was not lost on Les Arts Florissants.

---

3   Tina Silverman, Carla Perlo, and I had become lifelong friends in 1969 when we all served as counselors at Buffalo Gap Camp in Capon Bridge, West Virginia. Tina was the art counselor, I taught theater, of course, and Carla was running dance and synchronized swimming (yessiree, synchronized swimming). As it turned out, both Tina and Carla would be part of my personal and professional life forever.

The entire company had fallen in love with him, and so they took it upon themselves to convince the government of France to bequeath a Chevalier de L'Ordre des Arts et des Lettres award upon Ron, which he wore on the left lapel of his suit from that day forward. He couldn't have been more touched by the gesture.

The beauty of fundraising for the arts is that sometimes life and theater just come together like a hand in a glove. At the end of the first performance at the magnificent, old, wooden theater in Versailles, where in the seventeenth century, Louis XIV had seen this opera, as the cast took their bows, Maestro Christie stepped forward and stretched his arm out toward Ronald Stanton. Then the entire audience turned and applauded Ron for giving this gift of beautiful music to all of us. Of all the things Ron funded, and some of them were for a lot more money, I think the revival of *Atys* was the most gratifying for him. It was one of his greatest moments as a philanthropist. It was the perfect project for the perfect donor.

In fact, the *New York Times* ran a story about Ron Stanton's support, in which Joe Melillo summed up the impact of Ron's gift perfectly: "In our lives, on a daily basis, we rarely have the occasion to confront pure beauty. Here in the world of opera, of music drama, it is simply rare that you encounter consummate beauty. And that is the extraordinary truth, the authenticity, about 'Atys.' If you live in the world of aesthetics, that's what it is. The music, the singing, the décor. It all comes together in this extraordinary story about love, and you have a catharsis. You have this transformative moment. And, thank God, Ronald Stanton had it."

The best moments in fundraising, sadly, are always counterbalanced by terrible ones. It's part of the job, but sometimes I just wish I would have thought things through more carefully. One of the worst mistakes I ever made, one that really caused me to suffer, took place at the BAM opera house during the Dr. John gala in 2012. This was only a few years after the subprime mortgage bubble burst, and we found ourselves in the throes of a major recession. People had lost their homes. The banks had to be bailed out by the federal government, and consequently there was lot of distrust in corporations and financial institutions, which seemed to have skirted much of the responsibility for the crisis that they had played a large role in creating.

Programmatically, BAM was engaged in the 150th anniversary season and we had decided to launch a popular music program, which turned out to be a three-part retrospective of the music of the beloved New Orleans pianist and songwriter Dr. John.[4] As part of the series, we organized a gala around one of Dr. John's performances, which would

Above:
With my pals Carla Perlo and Tina Silverman and another kibbutz friend, Linda "Davie" Van Noojen, at Matt's bar mitzvah in 1993. It should be noted that Davie, on an earlier visit, attended a show at BAM with me featuring gospel legend Shirley Caesar. At one point during the performance, Shirley summoned all who were suffering physical ailments to the stage for "healing and laying on of hands." Davie had a shoulder injury from a swimming accident. She made her way to the stage with many others to be blessed and miraculously she was healed. It was fantastic. I saw it with my own eyes.

4   I had actually met Mac Rebennack, a.k.a. Dr. John (may he rest in peace), years earlier when he had performed as part of a summer concert series we hosted annually outside at the MetroTech office complex in Brooklyn. When I was introduced to him, Danny Kapilian, the series curator, said, "Dr. John, please meet Karen Brooks Hopkins, the president of BAM." The Doctor looked at me and said, "So you da president?" I replied, "Yes, I am," and he said in his New Orleans drawl, "Well, hello, darlin'!" and gave me a hug.

be followed by a Bourbon Street–style after party, where the revelry would continue late into the night. The decision was met with great enthusiasm, by our biggest supporters and by the large number of loyal Dr. John fans in the New York City area. In spite of the less than favorable fundraising climate, we had high hopes for the gala that year.

Given the recession and the pervasive rage against and resentment of Wall Street, I really should have given more thought to how best to acknowledge the corporate sponsor of both the 150th anniversary season and the gala, JPMorgan Chase. The tactful thing to have done would have been to thank the donor at the dinner, prior to the performance, in front of JPMorgan Chase's guests, our board, and their guests and friends. Instead, I chose to do it on the stage at the beginning of Dr. John's concert. There were 2,100 seats in that opera house and close to six hundred were filled by our gala guests. This meant that the other fourteen hundred people who showed up that April night were fans of Dr. John's music, but not necessarily lovers of BAM and likely not the biggest fans of JPMorgan Chase at that moment. So when I came out to acknowledge

the bank from the stage for sponsoring the gala, I was booed off the stage by a vocal group of Dr. John fans, shouting their dissatisfaction with corporate America and expressing their impatience, from the rafters, for the show to begin. I asked for the crowd to bear with me and to show some respect for our supporters, but the anger at banks was palpable, and as far as many of the Dr. John fans were concerned, BAM was guilty by association. Also, they clearly hadn't come out that night expecting to sit through a series of introductions and speeches thanking our sponsors. They had come, with all of the unbridled energy of the French Quarter, to hear Dr. John perform. They had paid for their tickets, and we were making them wait, and so when I walked out on the stage, smiled, and mentioned JPMorgan Chase, I was met with jeers, whistles, and boos—in my own theater.

This was a very low moment for me, perhaps the lowest of my career. I walked off the stage shaking and thinking that all I wanted at that moment was to go lie down. I wasn't used to being booed off the stage at BAM. I was used to feeling love from our audiences whenever I stepped out to make an introduction. Also, people weren't just booing, they were screaming, "Play the music! We don't wanna hear about banks!" I had badly misjudged what was needed that night. Since the event was open to the public, I should have been thinking beyond BAM and our wealthy patrons, about the issues affecting our audiences, but it was our 150th anniversary, and I was focused on making our supporters feel loved and appreciated and part of the BAM adventure. My oversight cost us a lot, not only relationships with both our valued audience members and supporters, but it also definitely had a negative impact on our long-standing relationship with JPMorgan Chase. Their executives were deeply offended. Who needs to be giving money only to be booed? People give money because they are looking for some kind of positive return. This is especially true when it comes to corporations, which give to organizations like BAM as an expression of corporate citizenship and a desire to be seen as a positive force for culture and communities. So getting booed at a major gala performance is naturally a showstopper for a bank, something that could have been avoided if I had simply thanked them at the dinner and after party, not in front of fourteen hundred Dr. John fans during the recession.

The mistake hurt all the more because I had encountered a similar situation, years before, with the cigarette company Philip Morris, the first big corporation to sponsor us. Philip Morris's support made BAM successful, as they were instrumental in supporting the Next Wave Festival from its inception. But, of course, smoking was extremely controversial, and I got hate mail about it. Executives from Philip Morris had been booed off the stage at a gala once, too. But since close to thirty years had passed between the Philip Morris and JPMorgan Chase experiences, I had forgotten what I already knew and had to learn the lesson again.

It took years for me to refine my ethical position on fundraising from companies that some people found objectionable. When this issue came up, I gave the following answer. If there is money available for a philanthropic purpose, then I want it to come to BAM. When it comes to the corporate world, whose hands are totally clean? Can we really make such distinctions? Also, let's take a look at the foundations. Where and how did the great tycoons, such as Andrew Mellon or Henry Ford, make their money? Were they free of controversy in their careers? Not for a minute. How were the great fortunes that support most American philanthropy accrued? This is how I look at the issue, after being criticized for soliciting support from corporations like Philip Morris. I wanted to use their contributions to make the world a better place, which for me was centered on the success of BAM. Since my departure from BAM, I have reflected on the ethics of fundraising, and now that I have stepped away, I can see more clearly the disdain some people have for the profession, especially as income inequality has accelerated wildly over the last twenty years. Others may have made a different decision, but during my career, I was in the heat of battle and, bottom line, I simply had to get the job done. These people were loyal and generous donors. I was and remain grateful for their support. However, as time has passed, some of these decisions weigh heavily on my shoulders.

CHAPTER SIX:

Expanding the Walls of BAM

n 1995, I served as executive producer of a sprawling citywide project designed to showcase and celebrate the multifaceted, multidecade career of the artist and international icon Ingmar Bergman. Since the prolific Bergman was not only an Academy Award–winning filmmaker but also a legendary theater and opera director and author, we believed that his vast output warranted a special New York event. Harvey had cultivated a relationship with the auteur, traveling regularly to visit both Stockholm and the tiny island Bergman lived on in Sweden, and we had presented many of his theatrical works with the Royal Dramatic Theatre of Sweden at BAM, including his unforgettable productions of *Hamlet* in 1988; August Strindberg's *Miss Julie*, Eugene O'Neill's *Long Day's Journey Into Night*, and Henrik Ibsen's *A Doll's House* in 1991; and Ibsen's *Peer Gynt* and Yukio Mishima's *Madame de Sade* in 1993. Over our nearly fifteen-year collaboration with Bergman, BAM exclusively presented all of his US stage premieres. Although he rarely traveled and never visited Brooklyn, Bergman trusted us and considered BAM his artistic home in America. Harvey worshipped the great director and considered him one of the most important artists in the BAM universe, not to mention the world.

The idea to mount an ambitious, comprehensive Bergman festival originated with Mary Reilly, BAM's company manager and director of artist services. She floated the idea to Harvey, but Harvey wasn't interested, since he was only focused on bringing the theatrical works to BAM. When she and I discussed it, however, I was extremely interested and decided to develop the idea into something BAM had rarely done, a 360-degree, citywide festival that would expand BAM's reach and recognition well beyond its walls while also expanding visibility for the sheer range of Bergman's abilities and accomplishments. Looking back on it now, the Bergman festival is one of my proudest achievements, a shining moment for the institution and for a master artist whose work deserved to be seen and experienced on the greatest scale in New York City.

One of the things that I learned from the Bergman festival is that when you have an idea that really can't be contained by a single institution, it presents a unique opportunity for building a coalition, not just of producing partners, but also of funders. When you join arms with other institutions, you exponentially increase your capacity to raise money. Large-scale collaborations between cultural institutions of all sizes and disciplines make a very compelling argument to donors, who know they will be getting more bang for their buck than when they invest in just a single organization. In the end, we convinced seven major institutions to join us, including the New York Public Library; the Museum of the Moving Image in Queens; the local PBS affiliate WNET (which broadcast a twenty-four-hour Bergman marathon); and the Film Society of Lincoln Center (which screened all of Bergman's films). The Museum of the Moving Image hosted an entire weekend with Sven Nykvist, Bergman's cinematographer. The New York Public Library at Lincoln Center displayed opera scripts with Bergman's annotations and direction. BAM presented Bergman's productions of Shakespeare's *The Winter's Tale* and Mishima's *Madame de Sade*

Peter Stormare and Lena Olin in the Royal Dramatic Theatre of Sweden/Ingmar Bergman production of *Miss Julie*, spring 1991.

with the Royal Dramatic Theatre of Sweden. In addition, BAM published a book, *Ingmar Bergman: An Artist's Journey on Stage, on Screen, in Print*. Collectively, we produced more than 350 events between May and September, including screenings, performances, lectures, exhibitions, and discussions with leading scholars, artists, filmmakers, and critics from Sweden and the United States.

Given the size and ambition of the festival, we pulled out all the stops in our fundraising efforts, leveraging our partners and Bergman's legendary stature to attract new donors to the mix and raise money on a massive scale. We approached just about every Swedish company we could identify, working with the Swedish consulate to gain access to them all, and—to our great delight—pretty much all of them got involved: Skanska (a large construction company); Skandia (a financial services company); a variety of Swedish banks; Visit Stockholm; Volvo; you name it. We focused on identifying every Swedish prospect in existence and enlisted their support for the festival, and through these efforts we were able to cobble together both program support and a very sizable marketing budget for all of the events. In the process, we also managed to raise money for BAM, underwriting portions of related operating costs and staff.

A big breakthrough in our fundraising efforts came when the Swedish vodka maker Vin & Sprit offered to make a substantial donation if the festival could be called Absolut Bergman, named after its most famous product. Our sources in Stockholm told us that Bergman was "pleased" with the idea of the festival. But they also made it clear that he would not attend. As the program and fundraising efforts started coming together, I flew to Stockholm to meet the great director in the flesh. Upon arriving in Sweden, along with our funders and partners, we announced the festival with a big press conference. As expected, Mr. Bergman was not there. In conjunction with our festival, it was also announced at the press conference that, in preparation for the screenings in America, the Swedish Film Institute had restored every Bergman film that hadn't yet been restored, and this amplified and built buzz around everything we were doing in New York.

After the press conference, I made the pilgrimage to visit Mr. Bergman, who was about eighty years old at the time. In spite of his age, he still maintained his rugged, handsome looks and the magnetism that had made him a legend. After spending only a few minutes with him, I could easily see how charismatic and charming he was (FYI, the man had five wives!). Being in the master's presence was intimidating, to say the least, and I think he sensed my nervousness. Nevertheless, he seemed excited about the festival and the events we were planning. After a somewhat strained but invigorating fifteen-minute conversation, I decided it was time to pop the fundraising question. "So, Mr. Bergman . . . as you know, a program of this size and importance requires a lot of support and we are so lucky that Absolut has stepped in and offered to underwrite the entire festival with the title Absolut Bergman. We are thrilled, of course. What do you think?" Bergman looked at me for what seemed like an eternity. Then, with a twinkle in his eye and just a hint of a smile, he dryly said, "Absolutely not."

Chastened but undaunted, I returned to New York straightaway and went back to the drawing board to figure out how to get the money we needed from Vin & Sprit and a variety of other companies. Eventually, we reached a compromise: it would be called the Ingmar Bergman Festival, Sponsored by Absolut. Yes, it was a less interesting title

Opposite, from top:
Börje Ahlstedt, Peter Stormare, and Gunnel Lindblom in Bergman's *Hamlet*, spring 1988.

The Bergman festival book: *Ingmar Bergman: An Artist's Journey*, 1995.

Ingmar Bergman and Björn Granath in Bergman's *A Doll's House*, spring 1991.

Following spread:
Scene from Bergman's *Hamlet*, spring 1988.

Pages 112–113:
Stina Ekblad and Anita Björk in Bergman's *Madame de Sade*, spring 1993.

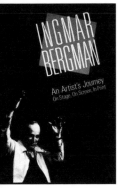

and they gave us less money, but we made up the difference by cultivating the full range of major Swedish banks and deepening Volvo's commitment. That's what fundraising is about: going for broke and then, after being rejected—time and time again—recovering quickly and moving forward on multiple fronts.

Bergman was uncompromising and exacting with regard to his vision and artistic integrity. In addition to putting his foot down about the sponsorship proposal, he was the only director who refused to let us switch from simultaneous audio translation to surtitles. He was not going to have people looking up and taking their eyes off the stage. And since he was Ingmar Bergman, you did not argue. Like Peter Brook, Bergman was a guru, and if you wanted to work with him, you had to do things his way.[5] This was both exciting and at times confounding, especially when it came to garnering financial support for his work. Just as we had done for Brook's *Mahabharata*, we set out to build a community of engaged and motivated funders to support both the festival and the productions at BAM. Our goal was to cultivate not just an audience, but a community of stakeholders who felt connected to the work and invested in its success. This had become the hallmark of our fundraising strategy, creating a bond between funders and artists that permitted us to raise more than anyone could have ever predicted. Years later, as a result of my efforts in support of the Bergman festival, I was awarded both the Dramaten Award—rarely, if ever, given to a non-Swede by the Royal Dramatic Theatre—and, from the nation of Sweden, the prestigious Commander of the Royal Order of the Polar Star.

Two years before the Bergman festival, we mounted a massive gala tied to Bergman's production of *Peer Gynt*, attended by King Gustaf and Queen Silvia of Sweden. The play, which lasted well over three hours, was far too long to be appropriate for a gala. To this day, I still don't know what we were thinking. But when it came to Bergman at BAM, logic didn't always prevail, like when we brought his theatrical work over for the first time in 1988. A Swedish bank called Swedbank had approached us with the money to bring Bergman's *Hamlet* to BAM. The bank was celebrating a special anniversary and, as a symbol of national pride, they decided to pay for a tour of the production. This was great except for that fact that the production was in Swedish (with no subtitles or simultaneous translation) and ran more than four hours; no one in New York wanted to take it on. It made no sense. Without hesitating, of course, Harvey said, "Yes, we'll do it. And we'll do it in the BAM opera house." I said, "Harvey, this time you've really lost your mind if you actually think people are going to come watch this play for four hours in Swedish with no subtitles." To which Harvey replied, "Don't worry. It's *Hamlet*. The audience knows the play." That was his response. And, his instincts were correct. We packed them in and sold the production out, standing room only. It was brilliant. Hamlet, who was played by Peter Stormare, wore dark shades and a long black leather coat. Ophelia was played by Pernilla August (who went on to play Shmi Skywalker in *Star Wars*), carried a

5   When Harvey told Mr. Bergman that we might not have enough money to present *Madame de Sade* again, in addition to the other shows on the bill, Bergman turned to Harvey and said, "I am sorry you can't go ahead with *Madame de Sade*, Harvey, because of all my shows, *Madame de Sade* is . . . well . . . perfect." You can guess what happened next. We certainly included *de Sade* that season as part of the festival. And, naturally, Bergman was right. It was perfect.

bouquet of nails instead of flowers in the famous "Good night, sweet ladies" scene. That first production came to pass because of Harvey's unflappable courage. He always bet on the artist. It also came to BAM because of Harvey's belief that people would step outside their comfort zone for something great. Over the years, I have observed that a thin line separates courage from irrational optimism, and Harvey always walked it. The Bergman productions at BAM and the Bergman festival were the stuff of legends, some of our crowning achievements as an institution. Years later, a group of BAM executives went to see a show on Broadway, a comedy, and one of the lines was a joke about BAM. "There's a production of *Macbeth* in Urdu in Brooklyn. Want to go?" We laughed—Urdu, Swedish, Georgian, or Japanese, we had them all. It was funny because it was true. And . . . it was also true that our young, adventurous audience stuck with us no matter what language was spoken onstage. Seriously, half the time our productions were confusing, even when they were in English! For our American audience, putting up with a Norwegian play, such as Ibsen's *A Doll's House*, performed in German by an all-male company from Berlin, was all part of the BAM experience.

Another of the more complicated projects that I initiated at BAM was a sprawling citywide festival involving one hundred artists and six venues over a ten-day period in 2009. It was called Muslim Voices: Arts & Ideas, and it seemed like a good idea, at least at the time. In the years following 9/11 and the US invasions of Afghanistan and Iraq, Americans had grown accustomed to intense airport security procedures, ongoing terrorist incidents, and a heightened war of words on the Internet and in the media, fueling a complete lack of understanding about the Muslim world and its relationship to the West— all of which threatened to destabilize much of our increasingly interconnected world.

While all of this was playing out, I received an invitation to attend a conference in Kuala Lumpur entitled "Who Speaks for Islam, Who Speaks for the West?" The invitation came from a gentleman named Mustapha Tlili, who ran an institute at New York University focused on this topic. I was already scheduled to be traveling in Europe a few days before the conference. Since my trip would be paid for, and I was curious about the intersection of these worlds, I decided to go, maybe learn something, and, at the very least, meet some remarkable people. I wanted to understand the issues that divided and united the West and the Muslim world and wondered if there might be a way, through the arts, to engage diverse audiences in crucial conversations that would increase understanding and compassion between fractured communities.

I arrived in Kuala Lumpur during the "cartoon crisis," when the Danish newspaper *Jyllands-Posten* published a number of political cartoons depicting Muhammad—an act that is forbidden in the Muslim world—and as a result, violent protests ensued. Hundreds of thousands of Muslims protested, and over two hundred people died, according to some tallies. Relations with the Muslim world deteriorated even further, and global hysteria began to take hold. As I took my seat at the conference, I could sense the fear that pervaded the room, the feeling of suspicion and uneasiness that underscored each interaction. The conference was global in scope, with over forty attendees from all over the world, ranging from neoconservatives to Muslim clerics to funders who wanted to facilitate dialogue.

Opposite:
The Muslim Voices festival. Even with fewer dervishes than originally called for (we couldn't get visas for them), the Sufis made a great impression, 2009.

I had been invited as a "cultural representative," since the goal of the meeting was to discuss the topic from many points of view.

As the two-day event unfolded and people came together to share their sometimes very divergent perspectives, the tensions in the room, rather than dissipating, only continued to mount. On the last night, a group of us, including Mustapha; Stephen Heinz, the president of the Rockefeller Brothers Fund, who was underwriting the conference; and I went out to dinner. Over several courses, we discussed how desperate we all felt about the growing divide, the cartoon flare up, and the seemingly unresolvable conflict in which the West and the Muslim world were now locked. As we talked, I proposed that BAM host a festival in New York, with many different institutions participating, along with a conference focused on culture, hoping that the arts might offer a different approach to understanding the conflict. We knew, of course, that a festival would not save the world, but it could be a transformative event, at which artists and audiences from both sides of the issues could learn and collaborate.

After attending many of the sessions in Kuala Lumpur, it seemed clear to me that one of the main reasons for the deep divide stemmed from differing perceptions of time. As the Muslim presenters spoke, I realized (from my Western perspective) that they were concerned and upset about historic events that had taken place hundreds, if not thousands, of years ago, while we in the West are completely locked into the present moment, with way less regard for the past. They inhabited a living history, with an ever-present consciousness of the past, while history for us was as old as the latest news cycle. This temporal dissonance between cultures stood at the heart of the crisis, and it seemed that perhaps the arts could provide a powerful, nonthreatening space in which to explore this divide and break down barriers.

Given the gravity of the issues before us, I felt confident that donors of all stripes would be eager to fund the Muslim Voices festival at the highest level. This was yet another mistake on my part. Upon returning from my trip, I met with Joe Melillo to discuss the project, and we agreed that BAM would serve as executive producer. Together we would invite a wide range of cultural organizations to participate, and I would attempt to establish a basic fundraising plan to launch the festival. Once that was achieved, the group would attempt to raise money together and if we were unable to find all of the necessary resources, each of the organizations would be responsible for covering their own costs. This was my next big miscalculation. The partners all had good intentions but, for the most part, BAM ended up holding the fundraising bag. However, despite the difficulties, the programming developed and an exceptional festival began to take shape.

The Metropolitan Museum of Art and the Brooklyn Museum, led by Arnold Lehman, curated and showcased wonderful pieces from their Islamic collections. The Asia Society planned an ambitious and exciting exhibit of Pakistani paintings, which was abandoned due to lack of funding and replaced with a video show. They also presented a terrific series of music events and talks. BAM co-presented an IMAX film at the American Museum of Natural History called *Journey to Mecca*, a dramatized documentary film about the first journey of the Islamic scholar Ibn Battuta to Mecca in 1325. The New York Public Library hosted several dynamic events including a conversation with Queen Noor of Jordan, led by LIVE from the NYPL host Paul Holdengräber. We added a range of European "consulate" type organizations to our consortium of partners, and one of them, the Austrian Cultural

Forum New York, organized a noteworthy exhibition called Behind the Veil.[6] Mustapha pulled together an impressive conference with participants who were experts in their fields. In Brooklyn, the Museum of Contemporary African Diasporan Art (MoCADA) and BAM hosted memorable events as well. The BAM shows ranged from a film and concert presentation featuring the great Senegalese Muslim singer Youssou N'Dour to a concert at which the New Orleans soul and gospel singer Craig Adams performed alongside Pakistani master qawwali singer Faiz Ali Faiz. The audience was on their feet every night. Finally, to deepen engagement, we also established consulate committees, community committees, and school and family programs, which added tremendous local gravitas.

The Muslim Voices festival was a tour de force in terms of programming and innovation, and yet everything about it was plagued with problems from the beginning. Despite grants from the Rockefeller Brothers Fund and the Doris Duke, Ford, Robert Sterling Clark, and Rockefeller Foundations, we simply didn't generate enough money, and the partners fought bitterly about every grant. In addition, the security restrictions at the time made the visas nearly impossible to obtain for many of these artists. In one case, the Moroccan Sufi show at BAM, ended up being short about three whirling dervishes. There was also a fair amount of disagreement among the festival's leaders. Zeyba Rahman, a very talented woman whom we had hired as chief curator of Muslim Voices, and Mustapha were constantly at odds with each other. And finally, the content of every piece had to be reviewed thoroughly to avoid political insensitivities, which turned out to be an extremely delicate and complex process.

To make matters worse, the myopic government officials in New York from each of the Muslim countries that participated in the festival were totally unhelpful because, while we were concentrated on showcasing work from a wide range of Muslim countries, they were solely focused on their own nation. Our goal in programming the festival was to try to acknowledge the global struggle and the tensions between the Muslim world and the West while not offending anyone, and it proved to be a delicate task, one that required heightened vigilance at all times. At one point, I forced David Harper, BAM's visual arts curator, who was helping the Austrians with their exhibit, to "recurate" several pieces in the show that Joe and I felt were a little politically heavy-handed. Overall, press coverage was good, but not extensive enough, given the scope of the event. Perhaps the most disappointing setback was that we didn't have enough money for the full-blown marketing initiative we had initially planned.

In the end, though, everything was very well attended. The Asia Society created a dedicated website that allowed people all over the world to take part in the events, and our funders were pleased that we pulled it off. But since everything, and I mean *everything*, about the project was fraught, I really had to question myself for taking it on. Yes, it was important. It was worthy. It was certainly ambitious, and for sure, it was one of those huge programs that enhanced BAM's reputation on the global stage. Looking back on it now, I must admit that it was crazy to undertake such a project. As BAM has proven time and again, sometimes that's what it takes to bring new approaches and ideas into the world.

Following spread: Faiz Ali Faiz and his ensemble performing with Craig Adams and the Voices of New Orleans during Muslim Voices: Qawwali Gospel Creation, spring 2009.

6   This consulate group was referred to with an unfortunate acronym, EUNIC (European Union National Institutes for Culture), but who am I to criticize their branding?

n the early eighties, one of our board members, Sidney Kantor, and his Chinese-born wife, Mary, persuaded Harvey to consider bringing what was then known as the Central Ballet of China to BAM. The Kantors visited China often, which in those days was rare for Americans, and Mary had powerful family connections in Beijing. The discussions went on for a few years until it was determined that I, along with Harvey, our then executive vice president Judith Daykin, and former board chair Paul Lepercq would join the Kantors on a trip to Beijing to meet Chinese officials and select the repertory that would be performed at BAM.[7]

We arrived in China and stayed in the legendary Peking Hotel, which at the time featured furniture that predated the revolution. A "tea boy" would sit on every floor of the hotel and could be summoned at any time of the day or night to pour hot water for tea. As I recall, this was the only amenity the hotel had to offer, and it pained me to see boys working all night serving tea to guests. We visited the Central Ballet of China in a dilapidated, aging theater in which the audience would wash fruit (which was the show snack of choice for theatergoers) in the lobby in large sinks. Most of the Chinese population at the time wore blue Mao suits, as fashion and Western pop culture were virtually nonexistent. The dancers were graceful and technically excellent, but there was no homegrown Chinese choreography to be found. Most of the repertoire was borrowed from the Russians, and so we had to work hard to find pieces that would interest American audiences curious about Chinese culture. As a gift to the company, we had brought boxes of gaffer's tape for them to use onstage to mark each of their set pieces. This type of tape was unavailable in Beijing at the time, and the company members greatly appreciated the gift.

As our trip unfolded, we met many wonderful people who hosted banquets in honor of our visit. Our Chinese hosts also arranged for us to visit the Great Wall and the Ming Tombs. It was a totally foreign world to me, one in which the language barrier was complete. No one, and I mean no one, spoke a word of English (except for the company liaison) and I had zero Chinese vocabulary. At one point, I somehow got lost at the Ming Tombs and was utterly unable to ask for directions. All I could do was stand there and wait to be rescued. Fortunately, our driver finally spotted me, the one lone westerner in the crowd, and I was reunited, after hours of total isolation, with our group.

On the final night of our trip, after all the agreements had been signed, we attended a fabulous farewell banquet with

---

7   Lepercq was a wild Frenchman who loved and believed in Harvey right from the beginning of his tenure at BAM. The Lepercq Space, home of the BAMcafé and many important programs such as Eat, Drink & Be Literary and BAMcafé Live, is located in the Peter Jay Sharp Building. After Lepercq's death in February 1999, his protégé, Francois Letaconnoux, and widow, Françoise Stoll-Lepercq, endowed many programs and capital upgrades for the Lepercq Space, enhancing its capacity to serve as a "living room" for the entire institution.

Paul Lepercq, ca. 1980.

beautiful dishes, Chinese delicacies, and a lot of bowing and toasting. Judith Daykin and I were seated at a table with several high-level male dignitaries. We tried to make conversation, but common words were few and far between. During the appetizer, I tried to tell an amusing story based on something that had happened on the trip. Despite my best efforts at pantomime, my presentation received no reaction at all. Then to my surprise, Daykin took over and repeated the exact same story in English to wild, rapturous laughter and applause. Somehow, they understood her perfectly, while I had failed to communicate even one word, and we were both speaking the same language! For years, she and I would get hysterical whenever we recalled that evening.

The ballet came to BAM for two weeks in 1986. They proved to be a huge success, and we even arranged a full American tour for them, which took them all across our country. In the end, I believe this early cultural exchange opened the door to China, just a crack.

Another memorable event on the global scene was when Joe and I went to Israel at the request of then borough president Howard Golden to put together a program at BAM for that nation's fortieth anniversary.

The Israelis, in their enthusiasm for our visit, organized a grueling program of shows and meetings for us from morning till night with no breaks, not even for meals. They kept feeding us cake and falafel on the fly as they moved us from performance to meeting to performance. It was there in the hallowed hills of the ancient city of Jerusalem that they almost broke Joe, who was generally calm, unflappable, and perfectly groomed. On the fifth day, he arrived in the hotel lobby for another early morning meeting and his hair was uncombed, his shirt not properly buttoned—even his socks didn't match! "Look what they've done to you!" I exclaimed. "Pull yourself together, go back upstairs to your room and don't return until you're Joe again, the one I can depend on. I need you, BAM needs you." I assured him, "You can beat this," and off he went, returning in a little while as a tired and stressed but perfect Joe.

As part of this nonstop cultural Israel blitz, we were taken from Elat to Rosh Hanikra, south and north, to see dance programs by rare and exotic small ethnic enclaves that dwelled in villages around the country. Joe was thinking that he might invite a group of them to showcase the range of traditional dances and cultures that could be found in the most remote locales of Israel. Finally, we arrived at a place far from the bright lights of Tel Aviv or the spiritual weight of Jerusalem. It was there in the wilderness that we saw the interesting and intricate movements of a little-known sect called the Circassians (also known as the Adyghe). After the performance, we had tea with the leader of the company. He was wearing his full, imposing traditional costume that was designed by the early generations of his ancient people, including a silky jacket covered in multicolored jewels, high black boots, a tall fez-like hat, and a sword dangling from his side. He leaned in close to us at the table and said in a hushed, reverential tone, "You know, my friends, we are a small and rare people. Aside from this community, there is only one other place in this world where you can still find Circassian."

"Wow," I said, "that is intense. Where are the rest?"

He looked at me carefully and said, "New Jersey."

A Festival of The Performing Arts

**TICKETS
ON SALE NOW**
at the BAM box office,
the West Side
Ticket Agency
(251 West 45th Street
Manhattan)
and Bryant Park
(42nd Street
West of 6th Avenue).

**CALL
TICKETMASTER**
212-307-4100

Brooklyn Academy of Music
30 Lafayette Avenue Brooklyn,
New York, 11217-1486
Information 718-636-4100

Presented by
**BROOKLYN ACADEMY
OF MUSIC**

In conjunction with the
Consulate General of Israel
In New York,
Department of Cultural
Affairs

and in association with
New York UJA-Federation's
Operation Exodus

Brooklyn Academy of Music. Jan 19 - Feb 2.1992

Consulate General
of Israel in New York

I S R A E L

THE NEXT GENERATION

Above:
Poster for Israel:
The Next Generation,
spring 1992.

Opposite:
Zhang Dandan and
Zhang Ruofei in the
Central Ballet of
China's *Giselle*, spring
1986.

I glanced at Joe, who gave me an eye roll and later proclaimed, "You see, Karen, as I have often told you, there is a very thin line between the local and the global." (Yes . . . very thin indeed.) [8]

When you work for a place like BAM, you never know where you might end up. In one particular instance, I was surprised to find myself in Krasnoyarsk, Siberia. That's correct—Siberia. Bruce Ratner, our former chairman, during his long, drawn-out battle to get the Barclays Center built on a large parcel of land very near to BAM, needed additional investment dollars and, somehow, this ended up taking him to Moscow and Siberia, via the participation of Russian billionaire—and enormous basketball fan—Mikhail Prokhorov. Of course, when I learned that a billionaire was "moving in" next door, I made it a personal quest to get him involved with BAM. It turned out that his sister, Irina Prokhorova, was not only an accomplished publisher, she was also running his foundation and wielded approval over all of his philanthropic giving. Mikhail was a famous bachelor who had made his fortune in Siberian nickel mines. There were various financial transactions he was involved in related to this business that he had successfully engineered, resulting in his massive wealth and inclusion in the group of Russian billionaires informally known worldwide as "the oligarchs." Because of the origin of his fortune, his philanthropic foundation was incorporated in Krasnoyarsk, Siberia. I, therefore, proposed an exchange project to Irina, and that was how Transcultural Express was launched.

Irina, to put it bluntly, was not an easy partner. She had, despite her deep intellectual capacity, a suspicious nature and a rather cold demeanor. My American/Brooklyn humor and informality wasn't exactly scoring points with her as I tried to negotiate this three-year endeavor. First, she wanted to ground the project in artistic events that would take place in both Krasnoyarsk and Brooklyn, and while we know that Brooklyn is in fact teeming with artists, the same could not exactly be said for Siberia. Somehow we ended up with a very good film and visual arts plan for the first year, but it proved to be a struggle every step of the way.

Since the project was complicated, it required a disproportionately large amount of staff time for what turned out to be a decent and generous, but not transformative, amount of money ($333,333.00 per year for three years, totaling a million dollars). I insisted that we allocate a percentage of the grant to cover administrative costs, a common practice in

---

8   Years later, we mounted another large-scale Israeli program called Israel: The Next Generation. This event featured both Israeli Jewish, Israeli Arab, and newly immigrated Ethiopian and Russian artists and performers. As part of our planning for the Russian company, Gesher Theater, we met with the great refusenik Natan Sharansky to get his point of view on the event. "We need a celebrity to tell our story," he said. Someone at the meeting suggested Paul Newman. "No," said Sharansky, "Newman is only interested in South Africa!" I meekly responded, "Natan, I think you mean Paul Simon, who is interested in collaborating with South African musicians, not Paul Newman." Sharansky dismissed my comment with a wave of his hand, exclaiming, "Newman, Simon, what is the difference?" I sighed. It was going to be a long meeting.

project-based fundraising. Irina rejected this idea outright, and our relationship, which was not exactly a sisterhood to begin with, deteriorated further. Irina suggested that Kirsten Monroe, a member of the BAM development staff who was leading the project, and I visit Moscow to meet with her panel of experts to decide how best to handle the problem. Following that meeting, we would all travel to Krasnoyarsk to take a look at the events connected to the first year's exchange. The so-called "experts" were all just desperate to curry favor with Irina and the foundation. It was like a visit down memory lane to the old Soviet Union. Predictably, on every major decision, the "experts" sided with Irina. Finally, after much debate, they agreed that each side (BAM and the foundation) would take a portion of the grant to cover their costs. This seemed bizarre to me since they, the billionaire funders, actually provided the cash to the foundation, but the process of working with them was so exhausting and bureaucratic that I finally agreed.

A few days later, we departed for Siberia. One stroke of luck in the whole series of events was that BAM had a parallel project with the State Department, Dance Motion USA, which was running at the same time as Transcultural Express. Dance Motion sent dance companies from all over the United States to international residencies, mainly in the developing world. During the time we were in Siberia, the fabulous Philadelphia-based hip-hop company Illstyle & Peace Productions was scheduled to perform as part of Dance Motion USA in Moscow, Ukraine, and Siberia, so we merged them into our Prokhorov project.

When we arrived in Krasnoyarsk, I was stunned by the landscape. Somehow, I had expected Siberia to be straight out of Solzhenitsyn—giant, empty, desolate patches of land covered by snow, ice, and gulags. Instead, to my surprise, it looked like Albany. I had served as Brooklyn regent on the New York State Board of Regents for the state's education department from 2005 to 2010, which required a monthly visit to Albany, so when I say Krasnoyarsk definitely resembled Albany, I know what I'm talking about. Our hotel was sparse and depressing, and the weather was gray and chilly. Being in Siberia and feasting on the delicacies of the region (fish and borscht) put Irina in a much better mood. I think the lack of pretension in Krasnoyarsk and the massive gratitude of the local population for the foundation's generosity to their city really cheered her up. When Illstyle—the remarkable high-spirited, athletic, African American dance phenomenon—hit the stage, and the Siberian teenagers went crazy and responded to them like rock stars, I actually saw Irina smile. Once again, the power of the arts had triumphed. Perestroika via hip-hop had cracked the Siberian ice.

The New York Times Magazine

NOVEMBER 2, 1986 / SECTION 6

The Avant-Garde Courts Corporations

The Brooklyn Academy of Music raises millions for its performance-arts festival.

By Cathleen McGuigan

KAREN BROOKS HOPKINS looked satisfied — so many people had wanted to attend this year. The chief fund-raiser for the Brooklyn Academy of Music, an institution usually known as BAM, Karen Hopkins was standing in what was once the academy's ballroom, spotting lots of important people in the crowd. They were so crammed around extra tables that the waiters could hardly squeeze by with their trays of duckling and champagne. Over there was Richard Gere, laughing it up with the painter Julian Schnabel. Dianne Brill, the Valkyrie of the downtown disco set, was table hopping. Candice Bergen and her husband, Louis Malle, were chatting with Bianca Jagger.

But it was not the sight of all the stars that swelled Karen Hopkins's heart that night. It was the fact that so many people from the staid corporate world were there. The occasion was last month's opening night gala of BAM's Next Wave Festival, the biggest assemblage of avant-garde performing art in the country, and dozens of businessmen had put on black tie and come to see the show. They had sat through the American premier of Merce Cunningham's "Roaratorio," a dance based on James Joyce's "Finnegans Wake," with a cacophonous score by John Cage, which included tape recorded barking dogs and crying babies. And then the business types had stayed for dinner. They seemed happy.

Karen Hopkins, whose official title at BAM is vice president for planning and development, could see executives from American Telephone and Telegraph, Schlumberger, Rémy Martin Amérique, Bankers Trust and Barneys New York. She could see real estate moguls. Three generations of chairmen of the board of Philip Morris Companies Inc. were there — Joseph F. Cullman, George Weissman and the current one, Hamish Maxwell. All these business people had given big money to the avant-garde event, but Philip Morris had outdone everyone else. The cigarette manufacturer is, in fact, the main corporate sponsor of the Next Wave Festival and has pledged it $500,000 over the next two years.

"I think this is the best opening we've ever had in terms of who is here," beamed Karen Hopkins, who spent the evening working the room, never sitting down to eat.

CHAPTER SEVEN:

Successful Fundraising in Twelve Steps

Here is the Karen Brooks Hopkins Twelve-Step Fundraising Program. You know that famous prayer of addiction recovery, "God grant me serenity to accept the things I cannot change, etcetera"? I have adapted it for fundraising. Here are my twelve steps—good luck!

THE PERSONAL SIX

1. Don't take it personally. It's not about you. Rejection makes you strong. Resilience is your mantra. You can do this. Stop whining.

2. Those who succeed in fundraising can do anything! She who brings the money has *a lot* of clout.

3. Remember, it's their money. They can do with it as they please. If your organization is chosen, give respect and show gratitude to those donors. Again, credit is easy—money is hard.

4. Good service is everything. No one gives you money to sit in lousy seats.

5. It's that extra touch that makes you great. Send a note when your donor is quoted in the *Times*, or even better, when their child is quoted in the *Times*. When you get good reviews, share them. I'll say it again: Good manners and common sense win the day.

6. Attention to detail makes a difference. Are your proposals and letters coherent and concise? Don't waste anyone's time. People are busy (especially in New York when they have to get to their next meeting or, more importantly, to lunch).

THE PRACTICAL SIX

1. Who do you raise money from? And what is it for? Define your constituents.

   a) **The Who**

   • *Foundations:* They are dealing with the big issues and trying to save the world.

   • *Corporations/small businesses:* They are dealing with their own issues and trying to improve their image.

   • *High-net-worth individuals and smaller family foundations:* These are proliferating—you want them as board members and donors. They don't have guidelines and sometimes they are also trying to save the world!

   • *Members:* These are your people. They live in your neighborhood and believe in your programs, and you want to keep them close and move them up the food chain. It's a cradle-to-grave operation—get them in as members and stay with them for life . . . and after life . . . bequests build great institutions.

   • *Galas and special events:* Yes, the seating and the menus are torturous but great honorees and glorious events build your organization's legend. Hosting an unusual fundraising event can win your organization many friends and donors. For example, on the hundredth anniversary of the opening of the Brooklyn Bridge, we hosted a fabulous celebration with fireworks on a New York City tugboat loaned to us by one of our board members. Our guests, including Caroline Kennedy and other New York luminaries, were pretty impressed when our tug elbowed all of the nearby yachts out of the way, giving us the best spot on the river to enjoy the show. Now *that* was a night to remember.

With Neil Chrisman, board chairman, in the *New York Times* Sunday magazine, 1986.

• *Government—city, state, and federal:* They have cut back their arts funding (notwith-standing special funds appropriated for post-pandemic recovery), but they are still there. Pay attention to those elected officials. They have power and they can deliver the big capital appropriations for buildings. (In New York City, capital funding has actually grown.)

• *Other:* Art, auctions, raffles, and all manner of crazy (but legal) schemes. Be creative! This is where new ideas are born.[1]

Pay attention to your projections and add the new prospects. This is your bible.

b) **The What**

• *General operating support:* The hardest money to get but the most essential. This is the cash you need to keep the place open, pay salaries, cover electric bills, maintenance, cleaning, etcetera. It's not sexy to the donors but it's the most desirable for organizations.

• *Project support:* Donors usually respond to this more than any other category. It's about the programs, new initiatives, special strategic capacity, building concepts. If general operating is the body, then projects are the beating heart of your institution. But . . . be smart when you develop a project budget. Allocate some of the funds to cover a portion of the administrative costs that actually allow the project to get done. This is how you have your general operating cake and eat it too.[2]

• *Capital support:* You know those names you see on buildings? Yes, capital support, generally from government sources and high-net-worth individuals, gets the buildings built and keeps your place looking good and working well for the public. These are generally big projects so make sure you are ready and can afford to run them once they are finished.

• *Cash reserves:* Every organization should have a reserve of 8 to 10 percent of its annual operating budget to cover the lean times and to have the capacity to borrow from itself with no interest or invest in a special unplanned project or problem. The trick here is to create rules—use it, then pay it back. Otherwise, it's not a reserve—it's just spent. Board members and some foundations will support cash reserves.

---

1   You never know when a unique fundraising opportunity may come your way, so it is essential to be open to all possibilities. For example, we were once gifted a stylish motorboat. It had been offered to several organizations, but since very few nonprofit leaders knew anything about accepting a boat donation or how to then turn around and sell it, all of them passed on the opportunity. I figured, why not accept it and take our chances? BAM's lawyer Ron Feiner knew a boat broker who explained the process, and our capable and always game CFO, Keith Stubblefield, learned how to deal with it. Sure enough, we sold it and Keith even arranged to have it transported to the new owner in Florida. Several years later, another donor actually offered us an airplane but the complexities of selling it proved too difficult even for us.

2   Sometimes institutional capacity building—just strengthening your entire operation—can be presented to the right donor as a project. Bruce Kovner, a fan of BAM Opera and a great philanthropist, offered us a multimillion-dollar grant if we could develop a business plan that would erase accumulated deficits, strengthen our balance sheet, build reserves, and ultimately make the institution stronger and more stable. This donation was transformative. The matching terms (3:1) were hard to meet but, in the end, we were better in every way. Bruce was a serious businessman with great financial skills. He knew that challenging us to address every weak component of our business model would make us so much healthier and more resilient.

- *Endowment:* The holy grail of fundraising. Don't take this on until you are ready. Endowment generates longevity and passive income and is the key to building a great institution. (Think universities, hospitals, etcetera.) Big gifts are the name of the game. You invest, you make more, and you live forever. Invade it, and it is gone. High-net-worth donors are the heart of an endowment effort. A good starting goal is to raise double your operating budget.

2. Doing the Research

You know what they say when you buy a house—it's all about location, location, location! Well, fundraising is all about research, research, research. Know your prospect: Be prepared.

3. The Meeting

a) Try to get a face to face. Find the personal connection, such as a board member, funder, loyal subscriber, your sister, your uncle—whoever can introduce you.

b) Attend the meeting and take the right people, not everyone you know. Be prepared (remember, research!). Show up on time and dress appropriately. Make your case and leave. Don't waste their time. But don't leave without lining up the next step.

c) Follow up: Send a thank-you note after the meeting that restates the next step.

d) Follow directions: if the next step is to send a proposal in three weeks—then do it.

4. Write Well

a) Donors have to read a lot of really boring stuff. Be concise, smart, efficient, and grammatically correct. Try to paint an exciting picture of your work and your project, but don't overdo it. Keep it real.

b) Wait a week then check in to ensure they have everything they need to act on.

5. Record Keeping

a) Keep track of everything: Records must be accurate, clear, and up to date. (I have seen organizational files that resemble a toxic waste site.) For example, did your prospect attend a show after you submitted your proposal? Did someone greet them when they arrived? The Internet was made for a detailed account of everything that happens. Use it.

b) Pay attention to your records: If you have not heard a decision, check the file regarding the timetable for closure, and if you should have heard something by now, check in—but don't badger or get hysterical. You may feel desperate, but keep it to yourself.

c) Remember those projections—keep them up to date.

6. Bravo! Congratulate the team!

a) You have gotten a contribution—nice work! Share the good news with your board and your colleagues. Receiving a grant is both a personal and an institutional success, so spread the love.

b) Thank your donors. Have a glass of wine. Go to sleep, get up the next day, do it again.

Bonus points: Yes, sometimes you have to take no for an answer. But only for a while. When and if it makes sense, try again! Remember what I said about delayed gratification?

- Repeat . . . Delayed gratification is the fundraiser's creed.
- There is a thin line between being aggressive and obnoxious. I know. . . I have crossed it myself. Try to stay on the aggressive side.
- Communicate—don't just take the money and run. Stay in regular touch. Share good news and invite frequently but don't email every day.

Extra bonus points: You are doing the Lord's work—hallelujah!

CHAPTER EIGHT:

Stepping Outside My Comfort Zone

Over the course of my career in nonprofit arts management, I have discovered that the experiences in life that push you outside of your comfort zone are the ones that catalyze the greatest growth and change. In 1989, during a period of great personal upheaval, as I was getting divorced and trying to remain focused on my eight-year-old son, Matt, and working endless hours at BAM, I got a call from a donor named Arthur Levitt Jr., a successful businessman who had served as the chairman of the US Securities and Exchange Commission during Bill Clinton's presidency. Arthur's father, Arthur Sr., had been New York State Comptroller for twenty-four years, and he and his family had long been supporters of BAM. I was sitting in my office, surrounded by piles of grant applications and prospect reports, completely consumed by my daily work, when the phone rang.

"Karen, I'm calling to change your life."

And I thought, *Okay, what is this?*

"I'm inviting you on an Outward Bound trip," he continued, "to go rafting on the Green and Yampa Rivers at the border of Utah and Colorado."

My mind began swirling with excuses, as I thought about all the things on my already overfilled plate, not to mention that I had never done anything even remotely outdoorsy before in my life. Arthur told me I was being invited as a guest and, after describing the trip in more detail, asked me if I wanted to go.

"Well . . . um . . . let me think about it and get right back to you. I'm honored to be asked, but you know, I should really give it some thought."

I hung up and weighed my options. *Okay, I spend my entire life sitting in the dark, watching shows. How could I possibly survive a rafting trip? Is this even in the realm of possibility?* But then I also thought, *On the other hand, I'm getting divorced and I am moving rapidly up the chain at work, gaining more leadership responsibility. Maybe a trip like this could be a breakthrough moment? Like it's karma and I have to go.* So, a few minutes later, I called back and said:

"Arthur, I'd really like to do this, but at the same time, I'm pretty nervous about it. Can you give me the names of some women who have done this type of thing before so I can find out what it was like for them?"

And he said, "Sure. Why don't you call Donna Shalala," who at the time was the chancellor of the University of Wisconsin at Madison, and soon thereafter became the US Secretary of Health and Human Services under President Clinton. I honestly didn't think she would take my call, but when she heard why I was calling, she actually did and she spoke very enthusiastically about her Outward Bound experience. So I agreed to go, but since I didn't want to completely humiliate myself, I hired a trainer who would get me in shape for the adventure—in order to go, I had to obtain a doctor's clearance, saying I was fit enough to embark on the journey.

Rapelling during an Outward Bound expedition in 1990. Can't believe I did this!

There were about twenty people on the trip, only three of whom were women, and nearly everyone was an accomplished banker or investor or had held major roles in government. I'd be lying if I said the fundraiser in me didn't see this as a major opportunity, even if a low-key approach was required! After all, we would be venturing off the grid, into a wild, untouched part of the country, where the concerns of our daily lives would be silenced by the beauty of nature and our desire to survive. There would be no communication with the outside world. There were no cell phones then, at least not the kind you could bring on a rafting trip. So, while we were on the river, we couldn't be reached, which gave us the time and the space to really get to know one another. The first day, I felt anxious about being cut off from the nonstop pace of Brooklyn and everything I knew. But, by the second day, I began to feel free, liberated from the need to plan every second of my life and empowered to be in the moment with a dynamic and fascinating group of people in an entirely different way. As the trip progressed, I found myself becoming far more reflective and engaging in profound personal conversations while pushing myself physically to do things that I had never before done, such as rappelling, climbing, and hiking long distances.

It was a stellar group, and the women formed an immediate bond, as the whole group took a few days to really come together. That said, it was also fun to see what caused people to gravitate toward one another. The New York Jews, of course, started hanging out, and, in spite of our surroundings, we talked nonstop about the big issues facing the city. I made a number of good friends with whom I'm still in touch today. The whole trip was a life-altering experience, because I had never before attempted to do something this challenging and for which I didn't have any natural ability or talent.

Being among other leaders made me a better leader but also revealed new insights about group dynamics. Part of every Outward Bound experience was to work as a collective. Everyone has to cook, tie knots, and perform basic tasks and chores on behalf of the group, and, though we were all leaders in our lives back home, we really learned to operate as a team. Over time, I found the best way to participate in the group and to play my part. I wasn't competitive because I was a terrible outdoors person, but I didn't humiliate myself either. Everyone was very nice to me and encouraged me to push ahead despite my concerns about the "athletics" of the trip.

On the first night, we each had to decide who was going to be what they called a "dunnage mate"—or buddy—the individual with whom you would pack your gear and work closely together with over the week. So I looked around and I thought, *Okay, this guy's a president of a bank. That guy's the foreign minister of his country. This guy runs a major not-for-profit. And this guy is a brilliant oncologist. Okay, we're outdoors in the middle of nowhere, anything could happen to a weakling like me, so I'm going with the doctor.* For once in my life I didn't just focus on potential funding, I focused on survival, so, based on my skills, or lack thereof, I knew I wanted to work with the guy who saved lives, not the one who had made a lot of money. I therefore befriended Dr. Samuel Waxman, a distinguished cancer researcher at the Icahn School of Medicine at Mount Sinai, and felt great comfort and safety having him as my dunnage mate. That first trip was remarkably beautiful and it opened my eyes to a world I had never thought I would see or be part of and, in that way, it did change my life. I must admit that I did invite the whole gang to BAM after the trip for a show and dinner and several of my pals actually did become donors.

The second time I went, again as Arthur's guest, on an Outward Bound trip, it was rafting on the upper half of the Grand Canyon, which was an experience like no other, the most radical contact with nature I have ever encountered. In the time between trips, I continued to train and started doing a daily workout, five miles on a stationary bike and exercises with leg and arm weights. My daily routine taught me that exercise could help me not only become stronger, but also more centered, providing a stability and equilibrium that has helped me weather challenges and organize my thoughts. I have Outward Bound to thank for motivating me to do it.

In spite of my efforts to get in better physical shape, the trip through the Grand Canyon was by no means easy, but it was jaw-droppingly gorgeous and well worth the effort. At a certain point, our rafts descended deeper and deeper into the Colorado, until we reached what is called the Vishnu Schists, or the basement rocks of the Grand Canyon, the oldest of which date back over a billion years. These rocks of the canyon are various colors, but they change the further you descend, growing darker as you go deeper, until you're at the Schists, which are black. It's one of the most dramatic things I have ever beheld. The Colorado River is freezing and a deep shade of dark blue. When you are rafting its waves, the rapids can grow pretty high and strong. At one point, we came to a side trail that led to a body of water called the Little Colorado, which was bright turquoise and warm. The Hopi Tribe believed it was the place from which all life originated. The change from cold to warm and dark blue to turquoise is just one example of both the dynamism and mystery of nature.

At another point on the trip, as we were moving through a particularly powerful rapid, I saw everyone on the opposite side of my boat go flying over my head, and I knew I was going to be in that water next. Getting tossed into a rapid can be pretty scary. You are basically being thrown into a vortex of spinning, cold water, and there is no assurance that you'll come up. But then, after a few moments of churning, you do pop up, and your friends haul you out of the water, and everyone starts cheering and laughing, which provides a crucial perspective that cannot be achieved in normal, daily life. That was the power of these trips, and why they had such an impact upon me. As I flew into the swirling waters, I was scared, but I had also faced my fears before and had the experience of the previous trip to bolster me in that moment.

In Outward Bound, there is a ritual through which all participants must pass, called a solo. The group is taken out into a remote part of the wilderness and then everyone is made to disperse for twenty-four hours and go off on your own. During that time, you are not supposed to eat, nor are you to read. Instead, you are expected to reflect and commune with yourself and with nature. They give you a notebook and encourage you to record your thoughts. When I did my solo in the Grand Canyon, I took the experience very seriously. It was frightening to be alone in nature, but it was also peaceful. I was able to slow down my mind and to be with myself. To be honest, I think I also fell asleep, but that felt important, too.

At the end of the trip, we walked the Bright Angel Trail on the south rim, which was over a mile, straight up the side of the canyon. Some people did it in two hours. I did it in six. It took me a long time, but in the end, I made it. And while hiking out of the canyon and returning to the surface, I felt a steadfast determination, an unflappable, relentless will

that was leading me to do something that was hard but possible. This was the ultimate lesson of these trips for me, that I could access that determination and discipline and apply it to other things that seemed scary or unattainable, that I had it in me to do things I didn't know I was capable of doing.

On the last night of the trip, we stayed at a hotel on the rim of the Grand Canyon called El Tovar, and there was a banquet, with toasts and revelry, celebrating all that we had accomplished. When it was my turn to speak, I recited a poem about our adventures that I had written during my solo, which had everyone clapping and laughing by the time I was done. I walked away from the experience transformed. Through my Outward Bound experiences—I later went on a third one—I learned about leadership, about teamwork, about embracing physical exertion and quieting the mind, about being alone and cultivating a reverence and appreciation for nature. Most of all, I learned the importance of stepping outside the familiar and facing my fears, something that shaped the rest of my tenure at BAM, as well as my work today.

Somehow I made it.

CHAPTER NINE:

Succession and the Godfather Lunch

At a certain point in the late nineties, Harvey began thinking about retirement. He was beyond seventy years old, and he had been at the helm for close to thirty-two years. His wife, Phyllis, was interested in seeing more of him at home. Harvey had also begun focusing most of his attention and energy on developing the district surrounding BAM, with the goal of transforming the neighborhood and Brooklyn into a vibrant cultural hub and an international home for artists. Over his tenure, Harvey had tirelessly championed innovators and avant-garde artists whose work had never been seen on a large scale in New York, and in support of that vision, we nurtured and grew an audience like no other, launched the endowment, greatly improved the physical plant, and opened the Majestic Theater (renamed the BAM Harvey Theater in his honor), among many other significant accomplishments. Now that BAM was on firm footing and the neighborhood was on its way to revitalization, Harvey wished to create a context for the institution he had built.

Around this same time, Joe and I began thinking about our futures. We'd both been at BAM for more than twenty years. So there was a lot of talk behind the scenes about the succession of Harvey Lichtenstein and what would happen when he stepped down. For all the stability we had achieved for the institution, the final few years of Harvey's time at BAM were still fraught with meltdowns and money problems. Harvey wasn't going to change. He always bet on artists he believed in, and this type of wagering of BAM's future against the success of individual artists and projects characterized his style of leadership from beginning to end.

One of the most notable crises occurred toward the end of his term, when the Ford Foundation authorized an auditor to take a thorough look at all of our operations and financial records as part of a grant we had received from the foundation. When the auditor, Tom Harris, got to work, he uncovered a number of problems in our finance department that probably had been perpetuating our money problems for some time. The biggest thing he discovered, to put it plainly, was that BAM was in a deep hole. As poor Tom tried to explain this to Harvey, the color of Harvey's face flashed crimson red, and he began interrogating the man, as if the bad news had somehow been his fault. I remember the guy looking like he was going to faint as Harvey began screaming at him. Tom started sweating. His hands trembled and he loosened his collar as he tried to find his voice. He kept attempting to clear his throat, and for a moment, it seemed like he might not recover. He asked if I could bring him a glass of water, and after I did, he finally found the will to speak, explaining carefully and in a totally straightforward, direct manner, how we had gotten into the mess. At first, Harvey acted as if Tom were our enemy, but he had actually done us a huge favor, because he was able to pinpoint irregularities that desperately needed to be clarified and improved.

Tom's biggest discovery had to do with the capital funds we were receiving from the

Above, from top:
With Harvey, dressed for a celebration of the Brooklyn Museum's director, Robert T. Buck, ca. 1990.

With Harvey at the book party for the publication of *Successful Fundraising for Arts and Cultural Organizations*, 1989.

Opposite:
On the roof of 30 Lafayette Avenue with Harvey and Joe.

city. As with all city money, there was a time lag between when the funds were awarded, deployed, reconciled, and finally hit our bank account. Because of this delay and in order to actually receive payments from the city (various compliance documents and assurances were required), our finance department had developed a system wherein BAM borrowed money against the city contract, so the capital projects funded by the city could be accelerated and move forward in a timely manner. This was okay, but, as Tom pointed out, when the money finally came in from the city, the interest on the loans wasn't covered, just the principal. The resulting shortfall generated a huge spending gap from the unpaid interest that had naturally accrued. This put us in a very difficult position, close to a million dollars in debt, and we had to solve it, which meant finding donors who would provide grants or loans to cover the interest in order to keep it from continuing to accrue. As usual, I was tasked with identifying the donors who would dig us out. So I set to work to find contributors who could help and, of course, this all exploded at the peak of our busiest period.

In addition to uncovering the mess, firing the vice president of finance, and digging into another do-or-die fundraising mission, we also had to find a new person to take on the job of straightening out BAM's accounting and banking systems. One of our board members, Marty Mertz, was a senior executive at Republic Bank. He suggested that Harvey hire Vincent Funke, a capable banking professional who had recently lost his job at Republic after many years due to a downsizing of their staff in New York. Vincent deeply missed the bank, had no interest in the arts, and his temperament was completely mismatched with someone as intense as Harvey. His personal life was also in disarray and it wasn't long before we sensed catastrophe with this hire. When Vincent didn't show up for work and couldn't be reached after a few days, police were called who went to his home on Long Island and found that he had committed suicide. It was devastating and, even though we barely knew him, the entire staff was shocked and saddened that something so horrible had happened to one of our colleagues. We then cycled through a few more finance vice presidents before Harvey promoted Peter Gee, our comptroller, and order was restored.

At some point during the course of these events, Harvey decided that he had had enough and would retire at the end of 1999, which triggered discussions at the board level about succession. Joe and I, who were very close and had been Harvey's deputies for decades, met to talk about the way forward. We resolved to join forces and propose to the board that we should both succeed Harvey, as managing both BAM's business side and artistic programs had become too large for one person to handle. Together, we knew the institution from top to bottom. Also, given BAM's financial problems, promoting us would cost the institution far less than a national search and a brand-new hire. We went to Harvey and asked him to champion our candidacy to the board. Not only were we his protégés, we argued, we were his legacy, because we believed in everything he had built. We would honor his vision for BAM and the surrounding area and do everything within our power to sustain and grow it.

Harvey went to the developer Bruce Ratner, our chairman of the board at the time, and tested the idea. With Bruce's endorsement, this succession plan started making its way up the organizational food chain. We appealed to the board to forgo a search, arguing that we would be compromised in our current positions if we had to compete for the jobs while executing our own. To our delight, the board agreed and Joe and I experienced the easiest succession in the history of a large cultural organization. It was a great moment for the institution, as well, because by backing us as the next generation of BAM's executive leadership, the board had ensured continuity of vision while avoiding the pitfall of founder's syndrome, wherein a visionary leader runs an organization into the ground by not planning for his or her succession or by not giving up control. We were the perfect stewards of Harvey's legacy, and yet we were both ambitious and independent minded enough to have our own complementary visions for how BAM could expand and evolve.

There was one notable hiccup in the process, when Harvey decided, even though he was stepping down, that he still wanted to lead a number of programs. Joe and I didn't know how to respond when he shared this news with us. We commiserated about how to handle it during a lunch with a very outspoken donor, Robert W. Wilson (not to be confused with Robert Wilson the artist). Unbeknownst to us, after the lunch, Wilson, who had developed a friendship with Harvey, called his wife, Phyllis, whom he also knew, and told her that Harvey's plan to hold onto control of certain BAM programs was a terrible idea. "Harvey has got to get out of the way and let those kids run the place," he told her. So with both Phyllis and Wilson leaning on him, Harvey not only graciously stepped aside, he continued to provide advice and counsel during all my years as president.[1] Joe and I were forever grateful to Mr. Wilson for the rest of our time at BAM (even when he steadfastly refused to donate a single dollar for projects he didn't like). In the end, after very little deliberation, the board named me president and Joe executive producer of BAM and we took over in 1999. A peaceful transfer of power had been achieved.

We honored Harvey with a spectacular gala, the crowning moment of which was the renaming of the Majestic Theater as the Harvey Theater, made possible by a three-million-dollar grant I had secured from the Doris Duke Foundation. We also called our colleague and BAM supporter Chuck Close and asked him to create a photographic portrait of Harvey, which still hangs in the Harvey Theater. Phyllis did not like the photo Harvey chose from Chuck's shoot. His choice was one where the "Boss" looked a bit scary, if I do say so myself. Upon seeing it, she exclaimed, "I never would have married that man!" So, we had to call Chuck and ask him to allow both Phyllis and Harvey to return to his studio to make a new selection. He wasn't thrilled, but he accepted the situation. As tough as Harvey was, he did not have the temerity to challenge his wife on this one.

For the gala, we also made a postcard book of Harvey's greatest artistic achievements. The book, *The Harvey Years*, was a perfect follow-up to a special *Harvey Newspaper* that we had created for his thirtieth anniversary at BAM, featuring stories and legends about Harvey from his tenure at BAM (and arranged for *New York Newsday* to print for free). Paul Simon came to the gala and performed a version of his hit "Mrs. Robinson" and when he sang out, "Where have you gone, Harvey Lichtenstein?" the crowd went crazy. There were also performances by some of Harvey's favorite artists, such as Trisha Brown and Philip Glass. And then, Harvey smoothly and gracefully transitioned from his role

1   As Harvey left the building on his last day, he turned to me and said, "You're the boss now. You must watch *everything*." This simple message had a profound impact on me. From a power outage on the BAM sign on Flatbush Avenue, to cigarette butts that weren't swept up in front of the building, to reading every line of every budget—I watched *everything*. Thank you, Harvey!

as the leader of BAM to the chairman of the BAM Local Development Corporation, which focused on the growth of the neighborhood and arts district surrounding BAM.

Right after Joe and I took over, the company Accenture assigned us a consultant, Constance "Connie" Cranos who donated her services to BAM, and we embarked on an extremely productive internal exploration of what we wanted to preserve from the Harvey years and what we wanted to change. We also used this time to solidify our process of working together, which became known as "the Karen and Joe show," establishing basic principles of our partnership, which didn't really change over the sixteen years we ran BAM. We agreed to be straightforward and honest with each other, showing respect for each other's roles at all times. The primary reason our partnership worked was that neither of us wanted the other person's job. While I wanted to help Joe shape large-scale initiatives, I certainly didn't want to be directly programming shows for BAM, and Joe certainly didn't want to be dealing with fundraising, finances, and the physical plant. We shared joint responsibility for marketing and always tried to speak in one unified voice to artists, our audiences, and stakeholders. Finally, we agreed that whenever we had a disagreement, we would shut the door and argue it out between us, rather than in the public eye.

Over the course of our time together, we worked hard to maintain these principles, which served us very well. We rarely competed or undercut each other, and we always tried to give each other space. Joe had an artistic agenda that I didn't always 100 percent agree with, but I supported it no matter what. If there were projects that had the potential to blow through their budgets and threaten our financial security, I would tell him, "It's costing too much." If there were things that were a problem for the institution, I would tell him, and vice versa. Most of the time, this strategy worked really well, and we avoided the financial roller coaster of the Harvey years, in which the artistic programming would sometimes lead to unnecessary fiscal insecurity in the name of serving artists' visions. Of course, if there was a large-scale project in which we both believed, something that would move the institution to the next level of glory, we would find a way to make it happen, even if it was complicated and even if it didn't make administrative sense. We had both learned from Harvey the importance of taking big risks on productions that were artistically brilliant and ambitious, the ones that advanced BAM's mission and brand more than a hundred other shows.

The first of these opportunities occurred in 2001. We had committed to producing The Next Wave Down Under, a minifestival within the big Next Wave, featuring over a hundred multidisciplinary artists from all over Australia. We were quite taken with the Australian artists, and at the press conference announcing the event, we had fun handing out Next Wave Down "Underwear" to all of the guests! This program was sailing along smoothly, until 9/11—the horrific terrorist attack on New York City that caused the collapse of the city's famous World Trade Center's Twin Towers and the death of over three thousand people. The catastrophe occurred a few weeks before the festival was set to launch. Many cultural organizations were canceling projects and going dark. But we decided to double down on the festival in spite of the odds that audiences might not be inclined to attend. We had a lot of support from the Australian government and their cultural leaders. In the end, only one artist decided not to come. The rest showed up, and after the first week of performances, the houses started filling up again. It was amazing to

Above:
Australian artists were featured in the Next Wave Down Under, Next Wave, 2001.

Opposite, clockwise from top left:
Harvey looking very impresarial. This shot graced the cover of a book of postcards entitled *The Harvey Years*, 1999.

Harvey in black tie.

Harvey at his desk.

Dancing at his gala, 1999.

The big *New York* magazine story in 1987. We had the cover.

Hirschfeld "does" Harvey for his retirement gala in 1999.

The Harvey Years

Harvey Lichtenstein
BAM President and Executive
Producer 1967—1999

Images from the
BAM Archives

Brooklyn
Academy
of
Music

A book of 30 postcards

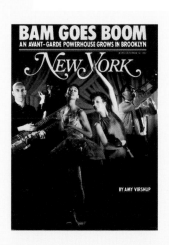

BAM GOES BOOM
AN AVANT-GARDE POWERHOUSE GROWS IN BROOKLYN
NEW YORK

BY AMY VIRSHUP

witness. In true form, New Yorkers refused to stay home (going out every night is in their DNA) and this incredible camaraderie with the Australians was on full display. To this day, I feel connected to the Australians because of their solidarity with us at a very low moment in American and New York history.

Joe and I also decided early on that we weren't going to produce off-site work, like many of the iconic productions of Harvey's time, such as Ariane Mnouchkine's *Les Atrides*, an adaptation of *The Oresteia* by Aeschylus, which took place at the Park Slope Armory and was an artistic triumph. The needs of the production and the venue had almost brought financial ruin once again. The fundraising highlight of *Les Atrides* was a glamorous dinner at Brooklyn's famous River Café, hosted by the CEO of the French company Elf Aquitaine, which was sponsoring the engagement. After the meal, attended by a hundred guests, we arrived at the armory only to find that Mnouchkine had decreed, "There will be égalité! No special seats for donors." So the high and mighty sat in the nosebleed section and the Elf CEO cursed at me in at least four different languages, leading with French and ending with general grunting from displeasure. It was one of those nights when I crawled home and got under the covers as quickly as possible.

Joe and I affirmed that our goal, first and forever, was to get people to come to our theaters in Brooklyn. We also resolved to keep working with artists who were central to Harvey's vision. These were, after all, BAM artists and we intended to keep it that way. We believed these luminaries were crucial to our mission, no matter whose curatorial imprint was on them. In the end, this was good for the institution. It provided continuity, and an even deeper level of integrity to the work. A new person might have come in and said, "I want a new regime. I don't want the same stuff as in the past," but we said, "We're going to keep the artists and projects that are the heart and soul of BAM, and—at the same time—we're going to introduce new artists and new work." And that is precisely what we set out to do, launching the early collaborations with the Sydney Theatre Company, featuring Cate Blanchett in Ibsen's *Hedda Gabler*, followed by her unforgettable performance as Blanche in *A Streetcar Named Desire*, directed by Liv Ullmann, as well as maintaining continuity with the past, including projects featuring the actor Simon Russell Beale and director Sam Mendes.

We also started thinking not only about individual artists, but also about large-scale, multiple presentations that would represent depth and showcase full bodies of work. We did things like present all three existing operas by Claudio Monteverdi under the banner of "The Monteverdi Cycle." The t-shirt read "I went the full Monte." We presented Peter Brook's *The Tragedy of Hamlet* and Simon Russell Beale in the Royal National Theatre production of *Hamlet* in the same season, back to back. That T-shirt read "2 Be or Not to Be." While Harvey was to some extent Eurocentric, Joe became global in his interests and tastes. Lincoln Center was now crouching behind us, presenting many of our past artists (often in new, big productions we could not afford), including many of the Europeans who worked in a contemporary vein, formerly the exclusive territory of BAM. The growing global community of artists demanded a larger vision so, in order to remain cutting edge, we had to keep innovating and pushing the envelope, and we committed ourselves to featuring much more diversity in our upcoming seasons than in the past. We also focused

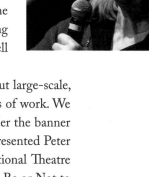

Actress Liv Ullmann, who directed Cate Blanchett in *A Streetcar Named Desire*, did double duty while at BAM, introducing some of her classic Ingmar Bergman films at the BAM Rose Cinema, 2009.

on local artists, creating more space and platforms for performers and creators from the surrounding community to be seen and heard. Community concerns were bubbling up as gentrification started to hit our Fort Greene neighborhood and nearby areas. At one town meeting, I heard BAM referred to as a "plantation." This literally blew my mind. I felt shame hearing those words and I vowed that night to change that perception. And while much more needs to be done, I focused on substantially ramping up racial and ethnic diversity as well as local representation among artists, board members, and staff, as well as providing more outreach programs to nearby residents.

None of this was easy. Harvey spent most of his more than three decades in Brooklyn trying to do one thing: get people to come to BAM. Consequently, he put nearly all of his indefatigable energy and talents into each production. He focused on bringing the most exciting artists to BAM, providing them with the resources to create masterpieces, and giving them a home. For Harvey, it was "great show, great show, great show." Joe and I were able to go larger, focusing on building a better, stronger, more equitable and resilient institution.

One of the other critical developments, around the time of Harvey's retirement, was the launch of BAM's movie business. Since we decided to get into the world of film exhibition, it made sense to renovate the physical plant of the Helen Owen Carey Playhouse, a former 1,400-seat concert hall adjacent to the opera house, which had limited potential for theatrical presentations, as it was originally constructed in 1908 to be only a concert venue with no wing or fly space. Since we had the Majestic (now the BAM Harvey) Theater as a second venue, we resolved to transform the Playhouse space into four cinemas. Once again, the architect Hugh Hardy, who had handled the Majestic renovation and many other BAM projects, took on the job. I decided to learn about presenting films and assumed responsibility for overseeing BAM's cinema, with the hope of turning it into a viable, long-term source of revenue for the institution. Before stepping down, Harvey had the idea of hiring the world-renowned art house programmer Dan Talbot, who ran the New Yorker Theatre and Lincoln Plaza, to select our films. Harvey always believed in following the best programmer, and Dan Talbot was the dean of independent film programming. But because he programmed theaters directly next to Lincoln Center, in the heart of the Upper West Side of Manhattan, film distributors would come to him, kiss his ring, and offer him their best movies. When he came to Brooklyn, he called the same distributors and they said, "Brooklyn who? Where? Forget about it."[2] This shook Dan to his core and caused him to pull out of the venture before we really took off.

After studying how other successful art house cinemas worked, we decided to dedicate one of our theaters to a standing repertory program and then use the other three theaters to present first-run independent movies. We hired Adrienne Mancia, former film curator at the Museum of Modern Art, to help program the repertory space, and brought on a young curator named Florence Almozini to assist her. At this point, I was working closely with Harvey on the program strategy with a view toward developing a fundraising campaign to support it. Harvey had miraculously convinced the city to give us four million dollars to

2   In Brooklyn, we say "fuggedaboutit," but in Los Angeles, home of the film industry, the common English usage prevails.

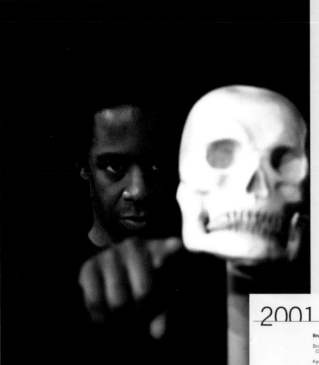

This page, clockwise from top left:
Adrian Lester in *The Tragedy of Hamlet*, spring 2001.

Scene from Peter Brook's *The Tragedy of Hamlet*, spring 2001.

BAMbill for *The Tragedy of Hamlet*, spring 2001.

Simon Russell Beale also played Hamlet in the production by the Royal National Theatre of Great Britain, spring 2001.

Opposite:
Cate Blanchett as Blanche DuBois in the Sydney Theatre Company production of *A Streetcar Named Desire*, fall 2009.

Following spread:
Scene from the Ariane Mnouchkine/Théâtre du soleil production *Les Atrides*, fall 1992.

convert the old playhouse space into the BAM Rose Cinemas, and Hugh Hardy found a way to preserve many of the theater's historic elements, including its beautiful ceiling and proscenium arch. All the same, we had no idea what we were doing in those early stages. We knew next to nothing about running a successful movie business. But Harvey was Harvey. He got the city money. Then I asked the real estate developer Jonathan Rose (a BAM trustee) and his wife Diana to provide the finishing funds, which resulted in the space being named the BAM Rose Cinemas.

Securing the money was relatively easy when compared to the process of designing the space. There were big arguments about little things, such as whether we would have cup holders in the cinema. The repertory programmers said, "No cup holders. It's disrespectful," while the business-minded people, like me, were saying, "We're having cup holders. It isn't a question. We have to. It's what movie theaters do these days! We are selling popcorn, soda, and water. This isn't even open for discussion." We called upon Michael Fuchs, who was chairman and CEO of HBO and had been on our board for a long time, for advice. Michael brought in a team of pro bono advisors who had run Sony's movie theaters and they told us all kinds of practical things, such as, "Don't put carpet on the floor under the seats. Paint that area, because you're going to have to clean up that soda, candy, and popcorn after every screening." A consultant named Gary Myer, who had worked with Landmark Theaters and Sundance, helped us create the beginning of a business plan, though we were still very much figuring things out on our feet. One of our key hires was cinema manager Efi Shahar, who had run the giant Lincoln Square movie complex near Lincoln Center. He knew all the ins and outs of the operation and only recently retired from BAM after twenty years.

In an effort to ground the cinema in the community, we decided to launch the repertory program with a Spike Lee retrospective. Spike grew up in the neighborhood, and his studio was just around the corner from BAM on one of the brownstone-lined blocks in Fort Greene. He was also a local artist who consistently held our feet to the fire and demanded that BAM build more bridges to underserved audiences and be more inclusive of the surrounding, mostly African American, community and its rich history. So it seemed fitting to begin with a retrospective of his films, especially as BAM began to make a significant commitment to strengthen community relations.

In order to distinguish the BAM Rose Cinemas from other movie theaters in the city, we resolved to adopt a number of innovative approaches. The first was to "personalize" the cinema-going experience as much as possible by inviting speakers to introduce films and participate in postscreening discussions and Q&As. These would include the filmmakers themselves, actors, and, in the case of documentaries, the subjects of films. This became a hallmark of our programming, a very theatrical way of driving people to our spaces, which was applied across all genres at BAM. Over the years, a remarkable roster of speakers came to our movie theaters. We launched significant series such as From Hanoi to Hollywood: The Vietnam War on Film. During that memorable program, Father Daniel Berrigan (the former antiwar activist, then in his nineties), entered the movie theater wearing his priest's collar with his clenched fist raised in the air as the audience rose to its feet. Another amazing group of films, all produced by legendary producer Ed Pressman, brought visits from David Byrne (*True Stories*) to Margot Kidder (who played Lois Lane in *Superman* and starred in the Pressman film, *Sisters*) to Oliver Stone (*Wall Street*). Retrospectives of films by Bill Murray, Robert Redford, and Susan Sarandon were presented, along with amazing foreign films and documentaries. Even Sacha Baron Cohen showed up at BAM fully decked out as his alter ego, Brüno, to meet our audience. These talks gave the BAM Rose screenings a real personality and our young moviegoers loved it. This approach also worked brilliantly in terms of tying the stage to the screen. If an artist, such as Liv Ullmann, Isabelle Huppert, Patrick Stewart, Ian McKellen, or Jeremy Irons, was at BAM working on a play, we simultaneously screened some of their films and asked them to participate in a discussion that usually included topics related to the play and the film. Our other strategy was to host itinerant community-based film festivals, which already had built-in audiences but had no permanent home base. These audiences often consisted of people who didn't normally come to BAM on their own, and we were thrilled to welcome them. We partnered and presented films with the African Film Festival, the Haitian International Film Festival, and the Brooklyn Jewish Film Festival, among many others. These festivals made sense from a business point of view, and also served to strengthen community relations. They drove new people into our theaters and they also came with their own films, many of which couldn't be seen anywhere else. The MET: Live in HD was another program of this type that was a big success for BAM. We persuaded Peter Gelb, the general manager of the Met, to allow us to be the first New York venue to have access to the screenings. Originally, Gelb only wanted to offer this program outside of New York, fearing it could hurt ticket sales at the house. With his permission, we forged ahead and even added a preshow brunch featuring an opera expert giving a talk about the production audiences would see that day. The Met screenings were so popular that, for a while, we presented the operas on all four of our screens. A major crisis occurred when some audience members who chose to buy popcorn were chomping during the screenings. A virtual war broke out between the popcorn eaters and the popcorn haters (those who insisted that the noise was a crime against the entire genre of opera). Finally, we decreed that certain screens were declared "no popcorn zones," allowing the munchers a space of their own where they could crunch to their hearts' content.

As our confidence as film presenters grew, we added popular family events, such as the annual BAMkids Film Festival (BKFF). Every screening sold out and the place was packed with little ones as young as two years old (accompanied by their parents, of course). BKFF was a popcorn sales bonanza, as you might imagine. In fact, this program was so successful, we added a full range of family friendly free activities in the lobby and live mini performances in the Lepercq Space. Senior Cinema for the elderly often kept the theaters full on weekday mornings and received generous subsidies from elected officials. We also added holiday events, such as a candlelight dinner and romantic film pairing on Valentine's Day.

Martin Luther King Jr. Day at BAM was particularly poignant on stage and screen. We hosted the largest celebration in the city, with music and a keynote speech in the opera

1. With Robert Redford.

2. Hilton Als and Sandra Bernhard.

3. Jim Jarmusch.

4. Harry Shearer.

5. Wes Anderson and Garth Jennings.

6. Benicio del Toro and Jiro Shindo.

7. Bong Joon-ho.

8. With David Byrne and Ed Pressman.

9. Bruce Dern.

10. Noah Baumbach.

11. John C. Reilly, Lawrence Jay Duplass, Mark Duplass, and Marisa Tomei.

12. Gena Rowlands and Peter Bogdanovich.

13. Laurie Simmons, Grace Dunham, Lena Dunham, Kyle Martin, Jemima Kirke, Alicia Van Couvering, Alex Karpovsky, and David Call, 2010.

14. Michel Gondry.

15. Sung-jung Jung and Oliver Stone.

16. Philip Seymour Hoffman.

17. With Spike Lee.

18. BAM Rose Cinema in the Peter Jay Sharp Building, 1998.

19. Susan Sarandon.

20. With Bill Murray.

21. With Steve Buscemi, agnès b., and Harvey Keitel.

22. Alicia Silverstone and Amy Heckerling.

house, along with many politicians in the city and state delivering remarks. Speakers ranged from Kofi Annan, then secretary general of the UN; to Congressman John Lewis, who had marched with King in Selma; to the mothers of slain civil rights workers Andrew Goodman and James Chaney. It was usually a very emotional day. The free opera house event was always followed by complimentary screenings of related civil rights documentaries that often featured guests. Most years, we filled our four cinemas with community members who welcomed the free screenings as part of the holiday.

While our repertory and festival programming came out of the gate very strong, the first-run side of the business rapidly went from bad to worse in those first few months. The main problem resulted from the arcane rules of independent film distribution. Because of our proximity to the Angelika Film Center in Manhattan, we were being "cleared" by film distributers. In the movie business, "clearance" means that if an independent film (this is not the case for commercial first-run films, which get wide distribution), is playing in one independent theater, it will not play in another independent theater within a certain block radius. Although we were technically outside of the required block radius, the Angelika was being run by people who did not want competition from Brooklyn. They had determined, and rightly so, that a large portion of their audiences were actually coming from our borough. And so we were, in effect, embargoed from showing the latest independent art house films. Even Dan Talbot, as celebrated as he was, with all of his power and prowess, was not able to break us free from the choke hold in which we found ourselves. This meant that in those early days we ended up playing the same movies for weeks and weeks and weeks. It was a train wreck. We played the Pedro Almodóvar film *All About My Mother* for a seemingly endless run that, after its initial success, pretty much dried up altogether. Many of us who were working at BAM at the time can laugh about it now, but as it was happening, we were absolutely miserable. We had made a huge investment in these movie theaters, and it was flaming out right before our eyes. As we bled money and our audiences dwindled, the board became hysterical and seriously considered closing the cinemas, just as we were getting started.

As the incoming president, I was tasked with trying to break this logjam. First, I set up a meeting with one of our board members, Nora Ann Wallace (who is now serving as Chair of BAM), at her firm, Willkie Farr & Gallagher LLP, which had a significant antitrust practice. Those lawyers agreed to explore whether it was legal for us to be cleared by the Angelika. They determined that we might have the basis for bringing a suit and they agreed to represent us pro bono. Next, I called Mr. Robert Smerling, who ran the Angelika, and set up a lunch to discuss the issue. Ron Feiner (BAM's entertainment lawyer and my future partner), accompanied me on what would go down in the annals of BAM's history as the "Godfather Lunch." Mr. Smerling chose the restaurant. It was an Italian place way over on the east side, replete with checkered tablecloths and huge hunks of cheese and olives on the table, reminding me of the scene in *The Godfather* in which the police lieutenant gets his head blown off, and Sollozzo gets assassinated by the young Michael Corleone.

As we walked into the restaurant to meet Mr. Smerling, we saw that we were the only people there. Right away, we started discussing the clearance issue, but then one of the waiters came over to take our order. "We're talking!" Smerling said forcefully and with a scowl, waving him away. The waiter backed away, rattled, and in the silence that followed, I saw my opening and went for it. "Mr. Smerling, with all due respect, the city has given us four million dollars to build these cinemas for the purpose of showing movies. We have to have them. We're a nonprofit. We're not even trying to make money. Your Angelika brand is so strong. You have all of Manhattan. You have eight theaters. How could we possibly compete with you?" Mr. Smerling thought it over for a minute, asked a few questions, and then made us "an offer we couldn't refuse." Angelika would release us from the clearance for an undefined "trial period," during which they would determine whether or not they had lost any market share or business because of us. We agreed to the trial and shook hands. Then, Mr. Smerling summoned the waiter and said, "Now, we eat!" Though I know it must have been in my head, I remember hearing *The Godfather* theme swelling in the background as we closed the deal. And from that moment on, the clearance was lifted. We never heard from them again.

Ron and I returned to BAM victorious and elated. We finally had access to movies, and so we began building a business, which turned out to be a crucial missing piece of programming that solidified BAM's status as a destination, a buzzing hub of cultural activity. The movies quickly became a critical component of BAM's success, bringing an additional two hundred thousand people into our buildings annually. The BAM movie business had the youngest audience, the cheapest tickets, and it kept the lights on 365 days a year. As the BAM Rose Cinemas gained traction, they ensured constant foot traffic and people meeting and spending time on our steps and in our lobbies every day. BAM was finally now active and filled with life all the time. The impact of this cannot be underestimated. It

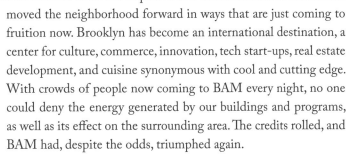

moved the neighborhood forward in ways that are just coming to fruition now. Brooklyn has become an international destination, a center for culture, commerce, innovation, tech start-ups, real estate development, and cuisine synonymous with cool and cutting edge. With crowds of people now coming to BAM every night, no one could deny the energy generated by our buildings and programs, as well as its effect on the surrounding area. The credits rolled, and BAM had, despite the odds, triumphed again.

CHAPTER TEN:

BAM Programs, Just the Highlights

One of our board members, Dan Klores, a former PR executive and manager turned filmmaker and playwright, represented the brilliant singer and songwriter Paul Simon for years. Dan brought Paul to shows at BAM, and Joe and I were thrilled whenever he attended our programs. While everyone in the world is, of course, a Paul Simon fan—I mean the guy not only wrote "The Sound of Silence," "America," "Slip Slidin' Away," "Mrs. Robinson," and about two hundred other great songs—many people had only seen him perform in large arena venues or at the historic Central Park concert in 1991. So, we decided to try and persuade Paul Simon to perform in the more intimate setting of our BAM theaters.

Ron had introduced me to Paul's album *Songs from The Capeman* when Paul was working on the piece as a Broadway show. Ron was representing the original director, Susana Tubert, who didn't stay with the show very long, but long enough for Ron to become completely captivated by the music. I, too, became obsessed with the story, the inspired Latin sound, the doo-wop aesthetic, and the great Paul Simon lyrics, co-written with the Nobel Prize–winning Caribbean/Saint Lucian poet Derek Walcott. Unfortunately, the production failed miserably on Broadway, but, in my view, its failure had nothing to do with the incredible music and lyrics. The theatrical components of the show just didn't hang together, and there seemed to be little camaraderie or cohesion among the creative team. Ron and I felt strongly that the towering achievement of this music needed to be liberated from the Broadway show, and Joe soon joined us in our quest.

Through Dan Klores, we reached out to Paul to see if he would be interested in mounting a concert version of *The Capeman* with the three-time Grammy winner and pioneer of Latin jazz, Oscar Hernández, leading the band. At first, it seemed like Paul was interested and that the idea was gaining momentum. Joe and I even had dinner with him to discuss it, and we were invited to a few meetings, including one memorable gathering at his apartment on Central Park. That afternoon, Paul invited Joe and me to his "guitar room studio." After getting a tour, we talked for a while, and he asked if we wanted to hear a new song he had written. It was surreal. Paul Simon was in his apartment playing and singing us a new song, and Joe and I were the only ones in the audience.

It was clear that the Broadway experience had been hard on Paul and, as a result, he was ambivalent about subjecting *The Capeman* to critics all over again. In any case, the initial heat of the original meetings soon faded, and it took a full nine years to persuade him to move forward with the project. Over those nine years, Joe, Dan, and I simply refused to let the idea die, and by the time we got the green light, it had morphed into something much larger, more interesting, and complex. My approach, whether it was fundraising or program conception, was to hang in until you manage to successfully bring a great idea to fruition. Nine years or twenty, we wanted Paul Simon to perform at BAM, and we knew it would be worth the wait.

With Alan Fishman, Joseph V. Melillo, and Paul Simon, 2008.

The full program idea that eventually materialized was much more than just restaging *The Capeman*. After a lot of back and forth, we concluded that the "BAMiest" thing to do was to celebrate the entire fifty-year career of Paul Simon, truly one of America's greatest popular singer-songwriters. It would be much more compelling to dive deep into his catalogue than to concentrate on one unusual piece or produce a "greatest hits" type concert. We proposed a full month of concerts to Paul, which he titled *Love in Hard Times*. The series, which he ultimately designed and curated, consisted of *Under African Skies* in the opera house, featuring all of his "globally inspired" works from albums such as *Graceland* to *Rhythm of the Saints*; *American Tunes* (which included a lot of the Simon & Garfunkel songs); and then, as promised, concerts of *The Capeman* at the BAM Harvey.

Once it was agreed that going big was the way forward, Paul, supported by the BAM team, which was led by Nick Schwartz-Hall, our line producer, proceeded to populate the concerts with a range of musicians who covered his songs in the most dynamic and engaging ways. David Byrne's version of "You Can Call Me Al" brought the audience to their feet and Grizzly Bear performing "Graceland" was notable for how different their interpretation was from the original. Josh Groban performed a sentimental and beautifully pure rendition of "Bridge Over Troubled Water."

Paul was a perfectionist. He brought Phil Ramone, the great sound designer and technician, into the process, which enhanced every performance. For me, of course, the greatest pleasure was watching the glorious music of *The Capeman* come to life. It may have been overly ambitious to present this wide range of concerts in such a short period of time, given the demands on Paul. He labored over every song. Many people came to all three shows, taking in the whole experience as if they were attending a film festival.

During the Broadway run of *The Capeman*, Paul and his co-lyricist, Derek Walcott, had a falling out, which severed their partnership. So when Derek came to *The Capeman* opening concert and joined us for the backstage toast, things felt momentarily strained, but everyone was thrilled by the show and rose above any former unpleasantness. Given the size and complexity of this endeavor, as well as the nine-year courtship, I would definitely qualify our month with Paul Simon as an incredible success.

Many of our board members couldn't understand why we didn't repeat the formula every year with a different pop star. Believe me, we wanted to. These shows were artistically brilliant, completely sold out, and represented an original approach to presenting popular music. After years of trying to convince Neil Young, Billy Joel, and a host of others to take it on, I came to understand how hard it was for a place like BAM to penetrate the world of rock and roll. There were legions of handlers and managers standing between us and the artists, making it almost impossible to broach the idea of a collaboration. As always, we had limited funds, and only 2,100 seats. We produced a smaller iteration of the idea with New Orleans legend Dr. John, but other than these two programs, we were unable to repeat the format.

When I think back on the process of producing those concerts, my respect for Paul Simon only increases. He certainly didn't have to take on a project of this scale, especially with zero economic upside for him personally, not to mention a huge time commitment. He just decided that he wanted to do it and then saw it through at the highest level. That is what great artists do, and also, hopefully, what great institutions, like BAM, enable them to do.

The Bridge Project

A nother ambitious undertaking, which expanded the global reach, brand, and reputation of BAM, was the Bridge Project. While Joe Melillo, like Harvey before him, was a global-arts-presenting specialist deep in his heart, he also had ambitions as a producer. Because we had successfully worked with the director Sam Mendes on several productions when he served as the leader of London's Donmar Warehouse, Joe approached him with the idea of developing a producing entity that would coproduce two plays a year for three consecutive years. The result was the Bridge Project, and our theatrical partner in the venture was the Old Vic, then headed by Kevin Spacey. The concept was to produce two classical plays (Shakespeare, Chekhov, etcetera) each season with a cast consisting of both British and American actors. The works would be performed at BAM, at the Old Vic, and at a range of international venues that would each contribute to the costs of creating each show.

Of course, this required enormous financial resources, but our vice president of development, Lynn Stirrup, and her British colleague at the Old Vic, Kate Pakenham, worked hard and were able to bring Bank of America in as the major sponsor for the three-year engagement. The first year was a great success, with outstanding actors from both sides of the pond involved, such as Sinéad Cusack, Ethan Hawke, and Simon Russell Beale. When the first season tour culminated with the performance of Shakespeare's *The Winter's Tale* in an ancient theater in Epidaurus, Greece, lit only by candlelight, for an audience of ten thousand people, we felt like rock stars.

The second year was more complicated, when lead actor Stephen Dillane delivered a nearly inaudible performance of *The Winter's Tale* at BAM and, by year three, the two-play schedule had clearly become too difficult for both institutions, especially given the extent of the tour. We resolved for the final year just to present one play, *Richard III*, starring Kevin Spacey. Bank of America agreed to the one-show season, given that Kevin wanted to embark on a sprawling tour that included several destinations beyond Europe, such as Hong Kong (China), Doha (Qatar), and Singapore. In spite of the inherent challenges of producing and touring new classical plays to far-flung locations, many of which did not have English as their primary language, the Bridge Project turned out to be a resounding success, in large part due to the theatrical brilliance of Sam Mendes and the leadership of Joe Melillo. In many ways, it redeemed Harvey's aborted train wreck known as the BAM Theater Company.

It was clear right from the start that Kevin Spacey was devoted to the role of Richard III. He showed up on the first day of rehearsal with his lines fully memorized and in top physical condition. I heard that he hired both a trainer and a chef to get him in shape for the part, and when we started work, he was fully prepared. The tour was well received everywhere, but even I, who was not on the front lines of the production, could sense trouble with Spacey as we brought the production to BAM, the final stop of the tour. He showed up two hours late to the cast party, seemed disoriented, made quick remarks thanking the actors, and left after ten minutes. The donors were deeply disappointed. Spacey also made a documentary about the show and tour, and BAM was barely featured or mentioned. Who could have known at the time that Spacey's fate, to be brought down by the #MeToo movement, would in some respects mirror that of his signature character, the self-destructive and villainous Richard III?

RadioLoveFest

WNYC–New York Public Radio rented the opera house in 2014 for the purpose of presenting two live performances of their popular show *Radiolab*, which featured Robert Krulwich and Jad Abumrad unpacking unique scientific phenomena and ideas in the most entertaining and heartfelt manner. I was on my way home one evening and decided to pop into the theater to see how it was going. Standing at the back, watching the completely sold-out performance, I was struck by the level of appreciation these radio hosts engendered in their fans. I was doubly struck by how inexpensive the production was because, after all, it was a radio show.

At that moment, watching an audience completely captivated by the sparse setting on the stage, I instantly saw the possibilities for a great festival. A partnership with WNYC that featured several iconic radio shows live could result in many positive outcomes. The shows had devout fans. The content potential (*This American Life*; *Radiolab*; *Wait, Wait . . . Don't Tell Me!*; *The Moth*; etcetera) was enormous, with one great show or host after the next. The cost to present, as predicted, was totally reasonable, and, best of all, BAM's name would be promoted on the radio endlessly by WNYC, the largest NPR affiliate in the country. For WNYC, the festival provided an opportunity to offer a series of terrific live

Above:
Kevin Spacey as Richard III in the Bridge Project, spring 2012.

Opposite:
Carin Gilfry and Ira Glass in "This American Life: One Night Only at BAM," RadioLoveFest, spring 2014.

Following spread:
The Bridge Project in Epidaurus, Greece. The ultimate Temple of Theatre.

shows to their members, who were generally only able to hear them on radio—a potential fundraising bonanza. It was, as they say, a win-win for all involved.

I called Laura Walker, president of WNYC, to discuss the idea, which she also embraced. American Express immediately came in as our initial sponsor, and we were off to the races. As partners, we sometimes struggled, since radio broadcast professionals and performing arts administrators often deal with deadlines in different ways (presenting live shows usually requires a much longer lead time than radio), but there was no question that audiences adored the shows, which were filled to capacity. When we launched the festival, we spent a lot of time talking, debating, and going crazy trying to come up with the right name for it. We tried hundreds of possibilities and had almost settled on RadioLive, which no one really liked, because it implied that radio wasn't usually live, which wasn't exactly true. In any case, Alice Bernstein, our executive vice president, was sending a memo about the project to all of the staff on both sides and, in a rare typographical mistake, she wrote "RadioLove" instead of "RadioLive." And that was it. Everyone at BAM and WNYC agreed that RadioLoveFest was the perfect name and so it came to be, through a happy accident.

Eat, Drink & Be Literary

One of my favorite programs came to fruition in an unusual way. As is probably apparent by now, I read everything that showed up on my desk, including brochures and annual reports from other cultural organizations that had BAM on their mailing lists. Usually, I scanned for fundraising ideas and immediately moved straight to their donor lists, but for some reason, when a pamphlet arrived from the National Book Foundation (NBF), which annually bestowed one of the most important literary prizes in America upon worthy authors, I was captivated by the depth and range of their programs.

Book clubs were reentering popular culture at the time, and it occurred to me that BAM and the NBF could create a new type of book club that would draw people together in large numbers to engage, over food and drinks, with the work of celebrated writers. I conferred with Joe, who liked the concept, and then I placed a call to the head of the NBF, in which I proposed that we develop an ongoing series that would include a buffet dinner with live music followed by a featured author reading from their work and then an audience discussion hosted by an expert moderator. The evening would culminate with a book signing and sales. In essence, we would, through this program, build and convene a vibrant community around literature, just as we had around music, dance, theater, and opera. The NBF loved the idea. They had access to some of the most talented writers in the world, and by then Fort Greene, Brooklyn, was ground zero for New York authors and editors, so we were able to mobilize the same literary population that often came to shows at BAM and lived right in the neighborhood to take part in this new kind of programming.

Joe named the series "Eat, Drink & Be Literary," and the program was an immediate success. The audience capacity was 250 people per event and the easygoing format of food, drinks, reading, and conversation radiated with warmth and good humor.[1]

Participating authors were given the option to read from whatever book of theirs they chose, which freed them to try new material or something special, often different from what they would read on the usual book promotion tour, even though we welcomed those texts as well. For over ten years, brilliant writers, from Paul Auster to Jennifer Egan to Joyce Carol Oates, Walter Mosley, Julian Barnes, Karl Ove Knausgaard, and Lynn Nottage graced our stage along with the talented moderators, such as the playwright Wendy Wasserstein and the *New Yorker* fiction editor Deborah Treisman. It was a literary tour de force. One of our

---

1   This crowd was literally obsessed with the program and arrived early to obtain the best seats in our Lepercq Space. People were so early that we started serving them wine in the lobby while they waited for the house to open. Believe me, the wine was great, too. Our donor, Joseph Steinberg, owned a fabulous California winery and he contributed his wonderful Pine Ridge reds and whites, which were as welcome as the great books.

generous friends, Martha (Marty) Rubin, loved the program so much that she endowed it with a five-hundred-thousand-dollar contribution.

There was, however, one event that proved a bit tricky, when the often-prickly, legendary playwright Edward Albee was our featured guest. Albee wasn't quite buying into the eating and drinking parts of the evening. When I went to bring him up to the stage, he informed me, in no uncertain terms, "Karen, if I hear anyone clinking a glass or silverware, I am out of here!" Before introducing him, I decided just to deal with it straight on. "My friends," I said to the audience, "our guest, Mr. Albee, has warned me that if he hears any clinking of silver or glasses, he is leaving! Please be on your best behavior." Not a clink was heard and Albee gave a splendid reading.

The evening was not over, however. There was a testy moment during the Q&A when a woman in the audience questioned why Albee had written a sequel to his famous one-act play, *The Zoo Story*, when, according to her, it was perfect as is. Albee was flabbergasted and asked her, "Madam, I beg your pardon, but whose play is it, anyway?"

She responded, "It's ours now, Mr. Albee. I think it belongs to the public."

"Oh, you do, do you?" responded an increasingly agitated Albee. The debate escalated from there, with the entire audience taking sides. I think watching 250 people become passionately incensed about *The Zoo Story* actually appealed to Albee, and I was pretty sure I saw a hint of a smile when he sat down to sign books at the end of the evening.

BAMart

The never-ending quest for money often led us to create new types of programs, and so it was with BAMart. To develop this idea, we reengaged our old friends and fundraising colleagues, Livet Reichard (Anne Livet and Steve Reichard), who were instrumental in bringing the visual arts world into the Next Wave Festival. Livet Reichard proposed publishing artist print portfolios as a way of generating funds. The concept was (1) find a donor or dealer to underwrite the production of a set of prints; (2) ask a series of great artists who loved BAM to donate the pieces; (3) print and sell a limited edition; (4) give the donor several sets for their own use; (5) give artists' proofs of each set to the contributing artists; and (6) keep one set for BAM and build a collection. We alternated between prints and photographs for three stunning editions, and the idea proved to be a great success.

This process worked well for both the portfolio and single edition prints. As always, the range of participating artists was fabulous, including Roy Lichtenstein, Julian Schnabel, Richard Avedon, Annie Leibovitz, and many others. The people who purchased these prints treasured them, and so BAMart became an important pillar of our annual fundraising. But that was just the beginning. From the initial portfolio concept, one of our board members, Dr. David Ramsey, came up with a new strategy: inviting an artist to put a "work" on the cover of the BAMbill every fall and spring. The artist would receive tremendous exposure in front of large audiences, and we would have the opportunity to sell the original piece. Important creations by Yoshitomo Nara, Philip Taaffe, Louise Bourgeois, and others graced our covers for decades, and this became another signature component of the BAM brand.

Opposite:
Another BAMart fundraising project was this Next Wave Swatch that played Philip Glass music as the alarm sound, 1994.

Following spread, from left:
Edward Albee headlines Eat, Drink & Be Literary, spring 2011.

Eat, Drink & Be Literary in the Lepercq Space, 2016.

Left:
When Louise Bourgeois designed this print, *Hamlet and Ophelia*, for BAM, she explained to me in a very thick French accent that the way print buyers could identify Ophelia was by her high heels. Hamlet's identity also seemed pretty obvious to me!

Opposite, from top:
Making yet another speech, 2013.

Andy Warhol and Merce Cunningham backstage, 1968.

"Carpet as Art" in the Opera House by carpet and textile designer Madeline Weinrib.

Following spread:
Poster by Keith Haring, also set designer for *Secret Pastures*, Next Wave Festival, 1984.

Pages 172–173:
Artist José Parlá spent all night painting his BAM Fisher Building mural *Gesture Performing Dance, Dance Performing Gesture* right on the wall, 2012.

Page 174:
The KAWS mural across the street with the David Byrne bike racks in front.

Page 175:
One of five windows featuring the lighting installation *Stars* by Leo Villareal, Peter Jay Sharp Building, 2007. Our staff refer to them as the "Leo Lights."

BAMart evolved into annual auctions,[2] during which we displayed the donated works on temporary walls in our lobby. These strategies filled our building with wonderful works of art while also filling our coffers with funding. It was the perfect merger of fundraising and programming. And since visual artists had been part of the BAM community from the beginning of Harvey's tenure, the works of major artists would also show up onstage (e.g., Merce Cunningham worked with Andy Warhol on *RainForest* in the early seventies; William Kentridge designed and directed *The Magic Flute*; and Keith Haring paired with Bill T. Jones and Arnie Zane in the dance work *Secret Pastures*). Inspired by the success of the auctions, we launched exhibition programs in all of our public spaces. One of my favorites was a show created by Dr. Lisa, a self-proclaimed psychoanalyst. She put her subjects on the couch, gave them a personalized therapy session, and wrote a diagnosis and prescription (which hung on the walls along with a photo of the "patient"). I was one of the people who was treated by Dr. Lisa and, no surprise, she proclaimed that I was a workaholic and suggested various remedies for my condition! We also commissioned a large mural by José Parlá, which gave the lobby of the BAM Fisher heart, while an installation by KAWS in the empty lot across the street on Lafayette Avenue, filled with decorative bike racks designed by David Byrne, gave it soul. The pièce de résistance, of course, were the amazing "Leo Lights," as we called them, or *Stars*, a light installation by Leo Villareal,

2   Annie Leibovitz often attended BAM shows and agreed one year to serve as chair of our art auction. I was walking around at the opening taking pictures with my old point-and-shoot camera. Annie saw me and asked to look at what was by then an antique device. She held out the camera, had me stand next to her, and snapped. "Now you have one of my pictures," she said. She made me feel like a celebrity. (You can see that picture on page 234).

illuminating the front of our historic Peter Jay Sharp Building at 30 Lafayette Avenue.

BAMart, with the assistance of the Robert W. Wilson Charitable Trust, led by Richard Schneidman, has now evolved and includes a magnificent public art program for the entire district, which will feature "Leo Lights," as well as other major pieces to be installed on each of BAM's buildings. The presence of these works announces to the world, "You are now in a place of art, a cultural district."[3]

Sundance Institute at BAM

At some point, in the early days of BAM cinema, Harvey was having dinner with Dick Fisher and his wife, Jeanne Donovan Fisher, and Robert Redford. Jeanne was on the board of Redford's Sundance Institute and Dick was chair of the BAM Endowment Trust. At dinner, they talked about doing something together, but it never materialized. Nevertheless, there was still a great deal of interest on both sides. So years later, when I was president and running the cinemas, I said to Jeanne, "Let's revisit the Sundance at BAM idea. Let's really do it this time, and think about what it could be." So, we met with Redford and Ken Brecher, who was then president of the Sundance Institute, and John Cooper, then deputy programmer, and we came up with the idea of a three-year initiative. Each year, we would present ten days of films from both the Sundance Film Festival and from theatrical events connected to the Sundance Institute. I wanted to call the initiative "SunBAMce." And they said, "No, we will call it Sundance Institute at BAM," which was a good decision in the end.

We held a big opening night premiere in the opera house that May, and then we ran films from 11:00 a.m. to 11:00 p.m. on the BAM Rose screens for the next week and a half. It was a completely immersive experience. Each January, we sent a whole team out to the festival in Park City, Utah, to work with the Sundance staff to program the BAM festival three months later. The festival got a lot of press and attention, and it was yet another example of our collaborating with a leader in the field, one that shared our mission of bringing bold, daring work to adventurous audiences.

3   Every aspect of how a cultural institution presents itself to the world should be thought about in terms of "art." This concept extends well beyond programming and marketing to every aesthetic choice concerning the way an institution looks and feels. For example, I have referred to the BAM art program as both a fundraising tool and a way to enliven all of our public spaces with paintings, drawings, and sculpture; selecting decor for our theaters was also part of this thinking. Therefore, when the opera house and our cinemas needed new carpeting, I reached out to a friend of BAM, the talented textile/carpet designer Madeline Weinrib, who had her own atelier at ABC Carpets in Manhattan. She was excited to design our historical theaters' flooring and donated her beautiful creations to BAM, adding luster to our spaces and reinforcing BAM's commitment to every kind of artistic discipline.

NOVEMBER 15·7PM, 16·8PM, 17·8PM

CRET
TURES

BILL T. JONES
ARNIE ZANE
CHOREOGRAPHY

PETER GORDON
AND THE
LOVE OF LIFE
ORCHESTRA
MUSIC

KEITH HARING
DECOR

WILLI SMITH
COSTUMES

© KHARING 1984

THIS PRODUCTION IS MADE
POSSIBLE IN PART WITH FUNDS
FROM NEA, NYSCA, CONSOLIDATED EDISON
AND OTHER CONTRIBUTORS

BROOKLYN
ACADEMY
OF MUSIC

PM. TICKET AND TRAVEL INFORMATION CALL 212·636·4100

Judith and Alan
Fishman
Space

Today at BAM: Celeste and J
                     4:50, 7:15, 9

Also, BAM was in a position, as it had been with so many other partners, such as WNYC and the NBF, to extend the reach of Sundance in ways that benefitted both institutions and moved us both forward. Sundance now had a home in New York, and BAM now had the imprimatur of Robert Redford and the highest level of independent films associated with our cinemas. It was yet another step in the advancement of BAM's visibility and the establishment of Brooklyn as the epicenter of all things hip and exciting.

At the end of the three years, we wanted to continue with the festival, but Sundance didn't. For one thing, Geoff Gilmore, their head programmer, never liked the idea. He just didn't see what was in it for them. Ultimately, John Cooper also felt it was too time-consuming and draining to go right from their own festival into Sundance Institute at BAM. He wanted to stop as well. I also think that they felt they could sell the Sundance brand to other locations, and it would be far more lucrative than working with BAM and having to be involved in fundraising for our events. This of course made some sense, when I thought about it from their perspective. On the other hand, we believed that BAM provided a platform for getting the best Sundance films in front of the New York public, as opposed to just industry insiders, who are the primary Sundance Film Festival attendees. But Sundance, after all, isn't primarily an audience-driven festival. It's a filmmakers' festival and market, which is largely about identifying great independent films and then buying, selling, and distributing them. We thought that the partnership had real potential, but, at the end of the day, it was probably much more successful for us than it was for them. It was still, however, a worthy program, and when it was determined we would not continue, John Cooper said, "You're ready now to start your own festival. Go ahead and do it." We had learned a lot over the three years and decided that was actually a great idea. Our staff was ready to jump in. We launched BAMcinemaFest the following year. Now we were free to cherry pick the best films not only from Sundance but also from South by Southwest, Berlin, and great festivals from all over the world. It was also an excellent showcase for the legions of Brooklyn filmmakers who were now part of the growing local artist community. Once again, we were ready to fly!

The three-year Sundance Institute at BAM program not only enhanced the BAM cinema program enormously through its film offerings, workshops, and general name recognition, it also brought us closer to Robert Redford. On the day we announced the partnership, the press was out in full force and all of Brooklyn (especially borough president and cheerleader-in-chief Marty Markowitz) were wildly excited.

Redford and his team were consummate professionals and most of the programs (screenings, workshops, talks, and even theatrical presentations) for the entire three-year run sold out. Following this positive experience, which resulted in the creation of our own two-week film festival, I asked Bob Redford to allow us to present a separate BAMcinématek retrospective of his films where he appeared as either actor or director. In addition to hosting a variety of screenings, we organized a showing of the classic Watergate film, *All the President's Men*, followed by a talk moderated by radio host Brian Lehrer and featuring Bob Woodward and Carl Bernstein, the real journalists who broke the story,

Above:
With Sally Field and Robert Redford, Sundance Institute at BAM, 2009.

Opposite, from top:
Installation in the Dorothy W. Levitt Lobby, Sundance Institute at BAM, 2006.

The BAM Rose Cinema, Sundance Institute at BAM, 2006.

along with Redford. But the icing on the cake was a program we put together that was one of those quintessential BAM special events, wherein we showed a different Redford film on each screen followed by a Q&A for the entire audience in the opera house.

On the day of the screenings, I introduced Bob before each film and he gave some context to each audience. Then, during the screenings, I ran around to each cinema to gauge reactions. When I entered cinema 1, Redford was kissing Jane Fonda in *The Electric Horseman* and the audience sighed. In cinema 2, he was bedded down in a tent with Meryl Streep in *Out of Africa*, and there was more sighing. In cinema 3, Bob was locked in a fierce embrace with Barbra Streisand in *The Way We Were*—an outpouring of sighs. And finally, in cinema 4, there was *The Natural* with Redford as Roy Hobbs, the doomed baseball hero who had, against all odds and in great physical pain, just smacked a homer over the left field wall. At that point, I heard someone weeping in the last row. It was Adam Max, our board vice-chair, crying his eyes out.

SHOWBILL ®

BAM

BROOKLYN ACADEMY OF MUSIC

PINA BAUSCH
TANZTHEATER WUPPERTAL

ARIEN

KONTAKTHOF

NEXT WAVE FESTIVAL • 85

CHAPTER ELEVEN:

The Water Gala, *The Hard Nut*, and the 150th Anniversary

One of the most famous fundraising events in the history of BAM was the great "Water gala" night. It took place in 1985 in conjunction with the opening of the third Next Wave Festival. One year earlier, we had introduced the groundbreaking German choreographer Pina Bausch and her company, Tanztheater Wuppertal, to New York with a trio of premieres, *The Rite of Spring*, *1980*, and *Café Müller*. Bausch and her works were well received, if not universally loved, capturing the attention of audiences and critics, reaffirming her as a serious force in modern dance. Bausch's dance-theater pieces were highly accessible, direct, psychologically rich, and emotionally dynamic. She worked collaboratively with her dancers, over long periods of time, to devise work through improvisation and the use of sense memories to explore emotions. The resulting performances featured not only movement but spoken dialogue, songs, vocalized sounds, silence, and theatrical spectacle, such as staging dance works in fields of flowers, between reeds, in huge piles of dirt, or immersed in water. The 1985 Next Wave Festival was set to open with one of her most ambitious spectacles to date, *Arien*, in which twenty-four dancers moved frenetically through three inches of water, kicking up spray in all direction. There was, at one point, a large (fake) hippopotamus onstage.[1] And for much of the Bausch piece, rain poured down from the rafters upon the dancers in an unrelenting deluge. The piece was so challenging to produce that it had only been performed at two other venues outside of Bausch's theater in Wuppertal, Germany.

As the old saying goes, when it rains, it pours. However, the inverse is also true . . . ("water, water all around and not a drop to drink"). New York was suffering from a pretty serious drought at the time. We couldn't obtain the water we needed in the city and had to purchase all five thousand gallons from a supplier in New Jersey. The day before the so-called Water gala, to our great relief, the first shipment of water arrived on time. The stagehands needed to test it first, before it could be piped onstage, and so they got out what looked like a fancy thermometer and inserted it into one of the gigantic tanks. As soon as it hit the water, the device practically melted. There had been a terrible mix up. Instead of clean water, the supplier had brought us tanks contaminated with toxic dry-cleaning chemicals. The polluted water had to be left in our parking lot and later guys in hazmat suits were brought in to move it off site to safe storage. The second shipment of water from New Jersey arrived too late for the dress rehearsal, and so the dancers had to conduct it dry.

1   This piece should not be confused with another work by the artist Martha Clarke, called *Endangered Species*, which opened at the Majestic Theater in 1990. That piece actually featured a real elephant, Flora, that lived in our parking lot throughout the run of the production. Suffice it to say, watching the elephant consume giant bales of hay on Fulton Street was the highlight of that particular show.

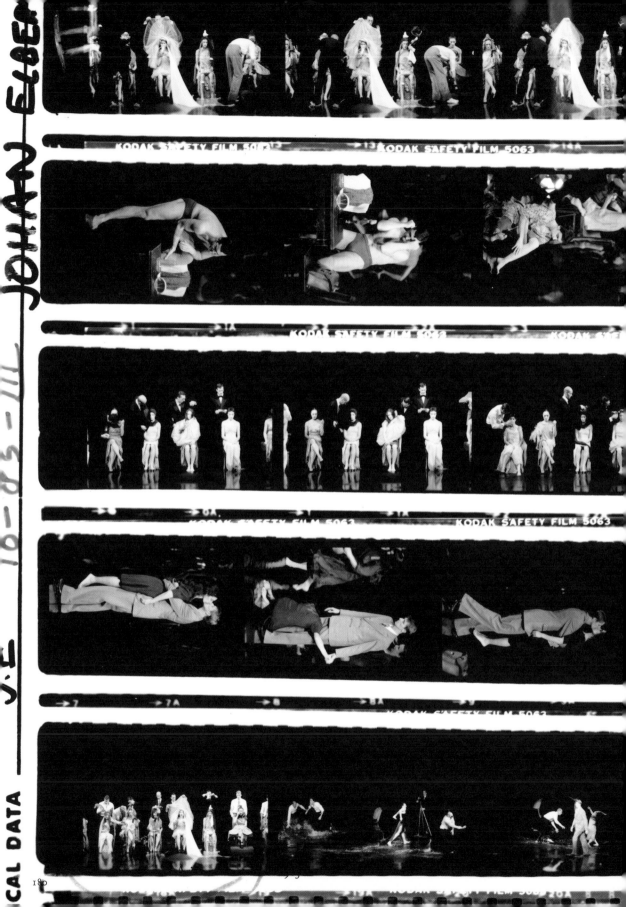

To make matters worse, in order to keep the dancers from contracting pneumonia during the three-hour rainstorm of recycled water, the second shipment had to be heated to 140 degrees Fahrenheit before it was pumped onstage, so it could cool down to 90 degrees for the performance. On the morning of the gala, the stage crew discovered that the heating system was not working properly. We now had clean water, but it was too cold for the performers. Fortunately, we had a board member who ran Brooklyn Union Gas; he marshaled his workers, along with a crew from their competitor Con Edison, to help save the day. They arrived with a variety of heating devices to get the water to the desired temperature. It was an all-hands-on-deck moment. We had production staff diving into pools of water under the stage to test the temperature, while gas and electric workers rolled up their sleeves and employed all their skills to help us make our deadline.

Ultimately, it took about ninety minutes longer than we had hoped to get the water heated. The main sponsor for the night was the French liquor company Rémy Martin. And so when the two thousand audience members, including five hundred black-tie gala guests, arrived at the opera house, the BAM development staff huddled together for a minute and made an executive decision: *Let's crack open the Rémy and pour them all a drink.* Harvey went onstage and announced that we had a "water crisis," and said there would be Rémy Martin for all in the lobby. By the time the show started, about an hour later, the entire audience was toasted, because, after all, we had all this free incredible Rémy Martin and the audience went through cases. It was a rowdy crowd that watched *Arien* that night for three hours before going off to the party afterward, which began close to midnight and was simply nuts. Everyone was there—as I recall—including Andy Warhol, Bianca Jagger, Richard Gere, and Calvin Klein, among many others. The mood, probably due to the Rémy, was incredibly upbeat. I'm pretty sure the painter Robert Rauschenberg was seen dancing on a table.

Another unforgettable story from the fundraising annals of BAM is the night of *The Hard Nut* gala. *The Hard Nut* was the choreographer Mark Morris's take on *The Nutcracker*. It was stunning, irreverent, and completely original, and it was our first Christmas extravaganza. Mark's greatest talent is his ability to integrate music with movement, and his utilization of the full Tchaikovsky score—something that few other choreographers had ever done—to create a radical new version of a traditional holiday staple revealed things about the original music that no other *Nutcracker* had touched. Inspired by the black-and-white cartoons of Charles Burns and featuring the Brooklyn Youth Chorus singing from the stage-right

Above, from top:
Harvey backstage in the Opera House basement dealing with the water crisis during the Tanztheater Wuppertal production of *Arien*, Next Wave Festival, 1985.

Bianca Jagger with Pina Bausch, 1985.

Following spread:
New York Times coverage of *The Hard Nut* gala, 1992.

box seats in the opera house, it was a bold, postmodern spectacle, full of drag and gender fluidity, which referenced all of the *Nutcrackers* that preceded it with irony, parody, and even respect. It was also very expensive, and in order to present it in the 1992 Next Wave Festival, we planned another gala—this time a holiday-themed post-performance party at Grand Central Terminal—to raise the funds we needed to cover the production.

The Hard Nut was a major opportunity for BAM. Finally, we had a show on our hands that was "contemporary and edgy," but not so weird that it would alienate a gala audience. It was a delightfully strange, tongue-in-cheek, cartoon version of the *Nutcracker* New Yorkers knew all too well. It served to reason that anyone who might come to *The Hard Nut* gala would be familiar with the Balanchine version of the ballet, which ran annually at Lincoln Center, and would likely be amused and entertained by Mark's interpretation. And, there was an added bonus that the gala chair was the legendary Anna Wintour, the force behind *Vogue* magazine and a friend and fan of Mark's. We quickly sold out all the tables and gala tickets and were excited to generate as much revenue and support as possible from Mark's holiday hit. Everything had fallen into place and all signs pointed to what would no doubt be a very successful fundraising event, perhaps one of the most successful we'd ever produced. The only problem was the weather.

On the morning of the gala, we woke up to perhaps the worst forecast in the history of mankind. A giant nor'easter, the likes of which the city had never seen, was barreling up the East Coast and bearing down on New York. It was pouring, hailing, and freezing. The winds were howling, and it was shaping up to be the most miserable day in eternity. We gathered early at BAM to discuss whether to cancel the gala. All day long, we went back and forth, arguing the pros and cons, never coming to consensus. At one point, while talking with Harvey and Nancy Umanoff, the executive director of the Mark Morris Dance Group (MMDG), on the phone about it, I ventured out onto the roof of the BAM opera house and felt like King Lear on the heath, with all of the elements spiraling down upon my head, conspiring against me. Finally, we decided we were just going to go ahead with the gala. It was too complicated to cancel.

Of course, the seating was completely screwed up, because we had no idea who was coming and who wasn't. People had been calling all day to find out if the gala was on or not. Given the extremity of the weather, we had no idea how people were going to get to BAM, let alone to the gala, but we threw caution to the wind (which was blowing at an unprecedented speed). By 2:30 p.m., we were telling people, "It's on. Get here any way you can. Late seating or never." So when the curtain went up that night, some people had actually arrived dressed in black tie and boots, drenched but miraculously present. We were so heartened by the tenacity of the crowd. The house was pretty empty at the start of the show, but magically—with that special Next Wave BAM karma—by intermission, the theater had filled up, almost to capacity. This was the pre–cell phone era, and yet word had spread that something extraordinary was happening that shouldn't be missed. People kept showing up and flowing into the space throughout the performance. Everyone was excited to be there. It was that thing that sometimes happens, when people transcend adversity together. Everyone shared a common bond that night. These are the moments as a fundraiser and leader you dream of creating but rarely do; the sense that we're all in this together, no matter what.

Suzanne Slesin

It Was Wild, Outside and In

Any academy of music in a storm . . . The night the toys invaded MOMA . . . Crying buckets over two boys and a horse. Make that two boys and three horses.

hurricane-like weatl
fashionable people
worrying about the d
houses. Their main
from Manhattan to **

At 7 P.M., 1,900 peo
Brooklyn Academy «
can premiere of Ma
Hard Nut," the icond
quirky version of Te
cracker." It had beer
Anna Wintour, the e«
rick McCarthy, the «
of Fairchild Publica
evening, were decie
really *had* to go on. A
with the Transit Autl
way train to take the
Grand Central Terı
formance party in the
room. But by midaft«
tem was still out of F

Ms. Wintour had n«
er in the day when

---

sticks, pecans and, of course, walnuts.

As the New York City Gay Men's Chorus, in red bow ties and ribbons, filled the 50-foot-high room with carols, Steven Meisel, Ross Bleckner, Ian Schrager, Lucie de la Falaise, Bianca Jagger, Anne Bass, Marc Jacobs, Oscar de la Renta, Blaine Trump and others were playing the usual musical chairs. Waiters with silver trays served them artichoke bottoms with globs of caviar, accompanied by potato salad and a few greens. And just when the main course should have made its entrance, lemon cake and raspberry ice cream appeared instead. More than one guest said he wished he had accepted the proffered seconds of artichokes and caviar.

"I'm off to have a steak right now," said Marian McEvoy, editor of Elle Décor magazine, as Mr. Morris, the guest of honor, did a couple of grand jetés across the room, beer bottle in hand.

The Night of the Living Toys

On their way to dinner at the Museum of Modern Art on Wednesday, 1,000 men and women were accosted by talking rabbits, the Tin Man and a princess on stilts. Having just attended the New York premiere of "Toys," a wacky movie starring Robin Williams and John Cusak that's set in a Frank Gehry-like toy factory, the scene didn't seem out of the ordinary.

The museum, however, did not look like itself, for vintage toys were on display on plexiglass pedestals and cartoon characters roamed the galleries. A big cuddly Barney, the dinosaur hearthrob of millions of children, was a wallflower. Apparently, no one had told him this just wasn't his regular crowd. "Who's Barney?" asked Ellen Liman, the chairwoman of the city's Advisory Commission for Cultural Affairs. "I came to see the Matisse show again."

On the second floor, Ralph and Ricky Lauren milled around dozens of red-cloth-covered tables that were set with yellow napkins tied with ponytail holders. Hardly anybody was in a rush to sit down — there was just too much to look at. Andrew Stein, the president of the City Council, was there, kissing people politician style, while L L Cool J, one of the stars of "Toys," who was dressed appropriately in combat boots, sidestepped a freckle-faced Raggedy Ann. And there was Frédéric Fekkai, the star hair

stylist. "An inteı
Fekkai would say
added, "I liked I
furry."

Walter Cronkit
busy helping them
Lazy Susan at thı
disappointed by
Cronkite said. Wh
interested in, ho\
Matisse show.

"Let's go," M
they tell us we hav

Horses for Cours

On Monday, th
three horses, actu
"Into the West" a
first part of a ber
programs in New

Harvey Weinste
amax Films, the
movie, which star
Barkin, for the ev

A dark fable, "
the adventures of f
"Now I know a lo

last Friday's
y of the most
York were not
n of their beach
was how to get
at rush hour.
expected at the
for the Ameri-
s's ballet "The
oreographer's
ty's "The Nut-
d go all day, as
ogue, and Pat-
vice president
airmen of the
ther the show
ey'd arranged
a special sub-
m Brooklyn to
the post-per-
stored waiting
e subway sys-

eassured earli-
seen what she

Anna Wintour was worried: if it rains enough, even a private subway train can be flooded.

called "desperate commuters" sitting on some of the 900 gilded ballroom chairs rented for the party, and she made a point to get out to BAM early. "I was the only person there for several hours," she said. But by 8 P.M. she had lots of company, as about 1,500 people made it to the auditorium. At intermission, everybody in the crowded lobby seemed to be patting himself on the back for getting there at all.

Kim Hastreiter, the publisher and co-editor of the downtown monthly magazine Paper, came with her group in a rented station wagon. "Like the Beverly Hillbillies," she said.

For Ms. Hastreiter, the journey had been well worth it. "The show was all so totally brilliant," she said, "especially the drag-queen fairies with their frozen-yogurt hairdos.".

After the performance, guests followed the call "Have your nuts ready" (the tokens for the evening were walnuts) as they were handed umbrellas and herded onto buses that took them around the corner to the Atlantic Avenue subway station, where they boarded the train for Grand Central and, finally, supper.

"We never see clean ones like this," said Esther Lorusso, the advertising manager for Alitalia, as she looked around the spanking-clean subway car. "It's like being on the monorail at Disneyland."

At Grand Central, jaded eyes were mesmerized by the gigantic regilded chandeliers in the refurbished waiting room, where Robert Isabell had made tower-shaped center-pieces of dried orange slices, cinnamon

---

lea," was all Mr.
e movie. Then he
air, so blond and

wife, Betsy, were
the shrimp on the
"I've never been
en tonight," Mr.
onkites were most
as looking at the

ite said, "before
our vegetables."

was a horse —
the screening of
feld Theater, the
ing for children's
y parks.
-chairman of Mir-
ors, had lent the
Byrne and Ellen

West" chronicles
and a white horse.
orses," Mr. Wein-

Scram, talking rabbit. Can't you see I'm communing with Matisse?

stein said. "They're Royal Lipizzaners. A male horse won't go into the water, so we needed three to make it all work."

That was news to Betsy Gotbaum, the Parks Commissioner. "It was a fantasy, and I fell in love with the horse," she said as she greeted guests who had made their way uptown to the American Museum of Natural History, where tables were set up under the shadows of prancing dinosaurs.

"I sobbed and sobbed," said Tupper Thomas, the administrator of Prospect Park in Brooklyn.

Stephen Rea, the Irish actor and star of "The Crying Game," who's currently appearing in "Someone Who'll Watch Over Me" on Broadway, was also teary eyed. "I cried buckets," he said. "But I'm sentimental. And I've got two little boys. Come to think of it, they would have been good in the film."

Maybe it was the herd of elephants in the middle of gallery that had many guests thinking of their children. "He might love it, but it would plague him," said Patsy Glazer, the director of public affairs for Seagram's, theorizing about her 6-year-old son Matthew's reaction to the film.

Ed Hayes, a Manhattan lawyer-about-town, was talking about his friendship with Ms. Gotbaum. A well-tended diorama featuring okapi (they're relatives of the giraffe) was in the background. "I'm Betsy's gardener in Bellport," he said, referring to the Long Island community where they both have summer houses. "It used to drive me crazy that she was the Parks Commissioner and that her yard was all messed up. So I planted trees and pruned shrubs."

Scenes from *The Hard Nut* gala, 1992.

Clockwise from top left: Front of *The Hard Nut* gala express.

Grand Central Station.

Guests en route to *The Hard Nut* gala at Grand Central Terminal.

Harvey Lichtenstein, Mark Morris, and gala chair Anna Wintour at *The Hard Nut* gala.

Guests en route to *The Hard Nut* gala at Grand Central Terminal.

New York City Gay Men's Chorus performing at *The Hard Nut* gala.

Since this was to be a holiday gala, we had arranged something truly spectacular. We had organized a special subway with the Metropolitan Transportation Authority (MTA) to run directly from Atlantic Avenue to Grand Central Terminal, where we were having the dinner. And we called it the Perlipat (a term used in the show) or, more simply, the Hard Nut Express. We decorated the cars with BAM signs in the windows, and as patrons entered Atlantic Terminal, we gave each of them a walnut as a token to get on the subway. We had our own track, and our own subway car. In spite of the raging nor'easter, which was flooding the streets of Brooklyn, the MTA agreed to go ahead with the plan because they, too, were now part of the event.

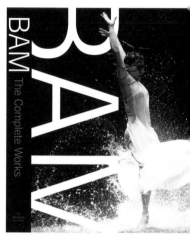

Everyone who had braved the elements to come to BAM was up for the adventure. After the performance, the crowd poured out of the theater and into the subway station, and we all boarded our train. Bing Crosby's "White Christmas" cackled over the subway cars' PA system. The mood was festive and the crowd was in high spirits. Because of the inclement weather, when we arrived at Grand Central, the majestic old station was virtually empty. We had the place to ourselves. So we walked up out of the subway into a vacant station, two and a half weeks before Christmas. As our guests entered the main concourse, the New York City Gay Men's Chorus, which we had engaged for the event—more than a hundred singers strong—serenaded them with Christmas carols. The grand concourse was theatrically lit to accentuate the sweep of the high clerestory arches and the shimmering zodiac, sparkling with stars. In the waiting room, where we held the dinner, the space flickered in the wavering light of a thousand votive candles. Between the sentimental notes of the Christmas carols, the glow of the thousand candles, and the unforgettable subway journey from BAM to Grand Central Terminal, many of the patrons were overwhelmed as they entered the station. It was one of those New York nights when the city lived up to its reputation as one of the greatest cultural centers in the world.

Mark and all of his dancers wore holiday outfits of red and green for the gala, and when he led his dancers in and paraded them through the space, moving gracefully and in unison, everyone leaped to their feet and cheered. Nobody argued about seating that night, as they usually did at galas, and for once, there were fewer complaints about the food. The whole night, from beginning to end, was illustrative of how the arts have the unique power to bring people together, even in the worst of circumstances. There was this feeling, as people talked about the event for weeks and months to come, that if you weren't there that night, you had really missed something historic. It became a badge of honor to have possessed the awareness and fortitude to persevere by attending the gala in spite of the terrible storm. *The Hard Nut* gala went down as one of the great social events of the decade.[2]

2   The Next Wave galas, with their imaginative locations and unusual shows, became part of the festival's legend. One year, in conjunction with another gala for Robert Wilson's show *The Black Rider*, we actually persuaded the director of the James A. Farley Post Office building, across the street from Penn Station, to allow us to host the dinner in their massive open atrium, where our dinner tables stretched from Thirty-first to Thirty-third Streets. As part of this event, we projected the words from historic love letters on the facade of the building. It was memorable.

BAM: The Complete Works, 2011.

Another time that all of the elements came together beautifully at BAM was our 150th anniversary year, which turned out to be an ideal platform for elevating our reputation, promoting the ascendance of Brooklyn, and, of course, maximizing fundraising. We started thinking about our approach to the celebration about two years prior to the launch. Our goal was, first and foremost, to present a transformative range of programs that reflected BAM's history and its future. To that end, Joe pulled out all the stops and programmed shows such as Robert Wilson's production *The Threepenny Opera*, featuring the Berliner Ensemble; the Merce Cunningham Legacy Tour; and the Dr. John retrospective, which bookended the Next Wave Festival and the winter/spring season. He also initiated a series of talks by iconic artists who had a long history of working with the institution, such as Meredith Monk,[3] Steve Reich, and Bill T. Jones.

Most important, however, was the publication of *BAM: The Complete Works*, a more than 350-page volume filled with essays, pictures, and time lines, the first book ever written about BAM from its origins in 1861 to the present. Each chapter represented a different era of BAM's history and was supplemented with personal reflections and essays by artists, board members, and community leaders. Of all the things Joe and I accomplished during our years of leadership, this book is among our premier achievements. The book told the story of BAM from a variety of perspectives—each chapter was drafted and structured by a different writer—pulled together seamlessly by our staff leaders on the project, our director of humanities, Violaine Huisman, and archive director, Sharon Lehner. *BAM: The Complete Works* delineated the organization's enduring role and influence on New York City and its lasting impact upon Brooklyn. From the presidents and first ladies who attended performances and made speeches, to tales of flood and fire, recession, depression, and redemption, BAM's longevity and survival is a testament to both the American spirit and Brooklyn grit. I urge anyone reading this book to pick up *BAM: The Complete Works* to see all of the great production photographs and stories. We were thrilled when the *New York Times Book Review*[4] selected it as the number-one holiday pick in December 2011. A feature-length documentary made by filmmaker Michael Sladek and screened on the OVATION network and WNET also enhanced the anniversary celebrations.

Another thrilling component of the anniversary was that, through the efforts of board vice-chair, Bill Campbell, and board member Thérèse Esperdy—both former JPMorgan Chase executives—and BAM's director of strategic marketing, Molly Meloy, we were able to secure a major million-dollar sponsorship from JPMorgan Chase for the 150th anniversary. This money gave us the freedom to be incredibly creative and expansive in our approach. So, in addition to the BAM book, we launched a pro-bono branding campaign

3   Meredith was a regularly featured performer in the Next Wave. Her breakthrough show at BAM was a piece she created with Ping Chong called *The Games*. When she reprised some songs from that show years later, I was sitting next to Joe in the opera house. Meredith introduced *The Games* by singing in her unique style the words, "Do You Remember, Do You Remember, Do You Remember." I turned to Joe and quietly mimicked her voice singing, "How could we forget? How could we forget? How could we forget?" Like her or not, Meredith's sound is truly unforgettable!

4   "The Joys of BAM," by Elsa Dixler, *New York Times Book Review*, December 2, 2011.

EVENING HOURS

A Line for Stamps (and One for Cocktails)

Brooklyn Academy of Music holds a dinner at the main post office in Manhattan, Nov. 20.

RIGHT 10:20 P.M.: About 750 guests at BAM's Next Wave gala dined in the lobby of the James A. Farley Building of the main post office, on Eighth Avenue in Manhattan. It was the first time such an event was held there. Dinner was served at tables that stretched from the 31st Street side of the lobby to the 33d Street side.

Photographs by BILL CUNNINGHAM for The New York Times

ABOVE 10:50 P.M.: PETER HELLMAN and FRAN KAUFMAN are served by a waiter at the gala's post-performance supper.

ABOVE 10:10 P.M.: Leni Schwendinger, an artist, projected images of mail carriers, letters, stamps and a world map on 18 of the 20 columns and on the stairway outside the post office.

ABOVE 10:25 P.M.: STEPHANIE FRENCH and JOHN KELLY were among the guests at the dinner.

ABOVE 10:35 P.M.: SCOTT OSMAN and JERYL MALLOY dine in front of one of the posters that decorate the main lobby of the post office.

ABOVE 10:30 P.M.: The dinner at the post office followed the American premiere of "The Black Rider," a pop opera that is a collaboration of Robert Wilson, William S. Burroughs and Tom Waits, at the Brooklyn Academy of Music.

ABOVE 10:25 P.M.: MARY SHARP CRONSON with KEVIN McKENZIE, the director of American Ballet Theater.

Above:
Gala guests entering the James A. Farley Building. The post office gala showcased that glorious landmark in a whole new light, 1993.

Opposite:
What a night! Dr. John's famous song says it all at the gala, 2012.

created by the bank's ad agency, McGarryBowen, and then, thanks to JPMorgan Chase, had the funding to execute it. The McGarryBowen team spent months at BAM talking to everyone, reviewing the programs and history and absorbing the general vibe of the neighborhood. Finally, on the day of the big reveal, our board leadership and executive staff convened in Bill Campbell's office for the presentation. It began with a powerful manifesto:

It can happen at a show. At the café.

It can happen three days later, while you're brushing your teeth.

It can happen anywhere, really.

This sense that you've been moved, altered.

The beauty is, it's different for everybody.

And that's what BAM is.

Yes, we are theater, and music, and art.

We are the Harvey, the Opera House, the BAM Fisher, the BAM Rose Cinemas.

Jazz. Drinks. Galas and Talks.

We are so many things, but the moment of impact.

That's the reason we're here.

And that moment, when it happens, you know it.

BAM. And then it hits you.

Cate Blanchett and Joel Edgerton revisited her on a rooftop in Clinton Hill.
Where did BAM hit you?

Sydney Theatre Company's A Streetcar Named Desire, BAM Harvey Theater, Nov 2009

BAM AND THEN IT HITS YOU

And then, though creative photo shoots that embodied the concept, the 150th anniversary sprang to life. The "BAM and Then It Hits You" campaign was a revelation. We bought placements on subway cars, dominated the advertising in the Atlantic Avenue subway station, showcased the photos at bus shelters, on postcards, and in all of our publications. We even ran a "Where Did BAM Hit You?" contest on our website, in which the winner won a free party on the Fisher roof. It was a tour de force campaign that won awards and recognition from the industry. For those of us in the room that day in Campbell's office, it was electrifying. As soon as the McGarryBowen team, led by Gordon Bowen, finished presenting the storyboards, the team was met with a standing ovation.

Our entire staff also got involved in devising components of the celebration. First, they formed a youth marketing committee wherein the next generation of employees from all departments got together and brainstormed ideas that would ignite our audience and reach an even younger demographic. Our audience analyses at the time showed that the median age of a BAM attendee was forty-four, about twenty years younger than Lincoln Center or Carnegie Hall attendees. We aimed to keep that trend moving downward in order to attract the theatergoers of the future. The youth marketing committee generated two great ideas, both of which we initiated. First, they came up with "Takeover," a late-night party, until 4:00 a.m., which would activate all of our venues with continuous activity. The cost was minimal. For twenty dollars you bought a wristband that granted you access to all venues all night, including a full series of music events that took place in the opera house, a club set up in Lepercq, and a video game lounge in the Hillman Studio[5] upstairs. The committee was also responsible for the film series in the BAM Rose Cinemas, including a "Lindsay Lohan Mid-Career Retrospective," which packed the theaters with young people. The three-dollar beers in the lobby didn't hurt, either. Our friends at the Brooklyn Brewery created a special designer brew for the 150th. They called it "BAMBoozle." The beer label was designed by the legendary Milton Glaser. We drank it for the full anniversary period. Needless to say, "Takeover" was a great success and we continued it for several years following the 150th.

Another member of our staff, Jonathan Bigelow, came up with a great professional development idea that connected our growing employee base in a unique way. He proposed that each year, beginning with the anniversary, we select one show, and for a few months leading up to it, each department would present its specific role in making that production happen to the rest of the staff. We called this excellent management tool and staff bonding exercise "Follow the Production" and it is still an effective team building strategy at BAM today.

Poster (featuring *Streetcar*) from the BAM 150th anniversary advertising campaign "BAM and Then It Hits You," 2012.

5   All of our rehearsal studios in all of our buildings were named by the Rita & Alex Hillman Foundation. Rita Hillman was an amazing woman who loved the theater and Harvey, even though she was a Manhattanite through and through. As Harvey used to say, "Any board that has Rita Hillman as a member can't be all bad." When she died, in her nineties, her grandson, Ahrin Mishan, took her seat on the board and became chairman of our education committee.

"*Your father and I have decided to give half your allowance to BAM.*"

CHAPTER TWELVE:

The Biggest Gifts

Sometimes you just get lucky. Generally, a fundraising strategy based on luck is essentially doomed. The odds are simply not in favor of an organization's leadership waking up one morning and finding that a hardworking secretary or the widow of Ray Kroc has just left you ten million dollars. Okay, it does happen, but not very often. Mostly, rejection and disappointment are your daily fare. However, once in a while, lightning strikes and, like magic, large amounts of money appear.

I had one of these out-of-body fundraising experiences on an otherwise normal, overcast New York day when I scheduled lunch with a loyal supporter and colleague, Susan Feder, who was program officer for the performing arts at the Andrew W. Mellon Foundation. Susan was one of those funders who was truly committed to her work. She diligently attended our shows and always returned phone calls, usually within hours. Mellon had been a supporter of BAM over the years, and the grants, particularly for BAM Opera, had been very generous. Given the cost of these shows, we needed all the help we could get! Opera was prohibitively expensive and terribly difficult to fund, especially if your audience, like ours, skewed generally younger and was not particularly wealthy.[1]

We had tried any number of approaches and partnerships to lower the cost but, in the end, presenting opera simply meant . . . more fundraising.[2] Thank God, Mellon "got" BAM Opera. They appreciated the fact that we were taking it on, presenting international productions that could be seen in few other places, and were outside of the mainstream repertory presented by most opera houses.

At the time of this particular lunch, Mellon had appointed a new president, who, serendipitously, happened to be a musicologist and loved opera. Luckily for us, Susan joined the foundation in 2007, and while I had met her at some BAM shows, this would be our first real "fundraising/get-to-know-you" lunch, which, among other things, provided me with an opportunity to tell her about our plans for the next season.

Rather than spending the entire lunch focusing on the struggle of raising funds for

1   As I always said to our board, "Opera is great. It's powerful and unique, but it is the money loser of all time. You lose more money presenting opera by intermission than you do presenting an entire season of theater."

2   Years earlier, Harvey had tried in vain to establish a partnership with James Levine (music director) and Joe Volpe (general manager) of the Metropolitan Opera to create a "mini-Met" series, which would feature contemporary and rarely seen operas that would not work in the large house at Lincoln Center, but would be perfect at BAM. I knew the project was doomed when we were invited to meet with Joe Volpe and his team at his office at the Met. Volpe sat in a large, solid chair in the center of the room. We were seated on a deep, puffy couch, which sank even lower under our collective weight. Joe Volpe appeared as a king in this setup and we "Bammies" were his lowly subjects. The body language declared the "mini-Met" would never see the light of day.

Victoria Roberts cartoon from the *New Yorker*, 1995.

opera (even though, of course, I engaged in a reasonable amount of whining on this topic), I asked Susan to make a special grant for our Muslim Voices festival, which was turning out to be a much harder fundraising lift than I had expected. Susan seem very open to bringing the Muslim Voices to Don Randel, Mellon's president, and, immediately following our lunch, Susan did approach Don and he agreed to a fifty-thousand-dollar Muslim Voices grant. But then something completely out of the ordinary happened. While Susan was in the president's office discussing Muslim Voices, she also found herself saying that, given the opportunity, she would like to make a large, transformative five-million-dollar grant to support BAM's vision related to opera, rather than throw that kind of money at the usual, more mainstream players, one of whom she was engaged with at the time.

Shockingly, Don turned to her and said, "Okay, go ahead and do both." These funds were coming from his special "presidential initiatives" budget, so it was icing on the cake, and not competitive with her allocation from the performing arts budget. She was stunned and called me immediately before he could change his mind! I was equally stunned and thrilled, since this kind of stuff only happened in dreams. It definitely was not the day-to-day grind of raising money (nickel by nickel, quarter by quarter, dollar by dollar . . .). Without knowing it at the time, that was the best lunch of my entire thirty-six years at BAM: the five-million-dollar lunch. And that's how it became known in BAM lore, from that day forward. The Mellon grant enabled BAM Opera to survive for years to come, and empowered us to present major operatic works rarely seen in New York. Needless to say, Susan remained a loyal BAM goer and friend, who also played a key role in my selection (after leaving BAM) as the first senior fellow in residence in the foundation's history. Ah, if only I could remember what we ordered for lunch that fateful day, I would have made it the centerpiece of my daily diet.

Over the last hundred years, the greatest partner to all of New York City's cultural institutions has been the City of New York. In BAM's case, the city saved the institution following a massive flood in 1977, when a water main broke, submerging the opera house up to the stage. Mayor after mayor, in partnership with borough presidents and city council leadership, have provided millions of dollars in capital support to maintain BAM's historic buildings and construct new facilities. Annually, city appropriations to cover various general expenses have also been a key element in BAM's survival. We are fortunate that BAM's facilities are all owned by the City of New York, because it has afforded us admission to an exclusive club, the CIG, or Cultural Institutions Group, consisting of thirty-four organizations in all five boroughs, that have this special relationship to the city.

The president of each CIG member organization is expected, at some point, to serve as its chair. My turn happened to come in 2001 as the city was experiencing perhaps its worst crisis in history up to that point, the horrific 9/11 attacks. Every New Yorker recalls that bright September morning. The primaries were that day, and many of us early risers were on our way to the polls when the incident occurred. Ron called me from his apartment. He could actually see the planes hitting the Twin Towers from his window and, of course, like all of us, he was confused and alarmed. As president of BAM, despite the chaos, I rushed to our building, not knowing, at first, the extent of the attack and, as the day wore on, trying to provide comfort to many of the staff who had showed up for work. That afternoon, I called the president of the nearby Brooklyn Hospital Center and offered our lobby as a triage center for the injured, should additional space be required. Sadly, there were few patients to be helped as most of those present in the towers at the time they went down perished.

After a few days, as the dust began to clear and Verizon restored phone and Internet connection, I convened the CIG organizations to discuss how we could be of assistance. Every member opened their institution's doors free of charge and many offered special programs and concerts honoring the firefighters, police officers, and other first responders who sacrificed their lives during the crisis. The impact of 9/11 took years to process, but I was proud of the way the CIG members stepped up to participate in the healing.

Brooklyn Remembers,
New York Rises

October 8, 2001
Brooklyn Academy of Music
Howard Gilman Opera House

A concert to benefit families of the victims of
the World Trade Center tragedy

Free admission; donations encouraged

Presented by:
Brooklyn Academy of Music
BAM Local Development Corporation
Brooklyn Philharmonic
651 ARTS
Brooklyn Museum of Art
Brooklyn Botanic Garden
Brooklyn Children's Museum
Brooklyn Information & Culture
New York Aquarium
Prospect Park Alliance
WNYC

On the first anniversary of the attack, then Mayor Bloomberg and his capable Department of Cultural Affairs commissioner (and former BAM employee), Kate Levin,[3] called on all the CIG organizations to commemorate the day. We decided to offer free showings of Woody Allen's film classic, *Manhattan*, in the BAM Rose Cinemas all day and evening. At each screening, when the audience heard the opening bars of George Gershwin's "Rhapsody in Blue" underscoring the stunning black-and-white image of the Twin Towers in all their former glory, everyone stood and cheered, and then bowed their heads in silence. We were all New Yorkers that day, paying homage to our damaged but resilient city.

It's hard to explain sometimes the grandeur of the city to outsiders, who see the grime, the traffic, the cost, and the general mayhem of daily existence in New York. For me, the city is and will always be the center of the world. Not only are my son and grandchildren proud Brooklynites, but the friends and colleagues I have known through my work at BAM are definitely the most creative people I have ever encountered in all of my travels. There is a life force, diversity, and energy in New York that provides a mix of the perfect ingredients to stimulate and encourage artistic output. New York City somehow embraces the best and worst of humanity. There is no middle ground. But if you like the "edge," there is no better place to live and work.

City leaders understand that the cultural offerings of organizations big and small are a crucial component of what makes New York great and gives it both its character and its competitive edge. That is why they embrace the cultural sector and support it at a higher level than any municipality in the country, well beyond the total budget offered by the National Endowment for the Arts.

3   Kate worked in our fundraising department at BAM right after she graduated from college. She was a great writer and her skill at authoring grants greatly impressed Harvey. Years later, whenever Harvey would refer to Kate, he always called her "the smartest person who ever worked at BAM." The fact that he would say this when I was standing next to him was not lost on me! But, truth be told, Harvey was right. Kate is very smart, and has had a great career working with organizations all over the world.

Program from *Brooklyn Remembers, New York Rises,* fall 2001.

Friends of BAM

open
new
doors

David Bowie & Iman
20th Next Wave Festival
Friends of BAM Chairs

Friends of BAM is a vital community of contemporary performing arts lovers who help sustain BAM's mission with annual membership contributions.

From the Next Wave Festival to a Spring Season of opera, theater, music, and dance; from educational outreach and humanities programs to independent film programming at BAM Rose Cinemas; from free BAMcafé live performances to programs the whole family can enjoy – you can discover the unparalleled, the unpredictable, and the unexpected at BAM.

With ticket sales covering less than half of BAM's expenses, and government funding uncertain, membership support enables BAM to achieve its artistic goals without compromise.

We hope you will join us as a Friend of BAM today and help BAM continue to present extraordinary arts programming season after season.

Membership is a wonderful way to enhance your BAM experience!

As a Friend of BAM, you'll receive great benefits that offer discounts and the "inside track" to BAM, including:

• Priority notice of BAM mainstage events so you'll always be in the know
• Invitations to working rehearsals for a "behind-the-scenes" look at the artistic process
• No ticket handling fees
• Private donor room access
• Pre-show dining reservation privileges
• BAMcafé, BAMshop, and BAMbus discounts

...and more!

PASSPORT

NEW MUSIC AMERICA
TENTH ANNIVERSARY

EXPLORER

THE

BAM

EXPERIENCE

JOIN THE FRIENDS OF BAM

When you join the FRIENDS OF BAM,

you will enjoy special benefits, and become part of the Academy's tradition of innovation, excellence, and diversity.

Innovation — reflected in BAM's presentations of new and unexplored approaches to contemporary and traditional performing arts.

Excellence — demonstrated in the risk-taking NEXT WAVE Festival, the daytime Performing Arts Program for Young People, and BAM's newest artistic initiative, BAM Opera.

Diversity — experienced through a wide variety of intercultural programs from DanceAfrica to theater productions from around the world.

Last year, BAM's creative excellence was specially recognized when the National Endowment for the Arts awarded a Challenge Grant to help launch BAM Opera. BAM Opera's inaugural season last spring received widespread critical acclaim and played to sold out houses.

Your support through the FRIENDS OF BAM will entitle you to exceptional benefits and privileges, and will make the difference in helping us reach our goal to match the NEA Challenge Grant.

Join us with your contribution today and enjoy privileges reserved exclusively for the FRIENDS OF BAM.

Mahagonny Songspiel
BAM OPERA, 1989

Japan's Traditional Dance - New
BAM Carey Playhouse, 1989

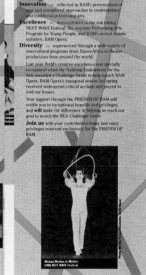

Michael Moshen in Motion
1988 NEXT WAVE Festival

Opposite:
David Bowie and Iman, ca. 1990.

Right:
A selection of BAM promotional and membership materials.

Sometimes a single donor can make a significant contribution to an institution from beyond the grave, but these gifts must be cultivated while the donor is still alive. The Next Wave Festival attracted a dynamic and diverse group of donors. The idea of presenting new work in all performance disciplines every fall was a shot in the arm of the New York cultural scene. Audiences loved the adventure of coming to BAM and not knowing what they would encounter.[4] The Next Wave was as provocative as it was fun. Yes, sometimes the shows could be excruciating, or pretentious, but they were always challenging, often very worthwhile, and, every so often, transformative.

Howard Gilman, a wealthy arts patron and photography collector, was one of those donors who naturally gravitated to the Next Wave. He came regularly and began to support us with annual grants of twenty-five-thousand dollars. His close friends included Isabella Rossellini and Mikhail Baryshnikov, whom he would bring to BAM whenever he could, adding to the glamour of the festival. While he especially liked dance and opera, he was also a huge animal lover and his spectacular White Oak Plantation in Yulee, Florida, was both an artists' retreat and an incredible wildlife sanctuary. When we presented Zingaro, the horse circus from France, in 1996, Howard was thrilled because the show featured both dancers and horses.

Zingaro was another crazy Harvey idea that involved transporting twenty-six performing horses from France and building a home for them in Battery Park, next to the tent where the show took place. We had to involve the US Department of Agriculture and the Olympic equestrian team to figure out how to bring the horses into the country and maintain a large animal population for over a month. In fact, Howard loved Zingaro so much that he purchased over a hundred tickets and brought all of his employees to the show for Christmas.[5] His office on Sixth Avenue was filled with art, and he had a private dining room and chef so it was a special treat when Harvey, Joe, and I were invited every year for a lavish lunch at which we would provide him and the other Gilman trustees a preview of the upcoming season.

Howard suffered from a chronic heart condition, and so his health was always a bit precarious. He passed away suddenly at the age of seventy-three while at White Oak, and the entire New York cultural world was devastated. This man was not just a donor—he was a fan and a friend with a broad palette of interests, and his demise left a gaping hole in the community of the arts.

A few months after his death, I asked the foundation's trustees to consider a five-million-dollar gift, namely, to endow the opera house in Howard's honor. They agreed and the Howard Gilman Opera House was announced at BAM. This was one of the first large spaces at BAM that was named after a patron, and we were particularly proud that the specific patron was Howard. When the naming was announced, the foundation and BAM threw a big, elegant dinner party on the stage of the opera house. The curtain rose

Opposite:
The *Next Wave Magazine*, featuring Zingaro, the French horse circus. The cut-off letters *WA* (versus *WAVE*) were part of our visual identity, 1996.

Following spread:
Tented arena set up at Battery Park City for Zingaro's *Chimère*, Next Wave Festival, 1996.

4   Or rather, they loved being at BAM, but getting there was often a challenge depending on traffic and if the subways were running.

5   Zingaro was a spectacle, with its magnificent horses and a large ensemble of dancers cavorting in a dark and mysterious pool of water lit as if by moonlight. The show was both as romantic as a fairy tale and as death defying as any high-risk circus act.

The Next Wave Magazine 1996

Brooklyn
Academy
of
Music

Wa

as guests took their seats for dinner, revealing the new signage displaying Howard's name. Many toasts were made in his honor. Of my own comments that night, I remember talking about how the beautiful and historic 2,100-seat opera house had opened its doors in 1908. More than a century had passed, and some of the greatest moments of theater history had taken place on that stage. Martha Graham danced her last performances there. Toscanini conducted his orchestra there. And when Rudolf Nureyev defected from the Soviet Union, his first appearance in the West was on the stage of the opera house. All that time, the opera house had waited for a name. The years had come and gone, thousands of artists and millions of audience members had passed through, but the place had remained nameless. "Clearly," I concluded, "this theater has been waiting for Howard." I then asked the guests to stand and give one final enduring standing ovation recognizing this man's wonderful life. Howard's portrait sits outside the opera house in the lobby. I would greet him every morning on my way to the office, and there were many days, I swear, I saw him wink and then tell me how much he loved the old opera house and all the crazy, unexpected things that had taken place on its stage.

I n 2005, I solicited the single largest gift of my career when I approached the Peter Jay Sharp Foundation about naming BAM's 1908 historic building at 30 Lafayette Avenue. The foundation was run by Norman Peck, a self-made man who grew up in Brooklyn, attended Princeton, and—thankfully, for us—loved BAM. Norman was friendly with the chairman of BAM's endowment trust, Dick Fisher, another self-made Brooklynite and Princeton alumnus, not to mention a major philanthropist in the arts and sciences who had been the CEO of Morgan Stanley.[6] I invited Peck to join the endowment trust and he soon became its vice-chairman. Over the years, he deepened his involvement at BAM, and in partnership with the chairman of our board, Alan Fishman, I worked hard to engage both Norman and the Peter Jay Sharp Foundation to make a major contribution to BAM (the foundation was endowed by the estate of Peter Jay Sharp, another great New York real estate man who was, of course, a Princetonian).

The foundation was a dream funder. It had a large corpus, was committed to supporting the arts, and functioned as one of the least bureaucratic foundations in the field, with

6   Dick was one of our greatest supporters and it is a tremendous source of pride to all of us at BAM that, upon his death at age sixty-eight, his wife, Jeanne Donovan Fisher, endowed the BAM Richard B. Fisher Building in his honor.

few guidelines, minimal tedious reports, and a very small staff and board. Opportunities like that rarely came along, when it was possible for a well-managed institution with a clear artistic vision to go to a funder, ask for a lot of money, and actually get it, rather than hearing a litany of rules and qualifications regarding what the foundation would and would not support. Norman had been giving us solid contributions for years. So when the renovation of the facade of our main building on Lafayette Avenue was well underway, the time seemed right to ask him for the big grant. I called him and said, "We would like the foundation to consider naming the building." Knowing Norman's passion for real estate, I proposed that he come out and take a look at what was happening to the building. It was the right moment for his visit, as we were cleaning up the facade, restoring it to its former "full color" glory, fixing the cherubs and other beautiful details that were hidden under years of New York City grime. The decorative cornice had been removed in the fifties when a piece of it fell off. It had been decades since the building received this kind of makeover, including a brand-new, undulating glass canopy, which added a modern touch to the old skin.[7]

A few days later, when Norman showed up at BAM, he stood in front of the building that housed our main administrative offices, the BAM Rose Cinemas, Howard Gilman Opera House, and Lepercq Space, and said, "Let's walk up the scaffolding to the top." My knees immediately buckled when I heard his words, as I have always harbored an irrational and overwhelming fear of heights. "What? Are you kidding?" I asked. "No," he said, "Let's go up." Okay, do I do this or do I wimp out? I thought. And then, after a visible moment of hesitation, I decided, All right, I'm doing it. I had heels on, not huge ones, but high enough that I had to steady myself after every step as we climbed up, up, up the shaky metal fire escape stairs and then onto a makeshift scaffold on the outside of the building. It took every last ounce of courage not to begin screaming at the top of my lungs as my stomach heaved and the street below began to swirl, but I managed to keep my cool through the vertigo attack, while Norman inspected the work around us, until I finally couldn't conceal my absolute terror any longer. After using all of my power and determination to reach the top, I totally freaked out while

Above:
BAM Richard B. Fisher Building (a.k.a. BAM Fisher) groundbreaking, 2010.

Opposite, from top:
CandyBAM by Vik Muniz during the Opera House facade restoration, 2002.

Peter Jay Sharp Building, 2017.

Following spread:
The audience got involved during the construction project to fix the facade. Everyone looked good in their "Building a Better BAM" hats (bonus points if you can spot Lou Reed!), 1996.

7 The facade project was years in duration and at one point the entire building had to be covered by a heavy drape for over a year, blocking out all natural light for those of us working inside. Passing by one day, local visual artist Vik Muniz mentioned to Joe that our building reminded him of a cake. So, when the heavy drape covering needed to be installed, we decided to make it an art project. We approached Vik, the Public Art Fund, and Target as sponsor, and *CandyBAM*, a delightful, pictorial confection painted on the drape, was featured on the building. During that time, *CandyBAM* inspired us to launch "BAMboo!," a massive free Halloween trick or treat party in the street in front of BAM, which has since become an annual, beloved neighborhood celebration.

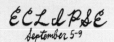

ECLIPSE
September 5-9

JONAH BOKAER   ANTHONY McCALL

Miriam
September 12-15

NORA CHIPAUMIRE

The Channel
September 19-22

DERRICK ADAMS

Next Wave of Song
September 28-29

IAN + CHAD   TAMAR-kali

Paris Commune
October 3-7

STEVEN COSSON   MICHAEL FRIEDMAN

Brooklyn Bred
October 11-13

MARTHA WILSON   DREAD SCOTT
JENNIFER MILLER   COCO FUSCO

Elsewhere
October 17-20

MAYA BEISER

Out Cold / Zippo Songs
October 25-27

THEO BLECKMANN WITH ACME   PHIL KLINE

red, black, & GREEN: a blues
October 31 - November 4

MARC BAMUTHI JOSEPH
LIVING WORD PROJECT

The Shooting Gallery
November 8-10

BILL MORRISON   RICHARD EINHORN

Dance Motion USA (sm)
November 14-17

TREY McINTYRE PROJECT

Untrained
November 27-December 1

LUCY GUERIN

And lose the name of action
December 4-8

MIGUEL GUTIERREZ
AND THE POWERFUL PEOPLE

Timber
December 13-15

MICHAEL GORDON
PERFORMED BY MANTRA PERCUSSION

All That Fall
December 19-23

GAVIN QUINN

Gesture Performing Dance, Dance Performing Gesture
mural

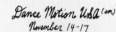

JOSÉ PARLÁ

BAM *Fisher*
inaugural season
Next Wave Festival September-December 2012
adventurous artists, audiences, & ideas

MITHUM BELGID 2012

Opposite:
Poster from the
inaugural season of the
BAM Fisher, 2012.

Above:
BAM Fisher, 2012.

I was up there, and Norman Peck practically had to carry me down to the ground. It was a low moment in my career, but I think it endeared me to him, because he realized the lengths I would go to to get the job done.

The Peter Jay Sharp Foundation made a twenty-million-dollar grant to name the building, and that gift was completely transformative, because it ramped up our endowment in a very serious way and also put us on firm financial footing. A small part of the contribution went to programs, a large chunk flowed into the endowment, and we also pulled a piece out for cash reserves, so that we would have access to our own liquid funds, permitting us to operate as our own "bank" when we needed one, rather than borrowing money and paying interest. The beauty of the story is that we already had an amazing historic building. We didn't need to build a new one, and the renovations had already been mostly underwritten with capital funds from the city. So we were in the rare position of being able to take the money and use it for things that we needed. It was a game-changing donation that, after years of financial instability resulting from betting on high-risk artists and productions, now ensured we would be able to build a serious endowment and establish an unprecedented level of firepower and stability. Though humiliating at the time, the story of Norman Peck carrying me down the side of the building turned out to be one of the greatest highlights of my career, as well as another crazy moment in the legend of BAM, illustrating the extent to which a true "BAMmie" would go in the never-ending quest to secure the future of our institution.

Peter Jay Sharp
Building, 2008.

BAM ENDOWMENT TRUST
Meeting of the Board of Trustees
Thursday, May 15, 2014 at 3:00pm

Hosted and Chaired by Timothy J. Ingrassia at
Goldman Sachs & Co.
200 West Street (btwn Vesey & Murray Sts.), Room 42C, NYC

1. **Meeting Called to order and Approval of Minutes from February 20, 2014**
   Timothy Ingrassia

2. **Presentation by WestEnd Advisors**
   Ned Durden, West End Advisors
   Mike Goldman, WestEnd Advisors

3. **Discussion of Investment Strategy, Asset Allocation, and Investment Results**
   Bank of America / Merrill Lynch Global Institutional Consulting Group
   James T. Ryan, Senior Vice President - Investments
   John Beriau, First Vice President - Institutional Consultant

4. **New Audit Committee Requirements**
   Nora Ann Wallace

5. **President's Report**
   Karen Brooks Hopkins

6. **Other Business**
   Timothy Ingrassia

<u>You are cordially invited to join us for this year's remaining BAM Board meeting:</u>
Tuesday, June 10, 2014 at 5:00pm (Followed by Annual Board Dinner) at BAM

220

CHAPTER THIRTEEN:

The BAM Board and an Endowment at Last

In the world of arts administration, there is no more important leadership group than the board of trustees. Board service is a noble service, which must be taken seriously by every individual associated with the organization. Board members are generally the largest contributors—in terms of time, money, and expertise—to the health of an institution. In addition, they act as ambassadors to the world on behalf of your organization and set policy at the highest level. Board members are also responsible for succession and ultimately for the long-term viability of an institution.

During the Harvey years, BAM attracted a few major board members who championed his cause at a time when Brooklyn was regarded as a foreign outpost. Members and leaders such as Paul Lepercq, Stanley Kriegel, Frank Weissberg, Rita Hillman, Seth Faison, and Neil Chrisman, among others, hung in with Harvey even when he self-destructed and drove BAM deep into debt. They believed in him and stood by him even during the darkest days because they understood that, despite some of his choices, he was kind of a mad genius.

When I took over as the organization's chief fundraiser in 1981, I became the key staff member to identify and recruit board members, since most of them evolved from donor relationships. Board members are usually three types of people: those who have a business reason for supporting an organization (i.e., their company is headquartered nearby); those who love the work (many board members came to BAM because of the Next Wave Festival); or those who feel that board service is the best way to build and enhance the community in which they live. We had many long-term Brooklyn boosters, such as Evelyn Ortner and her husband, Everett, who championed the brownstone revival in Park Slope; and Eugene Luntey, chairman and chief executive officer of Brooklyn Union Gas Company, on the board, who spent decades committed to BAM and our cause.

Over the years, our board expanded, and by the time I retired as president, we had over sixty members. This number is pretty unwieldy for basic business, so the real leadership of BAM was handled by a twelve-person executive committee. Nevertheless, the board naturally grew, as a result of the need for increased fundraising as well as diverse community representation, and there was both power and virtue in maintaining such a large board, as long as we kept all of the members engaged with our mission.

We did not believe in term limits and instead reelected our members on an annual basis. This strategy allowed us to retain loyal, generous participants and to ask those who were not actively participating to leave.[1] Our full board met for one and a half hours four times a year and each meeting consisted of a president's report, an executive producer's presentation of the upcoming roster of shows, committee reports (finance, education, etcetera), and a special presentation on a topic that was of interest (such as the Brooklyn

---

1   I used to often say that it didn't make sense to term limit people off our board who joined when they were young and simply turn them over to Lincoln Center and other powerful organizations, as they came into their wealth, years later.

Cultural District or a new capital project). All board meetings and committee meetings for the year ahead were meticulously planned and scheduled at the end of the prior fiscal year. Committees each developed work plans for the year in order to both engage and motivate their members and produce results.[2]

We set an annual contribution goal, and development staff were assigned to specific board members to help them achieve their goals, arrange their tickets, and generally keep them involved. We learned that it was much easier to work with members by generating a tightly defined annual plan rather than through open-ended calls for help and money. Therefore, our development team devised a strategy for each trustee at the beginning of the fiscal year and worked with them to achieve it.

In addition to power, influence, and wealth, diversity is a key factor in board composition that has sometimes historically been neglected by large cultural institutions. Of course, wealthy members are crucial, but a great board is truly reflective of both its community and its audience. Racial and gender diversity is essential, since the identity of the board is synonymous with that of the organization.

And, naturally, there is the issue of recruitment. How do we find and cultivate board members? This is, again, an issue of research. Logic dictates that for an arts organization, the most devoted fans come from the audience. Keeping a close eye on lower-level donors who increase their support over time, signaling their growing interest in the organization, is another recruitment tactic. And, a crucial strategy is for existing board members to invite their friends and colleagues and encourage them to get involved. This type of cultivation is the most effective common-sense plan for building solid board membership. For example, we had an outstanding board member, Donald R. Mullen, Jr. (former executive at Goldman Sachs), who would host fabulous dinners for his close friends and colleagues after shows that had a celebrity cast. We had to deliver the celebrities to the dinners and he delivered the "prospects." The process of getting actors like Geoffrey Rush, Fiona Shaw, Mikhail Baryshnikov, etcetera, to attend was often difficult and taxing for BAM's director of artist services, Mary Reilly, but, ultimately, she pushed through and got the job done. The results were plentiful and the dinners generally turned out to be great fun for both the artists and Mullen's guests. We identified great new board members through these events and raised a lot of money from everyone who participated.

2   Let's face it, sitting through thousands of board meetings, committee meetings, and various other endless gatherings, it's part of the life of a CEO, and most days I was booked solid. In order to listen while simultaneously passing the time, I often doodled on every scrap of paper in the vicinity. Sometimes my staff could determine the level of my desperation for the meeting to end by the frantic nature of the "drawings" I would leave on the table when the discussions finally came to an end. See p. 220 for examples!

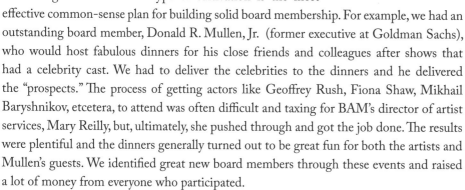

Mikhail Baryshnikov, Robert Wilson, and Willem Dafoe collaborated on *The Old Woman*, spring 2014.

At the end of each season, we would meet with board leadership and our governance committee to review each member's "performance," i.e., How many shows did they attend? What funds did they contribute directly or generate? Did they come to galas and special events? The board evaluation process was critical in terms of laying out an agenda for how we would work with that specific member over the coming year.

Board members, as leaders of the organization, had ongoing access to the patron desk for priority tickets and the best seats. When it comes to board cultivation and maintenance, good service is essential. An organization is only as strong as its board, and board members can easily be tempted to take their talents and assets somewhere else. Neglect them at your own peril! Regular communication is important. I would send out a short email to the members every Friday afternoon, updating them on the most compelling events of the past week, as well as upcoming programs.

As president, my relationship with the chairman was fundamental to the success of BAM. During my sixteen-year run, I worked with two chairmen. The first was Bruce Ratner, the legendary real estate developer who shaped the future of Brooklyn by constructing the MetroTech office complex in Downtown Brooklyn in the eighties[3] and the Barclays Center in 2010, among many other large-scale real estate developments. Bruce is a brilliant, high-energy, take-no-prisoners kind of guy. He bet on Brooklyn early and never looked back, no matter how tough it got for him. When he decided to buy the Brooklyn Nets (formerly the New Jersey Nets) and build the arena, a full-on war ensued, with various community factions for years, but Bruce and his deputy and successor, MaryAnne Gilmartin, stayed the course and saw the project through. Today, the Barclays Center is one of the most successful and welcoming large sports and entertainment venues in the US, having brought both local jobs and mass-market events to the area, even though enduring years of construction can be a hardship for those living nearby. Bruce was chair mainly during Harvey's tenure, but he facilitated the transition to the "Karen and Joe show" and continues to serve as a chairman emeritus of BAM decades later.

Alan Fishman, born and raised in Brooklyn, former Chemical Bank executive, self-made entrepreneur, and later CEO of the Independence Community Bank, succeeded Bruce and served as chair during almost all of my time as president. He and his wife, Judy Fishman, an arts leader in her own right who served as chair of Merce Cunningham's board, loved BAM and came to practically every show. I spoke to Alan every day. We worked on massive capital projects together, and he was a key player in BAM's relationship with the city. Alan also recruited both Bill Campbell and Adam Max as vice-chairs, and we, "the Fab Five" (Alan, Bill, Adam, Joe, and myself) functioned as a highly effective team, both in terms of leading the board, balancing the budget, and planning for the expansion of our facilities, and in shaping the Brooklyn Cultural District. On Alan's watch we finished

3   Bruce Ratner's decision to build MetroTech in Downtown Brooklyn was another great moment in the borough's transition. Every important Brooklyn organization wanted Bruce on their board, but BAM prevailed. When Harvey and I first met Bruce for dinner to talk about getting him involved, he laid his paper napkin on the table and on it drew a facsimile of how he thought our neighborhood would look ten years later. It was impressive and his assumptions proved, for the most part, to be correct.

the facade renovation of the Peter Jay Sharp Building on Lafayette Avenue, completely overhauled the interior and seating in the BAM Harvey Theater,[4] built the Richard B. Fisher Building next door, initiated the real momentum for the formation of the Brooklyn Cultural District, and generated serious money for the BAM endowment.

Also, at the time of my retirement, we had engaged in planning for BAM Strong, which combines the ground floor of the condo building at 230 Ashland Place, an empty lot, and the BAM Harvey Theater into one solid culture block on Fulton Street. This project, primarily funded by board member Brigitte Vosse, her ex-husband Bill Strong, and the city, solidifies the northern border of the district. Alan, needless to say, was an effective board leader for BAM and a great partner to me.

The third leader who played a transformative role in shaping BAM's future was Richard (Dick) B. Fisher, a longtime Brooklyn resident, chairman of Morgan Stanley and inaugural chair of the BAM Endowment Trust. Dick, felled by polio as a child, rose to the ranks of CEO of one of New York City's most legendary Wall Street firms. He had a great sense of humor, a fabulous eye for contemporary art, and a dynamic second wife, Jeanne Donovan Fisher. Neil Chrisman (an earlier chairman during Harvey's tenure) got Dick involved with BAM (again, it was the Princeton connection) and, as "BET" (BAM Endowment Trust) chair, he authored the original endowment investment policies and strategies that moved us into the big time as an organization with real resources and longevity. Dick was very ill on the blustery day that we cut the ribbon on the renovated facade at 30 Lafayette. From his wheelchair, he made an emotional speech about what BAM had contributed to his life. He was too weak to stand that day, even with the support of the two canes that were his constant companions due to the polio. He spoke with so much pride that we were all overwhelmed with a sense of grace in his presence. Dick died of prostate cancer at the age of sixty-eight in December 2004, and every year since his death until 2018, BAM bestowed the Richard B. Fisher award upon an artist who exemplified his spirit and his tenacity. That annual event, plus the naming of our magnificent Richard B. Fisher Building (BAM Fisher) in his honor, thanks to a leadership gift from Jeanne, keeps him very much alive at BAM, now and forever.

I n 2014, soon after I announced my upcoming retirement from BAM, I received an unexpected call from Joan Shigekawa, who was then deputy director of the National Endowment for the Arts. I had known Joan over the years when she worked at both the Rockefeller and Nathan Cummings Foundations, but she hadn't been to BAM very much since she took the endowment job in Washington, DC. She was calling with exciting news. BAM had been awarded the National Medal of Arts, and we were being invited to the White House to receive the commendation—the highest artistic

4   The original benches at the Harvey, selected by Peter Brook during our production of *The Mahabharata*, drove people crazy because they were so uncomfortable. For Brook it was an aesthetic choice. He didn't want people to be "too relaxed or inattentive" when they attended an important theatrical event, but the New York audience was fixated on this issue. We replaced the seats two times, finally achieving an appropriate level of softness and back support in 2014.

honor in the US—from President Barack Obama and the First Lady Michelle Obama.[5] Years earlier, Harvey had been awarded a medal from President Clinton, and now BAM, the organization, would receive this prestigious recognition. We were excited and wanted to share the honor with everyone at BAM, so we wrangled (gently) over the number of attendees we could bring to the ceremony.

Finally, we secured five spots, so that Joe, chairman Alan Fishman, vice-chairs Adam Max and Bill Campbell, and I could attend. But, as luck would have it, the award ceremony was scheduled right around the Fourth of July, when Ron and I had booked a beach trip to Montauk—our summer getaway destination—for the whole family, all of our collective kids and grandkids. Where there is a will, there is always a way, and when generous, enthusiastic board members step up, nothing can inhibit the path to success. In this particular case, Adam Max solved everything. He arranged for a private plane to pick Bill Campbell and me up in Southampton. We then flew to New York to pick up Adam and Alan, and then on to DC in time for the ceremony. And when it was over, he flew us all back. While I wasn't used to such luxurious logistics, I couldn't have appreciated them more at the time,

5 It was particularly meaningful to receive the medal from President Obama. On the day of his first inauguration, in January 2009, BAM opened its doors to the neighborhood and we simulcast the event in our lobby, in the Lepercq Space, and in all four of our cinemas. Our neighbors were ecstatic and the ceremony was a giant communal celebration.

Above:
Scene from the Lee Breuer/Bob Telson production *The Gospel at Colonus* at the Delacorte Theater, 2018.

Opposite, from top:
L–R: Medal of St. Olav, Norway (1983); the Order of the Polar Star, Sweden (2007); the Chevalier de L'Ordre des Arts et des Lettres, France (2006)

Lee Breuer, director; Bob Telson, composer; and Sharon Levy, producer at *The Gospel at Colonus* at the Delacorte Theater, 2018.

as they enabled me to be in two places at once, spending time with my family and with the president and first lady, celebrating BAM.

Our afternoon at the White House was glorious. We met the other medal recipients, including Linda Ronstadt, Julia Alvarez, and our old friend and collaborator Bill T. Jones. Our group was allowed to tour various areas, including the Blue Room and a gallery where we viewed portraits of former first ladies. I must admit that while Jackie Kennedy was elegant and graceful, Nancy Reagan looked fierce in her long red Halston dress. When I saw that portrait, her "Just Say No" campaign sprang to life in my imagination. For Nancy, in that flaming red gown, no meant no.

The ceremony itself was memorable on many levels. It was livestreamed, so all the kids in Montauk and my dear friends Tina and Carla were able to watch it unfold. We were all so proud and honored to be there on behalf of the institution we loved. When President Obama called my name, and I went up to the podium to receive the BAM award, we shared a moment. The president put his hand on my shoulder and said quietly, "You know, Karen, I've been there." I said, "To BAM—seriously?" "Yes," he replied, "for *The Gospel at Colonus* in 1983 and it was great." I was surprised and pleased that the then-young Barack Obama had made his way to Brooklyn for that unforgettable show. *Gospel*

was a retelling of Sophocles's play *Oedipus at Colonus*, set entirely to gospel music. Morgan Freeman played the title role of the preacher in 1983 when we premiered the work in the first Next Wave Festival. The show, created by Lee Breuer and composer Bob Telson, literally made the reputation of the Next Wave, and went on to be performed on Broadway and around the world for the next thirty-five years. Obama's appreciation of the show inspired me so much that, years later, following my retirement from BAM, I led an initiative, primarily supported by the Onassis Foundation (where I serve as a board member and senior advisor), to remount the work for six performances at the

Delacorte Theater in Central Park in partnership with the Public Theater.[6]

Working as a lifetime arts administrator does not often serve as a platform for winning prizes and awards. Harvey, Joe, and I were all very fortunate, since we had so many international relationships with artists, theaters, and government entities that we garnered a lot of recognition for

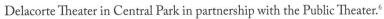

6   *Gospel* at the Delacorte was powerful. Lee Breuer was eighty-one and in fragile health, so time was of the essence (he died in January 2021). Many of the cast had been with the production for the full thirty-five years, so it felt like a family reunion. On our big night, Onassis's president, Anthony Papadimitriou, hosted a dinner under a tent right next to the theater for the entire arts community. Just as dinner was being served, a torrential rainstorm began and all the guests huddled under the covering. Everyone was concerned regarding our ability to open the show, but the gods of theater prevailed and, half an hour prior to curtain, the rain stopped, the clouds disappeared, and a beautiful calm evening settled over Central Park. The audience arrived and somehow we triumphed over another weather catastrophe.

our work. I was honored with the Medal of Saint Olav from Norway, the Commander of the Royal Order of the Polar Star from Sweden, and the Chevalier de L'Ordre des Arts et des Lettres by the Republic of France. Joe also received a venerable trove of global medals, the highest of which was a Commander of the Order of the British Empire (CBE) from the United Kingdom, a very rare and special honor. And, of course, Harvey, being the international presenting pioneer he was, received the Légion d'Honneur of France among many other decorations.

The ceremonies and decorations were all humbling and awesome, but it was the "Obama moment" that made me feel like a queen.[7]

There is simply no question about it. Great institutions have great endowments. A robust endowment provides short-term stability, long-term viability, reduces the strain of annual fundraising, and builds confidence among stakeholders that the organization will endure. The existence of a significant endowment tells the world that your institution possesses a bright future and is worthy of support. Yes, having an endowment for BAM was a necessity. Raising one was hard.

BAM, which opened its doors in 1861, had no endowment until 1992. That is a long time to wait for stability. The board of BAM, led at that time by chairman Bruce Ratner and vice-chair Alan Fishman, insisted that we embark on a feasibility study to assess the potential amount that could be raised to launch our endowment, and whether it might be within reach. We were all nervous about the work required, since meeting our annual goals was difficult enough, but at the board's request we hired C. W. Shaver & Company, run by Carl Shaver, and moved forward with the study. Carl, at the time, was a spritely elderly fellow with white hair and a sharp sense of humor.[8]

The study, which consisted of interviews and evaluations of potential donors, indicated that we had a shot at raising fifteen million dollars, which at the time seemed very ambitious. But, since this was a board-initiated effort, it was clear that individual members would have to step-up in order to reach the goal. We were thrilled when Bettina Bancroft, a shy but warm and enthusiastic board member, based mainly in Los Angeles, agreed to chair the campaign. Bettina was a member of the legendary Bancroft Family, which owned

7   Years earlier, when George H. W. Bush was president, then first lady Barbara Bush hosted an event for the arts community in DC followed by a dinner at the State Department. The occasion had been organized as a celebration of a landmark exhibition, *Mexico: Splendors of Thirty Centuries*, at the Metropolitan Museum of Art. I recall arriving at the dinner, shaking hands with Secretary James Baker and other dignitaries including Carlos Salinas de Gortari, the president of Mexico, who would be delivering the keynote dinner speech that night. Imagine my surprise upon learning that President Salinas's speech would be in Spanish and that English translation was only available by reading a printed card at the table . . . except the cards were only placed where men were seated. Women were obliged to ask the men they were seated next to if they could read along. Maybe the Bush administration officials didn't think women could read? Hmm.

8   It was Carl, who famously said of Joe Volpe, the stagehand who rose to become general director of the Metropolitan Opera, "well, every two thousand years, a carpenter gets a great job."

Dow Jones and published *Barron's* magazine. She was generous with her time and money, and willing to invest both in BAM, which helped us get off to a good start. Dick Fisher, also made a million-dollar gift and agreed to chair the BAM Endowment Trust board, which was another huge step forward.

Carl Shaver, in his wisdom, suggested that the endowment form a separate 501c(3) with an odd number of members (e.g., four from the BAM board and five unaffiliated with BAM) in order to make it harder for the board to authorize dipping into the coffers during a tough year. This suggestion proved not only critical to the integrity of the endowment, it also brought more committed business leaders into BAM, beyond those serving on the regular board, which, in turn, generated more possibilities for fundraising.

Our strategy for announcing the campaign was pure BAM. We put together a compelling case statement, the theme of which, developed by loyal staffer, Denis Azaro, was "Your Place in History." It was essentially a time line from 1861 to 1992, showcasing the greatest moments of individual artistry or leadership at BAM, ending with the suggestion that you, the donor, would have a place in BAM's illustrious history if you contributed to the endowment. The BAM board made significant contributions to the campaign, while we persuaded most of the members simultaneously maintain their annual gifts. The idea was to support both "the present and the future."

The biggest breakthrough came when Jessica Chao, then the program director at the Lila Wallace–Reader's Digest Fund, persuaded the foundation to give an initial

With Bettina Bancroft, board member and chair of BAM Endowment Trust, and her husband, Andrew Klink, 1988.

BAM is
the Brooklyn
Academy
of Music…

America's oldest performing arts institution…
Forging a new tradition in the performing arts…
Serving a diverse metropolitan population…
Sustaining a vital cultural heritage…
Encouraging the new…
Revitalizing the community…
Taking the risks that keep art alive.

This is BAM…
Yesterday
Today
And
Tomorrow.

1850's–1860's

Fall 1858: Philharmonic Society resolves to build Academy
January 1860: First Academy on Montague Street is dedicated—BAM has over $100,000 in subscriptions
January 15, 1861: Opening night performance
December 1861: First drama, *Hamlet*, is presented at BAM
February 1863: Two-week Sanitary Fair opens—$200,000 raised for Civil War relief
1863-64: John Wilkes Booth appears in *Richard II* and *The Marble Heart*

Henry Ward Beecher, a frequent lecturer at BAM. (Long Island Historical Society)

D'Oyly Carte poster for The Pirates of Penzance. (NYPL/LC, Music Division)

The original Academy on Montague Street.

Dear Friend of BAM:

In 1861, the Brooklyn Academy of Music opened its doors to a procession of artists and a tradition of community involvement that are unique in this nation's cultural life.

From the immortal Caruso's performances through the pioneering music-theatre work of Robert Wilson, BAM's artistic vision has been vital and enduring. Vital, because the Academy has always known that taking risks—on an artist and with an audience—is the basis for creating and presenting all good art. Enduring, because throughout its long history BAM has served the needs of its audiences and its community, and they in turn have responded to the Academy's needs.

BAM has always been what the community has made it. For the artistic community—local, national, international—BAM has been host, home and haven for the finest in the performing arts. For the civic commu[nity] BAM has provided a rallying poi[nt] the reforming and regeneration o[f] neighborhood and of Brooklyn.

The legacy described on t[he] pages is two-fold. BAM's cultural [heri]tage is second to none. But keep[ing] this artistic trust intact and avail[able] for decades to come depends on [your] involvement. If successful, this [fun]draising effort to match the Nati[onal] Endowment for the Arts Challe[nge] Grant awarded BAM in 1983 will se[...]

1870's–1880's

1872: Sir Henry Stanley describes his meeting in Africa with Dr. Livingston for the first time in public

December 1879: *H.M.S. Pinafore* receives its U.S. debut performance

May 1883: Brooklyn Bridge opens—President Chester A. Arthur & Governor Grover Cleveland host a gala dinner at BAM

December 1887: Boston Symphony presents first of many BAM seasons

1890–1907

March 1891: Edwin Booth gives farewell performance in *Hamlet*

April 1896: Eleanora Duse appears in *Camille*

January 1898: Brooklyn becomes part of New York City

November 1903: Original BAM building burns down

April 1904: Committee of 100 forms—proceeds to raise $1.3 million for new BAM

October 1904: First subway opens in New York

Your Place in History

The new Academy on Lafayette Avenue

Booker T. Washington lectures on behalf of Negro emancipation. (Long Island Historical Society)

Opera diva Nellie Melba gave frequent concerts during the 1890's. (NYPL/ LC, Music Division)

The Brooklyn Bridge at the turn of the century. (Long Island Historical Society)

Ada Rehan as Kate in The Taming of the Shrew *in April 1898. (NYPL/LC, Billy Rose Theatre Collection)*

the future BAM embraces, even as we celebrate the past.

BAM has weathered fire (in 1903) and flood (in 1977)—with your generous help. We come to you now not in crisis but with the exhilarating knowledge that our most deeply held convictions about the value and importance of the arts are being ratified by your curiosity and enthusiasm.

Now is the time, and now is the opportunity, to ensure our institutional future, so that the BAM legacy

can continue to meet and to shape the cultural challenges ahead.

Neil Chrisman
Chairman of the Board of Trustees

Harvey Lichtenstein
President and Chief Executive Officer

The National Endowment for the Arts Challenge Grant

In recognition of BAM's singular historic role and its outstanding contribution to America's cultural pluralism, the National Endowment for the Arts (NEA) recently awarded BAM a $600,000 Challenge Grant. To receive this award, BAM must now raise three times as much ($1,800,-000) in new and increased private contributions by June 30, 1987. This

1950s
1950's: Ethnic dance groups led by Jose Greco, Pearl Primus and Talley Beatty perform
April 1952: Merce Cunningham, Jean Erdman, Erick Hawkins and Donald McKayle perform on the same program at BAM

January 1955: 104-year-old *Brooklyn Eagle* folds
1955–56: Newly formed Brooklyn Philharmonia gives first performance at BAM
September 1957: Brooklyn Dodgers play last game in Brooklyn before move to Los Angeles

Marie Powers in the title role of Menotti's The Medium, *1955. (NYPL/LC Music Division)*

Rudolf Nureyev in Laurentia, *1967*

Katherine Dunham as Loulouse in L'Ag'Ya. *(NYPL/LC, Dance Collection)*

Leonard Bernstein, 1948.

FUND may be combined with annual gifts to qualify individuals for various BAM donor levels and their accompanying benefits.

What Sets BAM Apart?

Over the past several decades, the quality and diversity of BAM's traditional dance, music and theater presentations have earned the Academy international prominence. During the same period, the courageous and ar-

dent sponsorship which BAM has provided the nation's most important contemporary performing artists has attracted worldwide recognition. BAM is also widely respected as an urban-based arts center of major significance—one unfailingly dedicated to serving the needs of its surrounding community.

Today BAM has a unique role in America's performing arts tradition:

■ BAM is the nation's oldest continuously operating performing arts

center.

■ BAM's annual, three-mon[th] NEXT WAVE FESTIVAL has become o[ne] of the most exciting and popular co[n]temporary performing arts events [in] the country. The NEXT WAVE FEST[I]VAL enables America's pioneeri[ng] choreographers, composers, perform[ers] ing artists and visual artists, directo[rs] designers and architects to create ne[w] large-scale work, with selected pr[o]ductions receiving partial BAM fina[n]cial underwriting in order to to[ur]

1960's

1960: Brooklyn faces first population decline since 1700's

March 1962: Rudolf Nureyev makes U.S. debut at BAM with Ruth Page's Chicago Opera Ballet

1965–67: BAM's Jazz Series presents the big bands of Duke Ellington, Benny Goodman, Dave Brubeck, Louis Armstrong, Dizzy Gillespie, Count Basie and Glenn Miller

1966: Brooklyn Navy Yard closes

February 1967: Harvey Lichtenstein becomes Director of BAM

April 1968: Merce Cunningham presents first major New York season at BAM

October 1968: BAM presents The Living Theater under the direction of Julian Beck and Judith Malina

1968: Chelsea Theater begins decade-long residency at BAM, which inludes productions of *Yentl*, *Happy End* and the Harold Prince production of Leonard Bernstein's *Candide*

March 1969: Twyla Tharp appears for first time at BAM

April 1969: Robert Wilson presents the first of several theater pieces at BAM— *The Life and Times of Sigmund Freud*

October 1969: Eliot Feld's American Ballet Company and Maurice Bejart's Ballet of the Twentieth Century in their New York debuts

1969: The Polish Laboratory Theatre under the direction of Jerzy Grotowski in first American appearance

Trumpeter Dizzy Gillespie in 1980. (Alan Becer)

BAM Theatre Company's production of The Winter's Tale, *directed by David Jones. (Ken Howard)*

Le Sacre du Printemps *by Maurice Bejart's Ballet of the Twentieth Century*

...sea Theater's 1969 ...uction of Slave *... (Tomasso la Pera)*

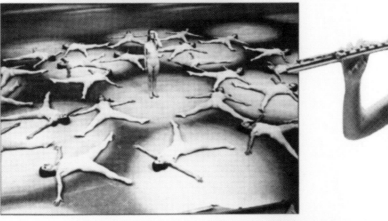

...ationally.

■ BAM has gained national and international renown for annually presenting all forms of dance—ballet, modern and post-modern—from cities across the United States and from nations around the world.

■ BAM has initiated active revitalization of its surrounding community through the establishment of a Local Development Corporation—an innovative move for a performing arts center. The LDC has helped spark a remarkable economic renaissance in the Fort Greene section of Brooklyn through renovations and other improvements in the neighborhood

■ BAM's annual commitment to minority arts presentation is comparable to that of other major cultural centers in New York.

■ BAM presents one of the oldest and largest daytime performing arts programs for young people. The program introduces over 120,000 students, from grade school through high school, to the world of live music, dance, theater and opera each year.

■ BAM has provided a home for the highly acclaimed Brooklyn Philharmonic Orchestra since 1954.

■ BAM has presented a popular and highly regarded chamber music series for over ten seasons, which is now broadcast annually on the American Public Radio Network.

This is BAM today: mixing the old with the new, serving its local community as well as a global artistic five-million-dollar grant to launch the effort. Wallace had been a relatively small donor, on and off, over the years, but Jessica was a real BAM fan and she delivered. It was my first really huge grant, and I traveled to the foundation by subway to pick up the five-million-dollar check, carrying it back on the D train, clutching my wallet tightly the entire ride. When I returned to BAM with the money, the development staff gathered in Harvey's office and I led the "ceremonial passing of the check," so the whole team could feel part of the accomplishment. And, make no mistake, it felt great.

A few years later, after we met the original goal of fifteen million, the campaign began to run out of gas, and I was stymied about how to maintain the excitement we had generated around the launch of the endowment. We hoped to continue to grow the funds, not only because we needed the money, because we wanted to achieve the general goal of having a solid endowment that was at least twice the size of the operating budget. So, at this point, I decided to interview a range of consultants and hire anyone who seemed to have fresh or compelling ideas. A man named Herb Weissenstein (formerly a vice president of development at Carnegie Hall) came up with a plan. He suggested that we bulk up the "bundling strategy," by asking every donor to add funds for the endowment to their annual contribution, no matter how small. His plan worked well and, once again, the always-thoughtful Denis came up with our case statement. This time the theme was "The writing is on the wall." The facade of the BAM opera house featured the names of great composers, etched into stone. So we decided to create a faux stone surface on the campaign brochure that would display not only the composers' names but our donors' names, as well. We also supplemented the printed case statement materials with an amazing short video—a novel concept at the time—created by the brilliant photographer and our loyal audience member, Annie Leibovitz.

Sadly, both Bettina Bancroft and Herb Weissenstein died very young and never got to celebrate the successful fruits of their labors. By 2015, after I had retired from BAM, several campaigns later, including a huge effort during the 150th anniversary season, the BAM endowment was valued at approximately one hundred million dollars.

This page:
Annie Leibovitz snaps a photo of the two of us with my old point-and-shoot camera.

Opposite:
Stills from the Annie Leibovitz film *The Campaign for BAM*, 1992.

Following spread:
BAM employee and illustrator extraordinaire Nathan Gelgud created a graphic biography of my entire career, 2015.

PHILIP GLASS

MERCE CUNNINGHAM

CHUCK DAVIS
DANCE AFRICA

STEVE REICH

LAURIE ANDERSON
daring and risk

The NeXt wave
gesture
art
MARK MORRIS

EIKO & KOMA

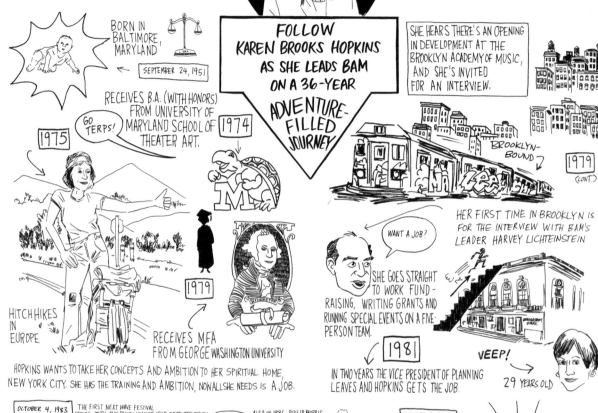

1988 — HOPKINS IS NAMED EXECUTIVE V.P. AND MANAGING DIRECTOR OF BAM.

PRINCESS DIANA ATTENDS WELSH NATIONAL OPERA'S FALSTAFF AND GALA.

SHE WAS WEARING A KNOCKOUT WHITE SATIN GOWN WITH BARE SHOULDERS COVERED BY A TINY BOLERO JACKET. THE TOP OF THE DRESS AND THE JACKET WERE EMBROIDERED IN METALLIC THREAD AND JEWELS. IT WAS INCREDIBLE. EVERYONE ELSE WAS WEARING BLACK (YOU KNOW NEW YORK!) AND SHE WAS IN WHITE.

$22,500,000

1993 — HOPKINS CHAMPIONS THE FIRST-EVER BAM ENDOWMENT CAMPAIGN, A DRIVE TO RAISE $22.5 MILLION THAT WILL BE SAVED, EARNING INTEREST TO SUPPORT THE INSTITUTION

KBH FAVORITE — BILLBOARDS BY THE JOFFREY BALLET, FEATURING THE MUSIC OF PRINCE

1989 — KBH MEMORIES

LES ARTS FLORISSANTS ATYS

1990

IN HURRICANE-LIKE WEATHER, ATTENDEES OF THE HARD NUT ARE TAKEN ON A SUBWAY TRAIN RESERVED FOR THEM TO THE GALA AT GRAND CENTRAL.

BAM REVENUE $12,473,604

1992 — THEIR TICKET FOR THE SUBWAY WAS AN ACTUAL WALNUT!

KBH FAVORITE

1991 — GRIOT NEW YORK GARTH FAGAN AND WYNTON MARSALIS

1995 — THE ROYAL DRAMATIC THEATRE OF SWEDEN RETURNS FOR A CITYWIDE INGMAR BERGMAN FESTIVAL

BERGMAN'S MADAME DE SADE

1996

HOPKINS IS THE EXECUTIVE PRODUCER, WHICH EARNS HER THE ROYAL ORDER OF THE POLAR STAR.

HOPKINS PUBLISHES HER BOOK ON FUNDRAISING, NOW IN ITS SECOND EDITION AND THIRD PRINTING

KBH GLASSES TIMELINE

1988   1989   1990   1999   2009   2012

1994-1996 — KBH IS CHAIR OF PERFORMING ARTS CENTER CONSORTIUM.

1997 — THE LEPERCQ SPACE — ONCE A BALLROOM, THEN MULTI-USE PERFORMANCE SPACE — HOUSES BAMCAFÉ

1998

KBH FAVORITE — STEVE REICH'S MUSIC FOR 18 MUSICIANS

FIRST LADY HILLARY CLINTON AT BAM FOR MLK CELEBRATION

1998 — BAM ROSE CINEMAS OPENS, MAKING BAM THE FIRST PERFORMING ARTS ORGANIZATION TO BUILD A MULTIPLEX IN AN ARTS CENTER.

BAM COMPLETES RENOVATIONS ON FAÇADE OF 30 LAFAYETTE AVE; NAMES FACILITY IN HONOR OF PHILANTHROPIST PETER JAY SHARP, RECOGNIZING $20 MILLION GIFT FROM PETER JAY SHARP FOUNDATION.

PETER JAY SHARP

2006 — ROBERT REDFORD INAUGURATES SUNDANCE AT BAM, BRINGING HIS PARK CITY FESTIVAL TO BROOKLYN FOR THREE YEARS OF FILMS AND EVENTS.

HARVEY LICHTENSTEIN RETIRES, SUCCEEDED BY HOPKINS AS PRESIDENT AND MELILLO AS EXECUTIVE PRODUCER OF BAM. TOGETHER THEY REIMAGINE BAM AS "DESTINATION BAM."

1999

BAM SIGN INSTALLED ON FLATBUSH AVENUE.

WHAT'S UP WITH THE SIGN?

2001

2005 — HOPKINS CELEBRATES 25 YEARS AT BAM

RECEIVES CHEVALIER DE L'ORDRE DES ARTS ET DES LETTRES

MAVIS STAPLES PERFORMS SONGS THAT WERE THE SOUNDTRACK OF THE CIVIL RIGHTS MOVEMENT

2008 — PAUL SIMON'S SONGS FROM THE CAPEMAN

KBH FAVORITE — KOYAANISQATSI 1999

BAM REVENUE $26,693,853

BAM MAJESTIC IS RENAMED BAM HARVEY THEATER IN HONOR OF HARVEY LICHTENSTEIN.

KBH FAVORITES

KBH HAIRSTYLES, A ROUGH CHRONOLOGY

EARLY 80s	LATE 80s	EARLY 90s	MID 90s	LATE 90s	MID 00s

(REPRISE OF EARLY 80s)

BAMCINEMAFEST BEGINS, FEATURING MANY BROOKLYN FILMMAKERS

2009

SYDNEY THEATRE'S A STREETCAR NAMED DESIRE WITH CATE BLANCHETT
KBH FAVORITE

YOUSSOU N'DOUR

BAM PRESENTS MUSLIM VOICES ARTS & IDEAS WITH THE ASIA SOCIETY, NYU, AND OTHER PARTNERS WITH EVENTS AROUND NYC.

BAM FISHER OPENS AT 321 ASHLAND PLACE WITH A FESTIVE COMMUNITY BLOCK PARTY

HOPKINS IS INDUCTED INTO CRAIN'S BUSINESS HALL OF FAME FOR HELPING "PUT BROOKLYN ON THE MAP AS A CULTURAL DESTINATION."

2014 — PRESIDENT OBAMA HONORS BAM WITH NATIONAL MEDAL OF ARTS IN A CEREMONY AT THE WHITE HOUSE

KBH FAVORITE

2010 — MARK MORRIS' SOCRATES

2011-2012 — BAM CELEBRATES ITS 150TH ANNIVERSARY OVER THE COURSE OF 16 MONTHS.

BAM 150 YEARS

BAM 150

BAM: THE COMPLETE WORKS IS RELEASED.

2013

2012

BAM 150 IS RELEASED, A DOCUMENTARY FILM BY MICHAEL SLÁDEK.

BAM REVENUE $62,200,370

THE STEINBERG SCREEN OPENS, MAKING THE BAM HARVEY THEATER THE LARGEST MOVIE PALACE IN BROOKLYN

HOPKINS RETIRES

BAM REVENUE $42,963,777   2011

BOOOOO

KBH MEMORIES

AT THE BAM 150 GALA, AROUND A DR. JOHN SHOW, HOPKINS THANKS AN EXTENSIVE LIST OF FUNDERS, AND SOME OF THE IMPATIENT AUDIENCE BOOS.

2015 — DURING HOPKINS' TENURE, BAM'S ENDOWMENT GREW FROM $0 TO $96,931,467; THE FULL-TIME STAFF FROM 94 TO 233; EVENTS PRESENTED ANNUALLY FROM 133 TO 812; AND BUILDINGS FROM 1 TO 3 AND COUNTING AS PART OF THE FLOURISHING BROOKLYN CULTURAL DISTRICT.

GELGUD 15

CHAPTER FOURTEEN:

Having It All, Losing It in an Instant

To say my job was all consuming would be a gross understatement. It was a twenty-four-hour commitment. Every day, I would get up at 6:00 a.m., make coffee, and read the *New York Times* and the *Wall Street Journal* so I had some sense of who was gaining and losing money, who was making and not making art, on any given day; who was alive, who died, who died and left money. After morning exercise, I would get dressed, perform my daily ritual of looking in the mirror, clenching my fist and saying, "Good morning, Karen, today you will raise a million dollars," pick up the heavy bag containing last night's reading, and then go to work. When I arrived, there would be meetings, fundraising calls, and issues that needed to be dealt with. I was also constantly interacting with the leadership of the board. At night, I would generally attend a performance, and often dinners and parties afterward. There were also regular donor events all over the city. Then I would go home and read the pile of proposals, reports, and periodicals for at least two hours before heading off to bed. This is all to say that, for thirty-six years, I maintained a schedule that made having a life outside of my job nearly impossible. As Harvey said, I worked like hell.

Though my career came fast and early, love came later. In 1989, years prior to becoming president, a colleague, Carolyn Stolper Friedman—a fellow arts fundraiser—and I decided to write a textbook on nonprofit fundraising for cultural institutions (this book, despite the fact that it was written pre-Internet, is still in print today).[1] As we attempted to negotiate with our original publisher, Oryx Press, I called Ron to ask him to review the contract. We got together to talk about the project and discuss the fine print. Ron was not only a good lawyer, he had great judgment and the kind of solid intuition that made him a valued advisor to his clients. I remember being impressed and charmed by him that day. Then, a number of years later, after both of our marriages had ended, we fell into a romance that rearranged my life and, eventually, many of my priorities. It turned out that Ron was the man I had been waiting for. Before falling in love with him, as an executive, I viewed love as a luxury that I simply could not afford. My first marriage had been based upon a strong friendship, one that still endures today, especially as it provided an amazing son, Matt Hopkins, and now years later, three granddaughters, but it had never been fulfilling at the level of my connection to Ron.

For decades, there had been no separation between my work life and my life outside of work (what little there was). All I had known were the walls of my office and the dark recesses of BAM's theaters and rehearsal spaces. Work was my center of gravity, the

Opposite:
The spectacular finale to the Karen gala with John Turturro, Alan Rickman, the Institutional Radio Choir, and a cast of hundreds, 2015.

Below:
My fundraising book! Proud it's in print since the eighties. Definitely ready for an update.

---

1   Our book, *Successful Fundraising for Arts and Cultural Organizations*, now in its second edition from Greenwood Press, has been used for thirty years as a text in fundraising courses in arts administration college programs all over the country. It's flattering to have a book that's been used by students for over three decades. But . . . it makes you think, isn't it odd that no one has written a new one? I guess thinking about the topic, let alone writing about it, just wears everyone out!

axis around which my universe spun. My son can bear witness to the consequences of having a workaholic mom. There were many conversations during his childhood that went something like this:

Mom: "Matt, do you want to go to BAM with me tonight?"

Matt (rolling his eyes): "No, Mom, I don't want to see the Indonesian shadow puppets again or *Einstein on the Beach*.[2] I just want to watch TV!"

Mom (actually surprised): Really?

Matt: Yes, Mom, really.[3]

It was always shocking to me that not everyone (even my own son) wanted to spend every minute at BAM. As our relationship became stronger and more intimate, Ron helped me see the world beyond those walls, and—over time—guided me toward new possibilities. When he walked into my life, my heart expanded, along with my perception of the world beyond BAM. I pursued him, but he was also drawn to me. We completed each other.

Ron was a funny, knowing, kind, and deeply empathetic man. Although he was by profession an entertainment lawyer, his real persona was more like that of an artist or a mystic. Just below the surface of his professional demeanor resided an anarchist with a deep inner life and a serious intellect. Once, when I asked him why he chose the field of entertainment law, he said, "I'd rather go to a Broadway opening than a real estate closing." Work for him was part of a whole. It wasn't everything.

Ron led a contemplative life, while I was more of a jump-in-and-do-it type of person. I would describe it this way. Whenever I went to the grocery store, I'd buy everything I needed as quickly as possible and put it away in five minutes, almost instantly forgetting what I had bought and moving on to the next task. When Ron bought groceries, he stacked them on the counter and bonded with them, carefully considering each item he had purchased. He was a person with a rich creative inner life. For example, he designed conceptual works of art, such as a series of American flag paintings made out of red, white, and blue Ping-Pong balls. His artwork was always filled with irony and humor. The pace of his life and his approach to living was inherently different from mine. Given the intensity

2   *Einstein* was a groundbreaking five-hour minimalist opera created by a brilliant artistic team including director and designer Robert Wilson, composer Philip Glass, and choreographer Lucinda Childs. Harvey was obsessed with it and Joe and I followed suit. We presented the work three times (following its debut in 1976 at the Metropolitan Opera). *Einstein* always sold out and contributed to BAM's reputation as a maverick institution.

3   For those needing more evidence regarding the impact of BAM on Matt's childhood, consider this: One afternoon, in 1998 or thereabouts, I brought Matt to my office after school. I had to do one last thing that day and I was between babysitters. I think he was about ten years old. The "thing" I had to do involved getting out a fundraising proposal at the last minute. This time the request had been written by a highly capable member of our development staff, Matt Bregman, but I wasn't completely satisfied with the document we were submitting. "Matt, Matt!" I bellowed to Bregman, who was at his desk several feet away from my office. Finally, he heard my rant and made his way to my desk. When Matt Bregman entered my office, young Matt Hopkins put his hand on Bregman's arm, looked at me, then at Bregman, and exclaimed with great empathy, "I feel your pain!"

of my job and the pressures of running a large cultural institution with an ever-increasing need for capital and more than 230 full-time employees, our relationship was complicated, to say the least. We often found ourselves struggling to find enough time to connect. Our life as a couple was constantly interrupted and challenged by the intensity of my career and, of course, the intense love and commitment we both had for our children (Ron had two, Daniel and Anna).

When we spent time together—mostly on the weekends and after performances and events—Ron encouraged me to slow down, to put away the budgets and proposals, and to be present with him, in the moment. He modeled a way of looking at problems—through compassion for the perspectives of others—that fundamentally changed the way I listened to staff, and even to my son. He helped me become a better leader, mother, daughter, decision maker, lover, and friend. He was my greatest advisor. Still, I remained tethered to my vast responsibilities as the president of BAM. When board members or funders asked for things, I couldn't say, "I'll get back to you later." No matter how spectacular a day we had enjoyed together, the work was always waiting for me. And sometimes this weighed on our relationship.

Since Ron was BAM's lawyer, he knew everything about the institution and how it worked. He understood what I was up against every day and was incredibly supportive. In many ways, our relationship made sense, though it was by no means a traditional one. We were both divorced and by the time I became president of BAM, our children were all grown adults. We maintained separate residences, carving out time on the weekends to visit our little beach place in Montauk, during which we hardly saw anyone else. We had a minimal social life because we relished every moment we had together. Our relationship was special and intimate and we knew how lucky we were to have such a deep connection.

For years, I continued working at a brisk pace, which over time brought a good deal of success and recognition. Of course, this was all wonderful. I certainly couldn't complain about people respecting and celebrating BAM or my career. I reveled in the excitement of my job and the life that it afforded. Ron felt much the same. He was thrilled for me and for the institution, and we reasoned that we had time to figure things out and plan for our future. At a certain point, however, I wished to enlarge the scope of my life, which included not only Ron, but also my son and his wife, Annie, and my grandchildren, so I began thinking about retirement.

The City of New York, which owns the BAM facilities, had a pension policy called the "rule of eighty-five." If your years of service plus your age equaled eighty-five, you could retire with a full pension. By the time I considered stepping down, I qualified. I felt that I had achieved certain things and could finally, for the first time, envision not working at such a crazy pace. Ron was ten years my senior and, twelve years earlier, had suffered a heart attack. We knew we didn't have forever, but we figured we had at least ten good years ahead. However, it was during this period of great intensity, in the year leading up to my departure from BAM, that Ron's health began to decline and the ground beneath us shifted.

First came the shortness of breath. We didn't really understand what was causing it, but we suspected it was angina from an earlier heart procedure. The doctors gave him some medication for that. His condition improved slightly, but not enough. Then he saw a

Following spread:
A "one of a kind" look
for the Peter Jay Sharp
Building on the night of
the Karen gala, 2015.

THE BROOKLYN

K

pulmonologist, who diagnosed him with pulmonary fibrosis, a condition that arises when lung tissue becomes damaged or scarred. Though the news was far from good, from our perspective, he had a chronic illness and, with oxygen therapy, he could continue to live reasonably well.

The additional oxygen worked, but walking long distances and climbing steps became increasingly hard for him. I had hoped that, after my retirement, Ron would come live in my Brooklyn brownstone in Park Slope but, given the staircases, that plan no longer seemed realistic. We decided to put off addressing where we would live until after I actually retired, giving us time to see how he responded to physical therapy designed for people with breathing issues and to a new medication, which had recently been approved by the FDA and had the potential to arrest the complications resulting from his condition.

Ron responded well to the physical therapy. The daily exercises helped him get into much better shape. However, the medication, which wasn't supposed to cure him but could potentially arrest the progress of his disease, proved incredibly taxing. The regimen required him to take nine pills a day, and the resulting side effects, such as terrible, unabating insomnia, were very hard on him. Over a period of weeks, after starting the new drugs, he developed a nagging and persistent cough, which we believed, based on the information about the drug, to be a side effect of the meds. In the days leading up to "the Karen gala," a giant party celebrating my retirement from BAM, Ron's cough worsened. Even then, we had no idea that it was the sign of something far more serious, no understanding of what would come next.

The end of my thirty-six-year tenure at BAM was finally in sight, and I had no choice but to dedicate nearly all of my attention to wrapping up the job and ensuring a smooth transition. The Karen gala would be my last major event at BAM, and I wanted to leave the institution on strong footing. In the days leading up to the gala, an unforgettable party including dinner at the Brooklyn Navy Yard and a performance at the Howard Gilman Opera House featuring Mavis Staples, Rufus and Martha Wainwright, Steve Reich, and tributes from artists, donors, administrators, city offices, and close friends—I put my energy into ensuring the evening's success. The development and press office at BAM worked to make sure I looked my best. It was a special thrill getting decked out for the gala. The fashion designer Kate Spade gifted my white leather dress with shoes and bag to match and Tiffany & Co. loaned jewelry for the occasion. I was particularly pleased when the dresser at the Kate Spade atelier looked at me and said she needed to bring in dresses that were two sizes smaller than they originally were told!

The evening would culminate in the announcement of a new space between Ashland Place and Flatbush Avenue—the "BAM Karen"—which would potentially house three cinemas; the Samuel H. Scripps Education Center, a large education space; and the BAM Hamm Archives. Looking back now, my fragmented memories of those last weeks as president all run together. There was no past or future. Everything dissolved into an eternal present, with the day of the gala, April 28, 2015, looming large.

I remember that Ron and I spoke before the gala. He had been using an oxygen machine at home, when needed, and—only recently—had begun taking portable tanks

with him when he left his apartment, since he was finding himself requiring extra oxygen for climbing stairs and walking long distances. In his characteristic way, he assured me over the phone that he was fine because, even if he wasn't feeling his best, he wanted everything to be perfect for my big night.

When I arrived at the Brooklyn Navy Yard, I found Ron sitting on a log near the entrance with one of our staff members, Louie Fleck, tending to him. I knelt down and asked with concern, "What's going on?" He said he had fallen and twisted his ankle as he stepped out of a cab en route to the gala. He couldn't walk, due to the pain, and needed a wheelchair. A swarming mob of people—nearly twelve hundred—were filing past us into the venue for cocktails. Staff and board members were shouting my name, beckoning me to come inside for photographs. I dispatched Louie to bring back a wheelchair from BAM, looked Ron in the eye, and asked, "Are you okay?" He nodded stoically and told me to go inside.

The party was flat-out crazy. People were spilling into the Navy Yard on both sides— by car, by bus, and by boat. The weather (despite all of the rainy, snowy, miserable galas of the past), turned out lovely. The next thing I remember was sitting at the head table with Ron in a wheelchair beside me. I stood and started working the room and greeting people, circulating among board members and friends in what seemed like one collective embrace. When I returned to the table, Ron waved me over and quietly said, "It's not my foot. I'm having trouble breathing." He had used up the portable tank and was out of oxygen. "I'm okay as long as I'm sitting down," he continued. Then, gesturing to his son beside him, "Don't worry, Dan will help me."

I asked, "Are you sure?"

"Yeah," he said, without hesitating. I squeezed his hand and told him that after the performance, I'd have the private car service I'd been assigned for the night take him home.

The rest of the evening was out of a storybook. I remember the crowd cheering and people whistling and shouting my name. When I arrived at the opera house for the show, I discovered my name displayed in lights. Steve Reich, Rufus and Martha Wainwright, and Mavis Staples (one of my idols) rocked the house. There was also a video featuring Paul Simon, who sang and sent a personal message. The show hosts were good friends and men of the theater: John Turturro, a local Brooklynite who had performed at BAM throughout my tenure; and the great British actor Alan Rickman.[4] The stage had been decorated with thousands of balloons. I couldn't believe it. At the after party, they served slices of chocolate babka and Diet Peach Tea Snapple, two of my favorites. And the staff presented me with a touching handmade book filled with memorabilia from my time at BAM. The entire evening—overflowing with love and affection—reached its climax with the announcement of the BAM Karen building. It was, without question, the highlight of my career, and the greatest moment of my life, next to the birth of my son.

Ron did not stay for the after party. He left right after the performances with his son. Naturally, I was worried about him all night and called as soon as I got home, around 1:00 a.m. He was okay and felt better after getting home. I sensed something was wrong, but

4 My dear Alan, brilliant performer, director, and good friend to BAM, passed away on January 14, 2016. We had no idea he, too, was gravely ill on the night of my gala.

didn't fully process it that night, my mind still reeling from the gala. The next day, Buzzy O'Keeffe, the owner of the River Café, planned to hold a retirement lunch for people who had come to my gala from out of town. So I said to Ron, "If you feel better, you can come to the lunch." Silence. Then, Ron said, hesitantly, "I think I should go to the hospital." Not hearing him, I gently pushed back, "Well, why don't you wait and see?"

"Karen," he definitively replied, "I'm not coming to the lunch."

The next day, while I dined at the River Café, celebrating with friends, Ron was admitted to Mount Sinai. After the lunch, I rushed off to see him. Just when I arrived at the hospital, I got a call from Chantal Bernard from our fundraising department, who had arranged for me to borrow and wear beautiful and expensive Tiffany jewelry for the gala night. Chantal was in a panic because a seventy-five-thousand-dollar diamond necklace, which I hadn't selected or worn, but had gone home with me to try on before the gala, was missing. I immediately began freaking out as I realized that I had dumped all of the paper boxes from my outfit in a trash can on the street, and trash collection was scheduled that day.

I immediately called my friend Tina and her husband, Alan, who had been staying at my house for the gala. They were—thank God—in a car service on the way to Manhattan, but hadn't yet reached the Brooklyn Bridge. "Tina!" I said, "Turn around, go back to Garfield Place, go back to the gray trash can on the side of the pharmacy on Seventh Avenue, dig through the trash, and find that necklace!" Tina, now as fully frantic as I was, implored her driver to turn around and speed as fast as he could, back to my house. They came to a screeching halt on Seventh Avenue and Garfield. (The driver was now fully involved in the drama.) Allan, Tina, and the driver started rummaging through the trash, as I yelled through the phone delineating the list of all the stuff I had tossed in that can. To make matters worse, Allan said he thought he heard the grinding brakes of a big sanitation truck at the top of the street. We were all now in an advanced state of hysteria. As luck would have it, there, lying peacefully on the bottom of the can, wrapped in soft blue velvet, was a magnificent sparkling diamond necklace, waiting to be found and returned to its home on Fifth Avenue. Tina gave the driver a huge tip. Another crisis had been solved just in the nick of time.

Minutes later, I went into the hospital to visit Ron in the cardiology unit and learned that he had been diagnosed with pneumonia. His doctors took him off his meds and started him on steroids and IV antibiotics. The rest of the day, full of ups and downs, was punctuated by moments of crisis, followed by periods of relative calm. As the medication kicked in, it seemed like the worst might be over. Over the next few days, he slowly stabilized. His oxygen levels were still low, but not getting worse, and the nurses were able to sit him up in a chair, and—eventually—take him for a walk around the cardiology unit. Finally, the doctors said that he was out of immediate danger. Ron, our kids, and I all breathed a collective sigh of relief.

For the next week, I split my time between BAM and the hospital, going uptown each day to visit Ron for long stretches, while trying to stay ahead of the post-gala follow up. Things finally seemed to have calmed down on both fronts, but it was difficult to focus on anything. By this point, I was spent, emotionally and physically. Finally, at the end of the week, the doctors decided to send Ron home. He was still pretty sick and would need a

more complicated oxygen machinery and and visiting nurses, who would come regularly to monitor his condition and oversee his medications. Nevertheless, the pneumonia seemed to be clearing up, though he would get winded quickly just from walking around the room. I went to stay at his apartment. He was doing better, but there was a long way to go. He seemed well enough that I went into work the next day for a few hours. There was still so much to wrap up before I left BAM, and Katy Clark, a former orchestra manager and classical musician, took over as the new president,[5] and I hadn't found time to regroup after the gala and plan for my final six weeks.

Over the weekend, a visiting nurse came and listened to Ron's chest. "Your lungs sound clear," he said. "The pneumonia seems to be gone." So we thought Ron was finally safe and even started allowing ourselves to indulge in fantasies of fulfilling the postretirement plans we had made long ago. Ron and I had traveled extensively during our years together and that summer after my retirement we were scheduled to visit Greece and Israel. It seemed after the encouraging report from the visiting nurse that with enough physical therapy, Ron might still be able to travel internationally. With a little luck, we might even enjoy those ten good years together, after all.

Later that night, around 10:30, I was reading the 2016 BAM budget in bed, trying to prep it for the new president. It was massive, pages and pages. I turned to Ron, who was watching TV and working on his computer, and said, "Do you mind?" And he said, "No." A few minutes later, he sighed and said, "I just want to go to Montauk and sit on our deck." So we resolved to visit our place as soon as he was well enough to make the trip. I said, "I'm going to sleep. Are you ready?" And he replied, "In a little bit." Right before I fell asleep, Ron said, "Could you turn my oxygen up to ten?" And I said, "Yeah . . . but the guy who delivered the machine said if you have to turn it up past eight, you should go to the hospital." Ron was not the kind of person you nagged. I nagged everyone else in my life, but never nagged him. "Believe me," he said, "I understand this equipment better than he does. Just go turn it up to ten." So I did.

It was around midnight that I heard him gasp. I bolted up and frantically asked, "Ron, are you okay? Are you okay?" But he didn't respond. I shook him and tried to wake him. Then I called 911. The operator told me to start compressions. And I said, "Just get here!"

"Are you refusing to comply?" the operator asked. And I said, "I'm not refusing to do anything. Just get here!"

I ran over to the oxygen machine to make sure it was working. The mask had slipped from Ron's face. I pushed it back up while simultaneously trying to administer the compressions. His leg had fallen to the side as well, and when I went to lift it, it was heavy. I shouted, "Ron, Ron, wake up!" But I couldn't wake him. When the medics arrived, less than five minutes later, I yelled, "Please, please come in here!" And they rushed into the room and intubated him. While they were working on him, they told me to go into the other room. And I was relieved to do as they said.

Then they came back out and said, "We're going take him to Bellevue." So I thought,

5   Joe Melillo retired from BAM in 2018 and was succeeded by David Binder, a talented Broadway producer and festival curator, completing the full transition of our executive team. Katy Clark resigned from BAM at the end of 2020.

Thank God they've revived him. "Can we take him to Mount Sinai?" I asked.

"No," they insisted, "we have to take him to Bellevue."

I said, "Okay, we'll take him to Bellevue." I didn't care as long as he was alive. Then, two minutes later they returned and said, "We're sorry. We can't do anything for him. He's gone." And I cried "Please! You have to bring him back!" But they couldn't, and I knew it. He was gone.

It was only twelve days after my gala. The moment of freedom had arrived and suddenly our future together was shattered. It was the cruelest thing. For the first year after his death, I would crawl into bed at night—the proposals and budgets no longer piled up beside me—and think, Where are you, Ron?

We were so close to having it all—the pension, children, celebrated careers, and time to be together. It disappeared in an instant. People say that things happen for a reason, but I really can't see any logic in it. For that first year following his death, I struggled with the same questions. How do I go on from here? What has value now? Had I known what would happen, would I have retired? Could I have done more for him while he was alive? Some days, I want my old life back. Some days, it all seems like a distant memory. And yet, I'm still here, riding my bike, lifting my weights, reading newspapers and magazines, making my crazy clippings and notes. The pile is smaller, but we are who we are, and I carry on, continuing to do what I've always done.

After Ron died and I retired from BAM, I found myself unmoored, suffering deeply from the loss of two of the key anchors in my life. It was confusing, amid the grief and uncertainty, and hard to find a comfort zone. My son, Matt, was wonderful, and he and his wife, Annie, made sure that I saw my three granddaughters, Adrienne and Natalie (then four years old) and Caroline (then one), as often as possible, which lifted my spirits more than

Above:
Rufus and Martha
Wainwright in A Kate
McGarrigle Tribute:
Kate's Kids, spring
2013.

Opposite:
DJs Andrew and
Andrew with Rufus
Wainwright and Jörn
Weisbrodt, 2015.

anything. My friends were also great and rallied around me, especially Tina, who stayed by my side for two straight weeks following Ron's death. Despite this support, I was anxious about summer, which was approaching quickly, and with it the long hot months that would stretch out with no end in sight. I wasn't sure if I had the nerve to go to Montauk, where Ron and I had spent so many wonderful years in our little "unit" right on the ocean, but I felt compelled to escape the city.

Because of BAM's long-term relationship with Robert Wilson, I had become friendly with his executive director at the time, Jörn Weisbrodt, who was married to Rufus Wainwright. Rufus and Jörn also had a place in Montauk, and Ron and I were regular guests at their home,[6] where Jörn prepared fabulous meals of fresh fish on his huge green barbecue grill, the Big Green Egg. Jörn and Rufus's wedding was at their house (and included Rufus's sister, Martha Wainwright, singing her rendition of a Rufus classic, "Montauk," from the roof of the house; a feast at the famous Montauk outdoor restaurant, Clam Bar, followed by an after party at the old Shagwong, where Sean Lennon led the guests in a spirited rendition of "YMCA"). As our friendship grew while I was still at BAM and Ron was healthy, we talked about launching a series of program ideas for BAM and a new collaboration between BAM and Luminato, a multidisciplinary arts festival in Toronto, where Jörn served as artistic director.

One of our big events that involved the Wainwrights was a BAM series timed to occur alongside the release of a Nonesuch recording called *Sing Me the Songs That Say I Love You*. It was a tribute album that Rufus and Martha had devised, featuring songs written by their late mother, Kate McGarrigle. The siblings were joined by many friends and family members for two performances in the Howard Gilman Opera House, alongside a screening

of a documentary made about the project and several other events. Proceeds from the show supported the McGarrigle Foundation, which Rufus had launched in Kate's honor. Everyone in the audience received a free copy of the CD (courtesy of Nonesuch, where my old friend from the early days at BAM, David Bither, now served as a senior executive). It was one of those BAM events where a deep connection was forged between the performers and the audience.

Between the professional association and our shared love of Montauk, Rufus and Jörn had become my close friends, and so, just two months after Ron's death, they asked me to join them for Rufus's birthday celebration at the Kennedy compound in Hyannis Port, Massachusetts. I was a little nervous about going away so soon after losing Ron, but spending time alone in Brooklyn only exacerbated my grief. Rufus was a friend of Kathleen "Kick" Kennedy, one of Bobby Jr.'s daughters, and that was how we came to be invited. The first night we were asked to dinner by Ethel, Bobby Kennedy's widow. Each family member had their own house in the compound, and Ethel's was filled with Bobby and Jack Kennedy memorabilia. It

6   Rufus and Jörn had a lovely swing on their deck. A perfect Montauk night for me was drinking wine and watching Jörn barbecue while Ron was swinging and Rufus was singing!

was impressive. The food was less inspiring, and I remember thinking how odd it was with all the Kennedy wealth and hospitality that we were dining on a clump of meat and frozen French fries. Aside from the cuisine, however, the weekend was soothing, as various Kennedy members came and left, arriving and departing on sailboats. It was interesting that every family member from all the various generations present possessed that same toothy Kennedy smile and look that identified their tribe.

On Rufus's birthday, July 22 (the date is inscribed in my brain because my twin granddaughters, Adrienne and Natalie, share that birthday with Rufus), we all gathered in the center of the compound to celebrate. At that moment, Bobby Jr. initiated all of us into a Kennedy family birthday tradition. It was called "the Circle of Love" and consisted of a short speech made by every person in the circle saying something that they loved about the individual whose birthday it was. I think Rufus was a little embarrassed to have so much love coming at him from all sides, but it was truly a touching and moving ceremony. And, of course, when I made my tribute to Rufus, I thought of Ron, his love of family, how much I missed him, and what he would have said in the circle. At that moment, I felt Ron's presence very strongly and I recalled the beautiful concert and record Rufus had made in honor of his mother; so I told Rufus, in the circle, what Ron would have said: that we loved him, "because, in addition to his remarkable talent and compassion, he was a wonderful son."

Left:
Ping Pong Ball Art by Ron. This piece is called *The Dow Jones Industrial Average*.

Opposite:
With Ron in Havana, our last trip together, 2015.

This page, clockwise from top left: Matt's band, Kidding on the Square, filled the house at BAMcafé Live, 2011.

At Matt's wedding, 2008.

With Annie (my daughter-in-law) and Adrienne, Natalie, and Caroline (my granddaughters) and son, Matt, with the Cookie Monster at BAMkids Film Festival, 2015.

With Ron at my fiftieth birthday.

With Annie and Matt at a party celebrating my French medal, the Chevalier de L'Ordre des Arts et des Lettres.

Opposite, clockwise from top left: With Ron in Hong Kong.

With Ron at the rehearsal dinner for Matt's wedding.

With Ron at my gala.

With Ron at a BAM opening party.

With Daniel and Meri Feiner; Anna Feiner, Ron, Matt, and Annie Hopkins at the Hoover Dam on a family gambling trip to Vegas.

CHAPTER FIFTEEN:

DanceAfrica and ¡Sí Cuba!

The DanceAfrica Festival at BAM, which began in 1977, wasn't just a program; it was a force. Charles (Chuck) Davis, dancer, griot, teacher, all around leader of people and champion of the arts brought the show to BAM and changed the Memorial Day weekend in Brooklyn forever. Harvey, and one of his finest program deputies, Mikki Sheppard, wanted—particularly in light of the neighborhood demographic—to put work on BAM's stages that reflected racial diversity. Chuck Davis's *DanceAfrica* brought that and so much more. The program, which began as a small showcase of African American dance companies in the Lepercq Space, has spanned four decades and remains the centerpiece of Memorial Day weekend in New York.

To truly comprehend the scope of this event, it is important to understand the magnitude and charisma of Chuck Davis. He was a huge presence, well over six feet tall. He always wore the traditional multi-colored African robes and headwear that defined him as a both Chief and inspiring leader. He had huge hands, long arms and emanated a warmth that touched everyone he met. First and foremost, he was a cheerleader for African dance. He believed that dance was not only the way to bring people together; it was the way to make them feel proud of and connected to their heritage. He was from North Carolina and his southern hospitality, combined with his knowledge of African traditions, defined the personality of *DanceAfrica*. He introduced each show and *DanceAfrica* gathering with the "Ago," a greeting from the Ghanaian people of West Africa. He would bellow "AGO" or "listen" and the audience, at his instruction, would faithfully bellow back "AME!"—"I am (we are) listening." Over the years the program kept growing and expanding both inside the building, outside on the streets around BAM, deep into Brooklyn and then to cities all over the United States (led for many years by Tamara McCaw, Director of Government and Community Affairs and Dewonnie Frederick, Community Affairs and Bazaar Manager).

At BAM, the DanceAfrica Festival is overseen by a distinguished Council of Elders who worked with Chuck all year long to select themes for the festival, and provide education programs related to dance and other African heritage events. We all referred to Chuck as "Baba" or "Father" in many African languages, and he made us feel like we were all his children. Every Memorial Day, our former parking lots—now open revitalized public spaces or sites for new buildings, became an enormous African bazaar, with over 250 craft, food, and clothing vendors. It was common for close to fifty thousand people to attend the bazaar every year. Inside the Howard Gilman Opera House, the five performances scheduled for that weekend were always sold out. Every year we showcased not only African American companies, but also a company that came to BAM from a nation in Africa. You could hear the drums all the way down Flatbush Avenue. There were master classes with the visiting African companies, related films in the BAM Rose Cinemas, talks, an emerging choreographers fellowship and scholarships for youth supported by the SHS Foundation,

Opposite:
Chuck Davis in
DanceAfrica,
spring 2013.

dinners for the Elders, an official Memorial room, events at Weeksville Heritage Center,[1] the African Burial grounds in Manhattan, and a massive education program.[2]

The education program consisted of an in-depth partnership with Bedford Stuyvesant Restoration Corporation (often called BSRC or Restoration). It is the oldest community development corporation in the country having opened in 1967, through the efforts of Robert Kennedy and Franklin Thomas, who served as the organization's first president. In 1996, I decided to pay a visit to the Rev. Dr. Emma Jordan-Simpson, a senior executive at Restoration. It seemed strange that we didn't know each other, given that both BAM and Restoration had been important organizations in their respective communities for decades. At our meeting, Emma, Jayme Koszyn (BAM's then director of education and humanities), and I cooked up a partnership that has become an integral part of the festival for over twenty-five years. We decided that each season, a group of young people would study the traditions and mores of the African country represented at that year's festival, and learn a dance, which they would perform alongside the professional dancers on the opera house stage. The participants maintained good grades at school, attended all rehearsals, and remained fully engaged in the program, from beginning to end. The experience has been transformative and powerful, as hundreds of children have participated this initiative. Each year, the selected African company would come to BAM a week before the festivities to work directly with the young dancers. As part of the program, the students would make their costumes, learn their roles, and work diligently under the supervision of the Elders, Chuck, Peggy Alston, Karen Thornton, and the dedicated team at BSRC led by Indira Etwaroo, to produce work of the highest quality. The professionalism and style of these student performers has been off the charts. They have been invited to perform in many places beyond BAM and they (the BAM Restoration Dance Company) are a source of enormous pride to BSRC, BAM and all of Brooklyn.

Over the years, Chuck, bubbling with enthusiasm for each individual festival, also came up with some extravagant special additions to the program. There were a few particular festival events that I always recall joyfully. One time Chuck actually conducted a traditional African wedding ceremony onstage. He joined his loyal assistant stage manager, Normadien Woolbright, and N'Goma, our stage manager, in holy matrimony that day with the entire audience of over two thousand people in the opera house as witnesses. The couple is still together, and I have fond memories of their wedding day. In 1983, for the sixteenth anniversary, Chuck organized a group African American motorcyclists, called the Imperial Bikers Motorcycle Club, each rider bearing a flag of a different African nation, to

---

1   The Weeksville Heritage Center documents and preserves the historic site of Weeksville in Central Brooklyn, one of the first and largest free Black communities founded in pre-Civil War America.

2   The SHS Foundation became a very important contributor over the years. Harvey had known the donor, Sam Scripps, for decades. He was a portly man with a grey ponytail and a heart of gold. He loved theater, gamelan music, and modern dance. Sam was more eccentric then your usual board member, so when he passed away we were delighted that his executor, attorney, and family advisor, Richard Feldman, took his seat on the board and continued Sam's philanthropy. Richard supported the DanceAfrica Festival and these contributions allowed us to expand and deepen the entire program while simultaneously channeling Sam's spirit in the most sincere way.

Opposite:
Posters for the
DanceAfrica Festival,
1979–2012.

BAM AND THEN IT HITS YOU

DanceAfrica accompanied her on the ride home. Where did BAM hit you? Join in on Facebook.

L'Acadco: A United Caribbean Dance Force in DanceAfrica, BAM Opera House, May 2005

BAM 150th Anniversary sponsor CHASE

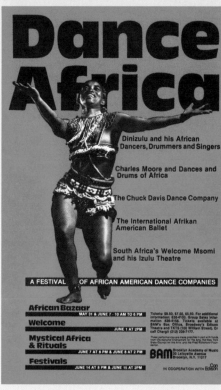

drive in formation from Harlem to the steps of BAM. They were joined by the Council of Elders, artists, and dignitaries for a libation pouring ceremony, for which we commissioned the famous Brooklyn baker, Cake Man Raven (Raven Patrick De'Sean Dennis III), to bake an enormous red velvet cake in the shape of Africa, and we opened the doors for a huge public cake party. We also sometimes featured marching bands and teen break-dancers performing in front of the building. Baba Chuck loved the annual Brooklyn celebration but he wanted to spread the *DanceAfrica* message of "peace, love, and respect for everybody" far and wide. By 1987, Carla Perlo (my dear friend and camp co-counselor from 1969) had launched DanceAfrica DC at her organization, Dance Place, in Washington's Brookland neighborhood. With some urging from me, she took on the role of national coordinator, and we got an NEA grant to take the program all over the United States. We ended up touring the festival and adding local companies in each of our five destination cities around the nation. Many of those festivals and some new ones still exist today.

One year I arrived at BAM on the final day of the festival to see that police had cordoned off the area and that everything had been shut down on Lafayette Avenue. I dashed up to the door of the opera house, apprehensive about what might of happened, and learned that a gigantic swarm of bees had escaped from their owner's hives and had taken up residence on the canopy of the opera house. There were millions of them. Even the bees couldn't resist the sound of the drums.

Baba Charles "Chuck" Davis left this world at the age of eighty in 2017.[3] The entire community and dancers all over the world were heartbroken. Fortunately, two years prior to his death, and with his blessing, BAM, led by Joe and then vice president of education and humanities, Stephanie Hughley, had mounted an effort to find a new artistic director who would continue his work. The accomplished choreographer Abdel Salaam has picked up the mantle, and *DanceAfrica* continues stronger than ever.

Over the decades of its existence, my favorite *DanceAfrica* visiting company was Ballet Folklórico Cutumba from Santiago de Cuba. Once in a while, Chuck wanted to bring a company from the Diaspora, rather than from Africa, and so we featured Afro-Cuban and Haitian performers on occasion. Cutumba performed this intense rope dance that was totally original. The piece featured twenty dancers moving at lightning speed, weaving their way in and out of a series of ropes dangling from a pole, which culminated in the creation of an incredible pattern, which somehow, miraculously, unraveled. I cannot imagine how they learned this dance, but it thrilled our Brooklyn audiences to no end.

Working with Cubans, because of the political situation, was extremely difficult. There was one entity there, the Ludwig Foundation, run by Helmo Hernández who was able to

Chuck Davis organized the African American motorcycle club in 1993 (the DanceAfrica Sweet 16) to ride from Harlem to Brooklyn with each bike displaying the flag of a different African nation.

3   When Ron passed away, Chuck, at my request, chanted the traditional African blessings for the dead at his shiva, the Jewish custom of honoring the life of the deceased, which was touching and heartfelt. When this great man died only two years later, I was honored to pay tribute to him onstage at the Howard Gilman Opera House on the Saturday of the festival. I asked the audience to stand as I told the story of what Chuck had done for Ron, and then I recited the mourner's Kaddish in Hebrew from my own ethnic tradition as a tribute to my dear friend.

negotiate cultural exchange projects with the United States. Helmo made arrangements for Cutumba to perform at the festival, and his capable director of Dance Programs, Fernando Sáez, managed all of the logistics and travel.

A few seasons later, political tensions between Cuba and the US began to ease, and Joe decided to bring the famous Ballet Nacional de Cuba, led by the world-renowned prima ballerina, Alicia Alonzo, to BAM. It turned out that some of our other colleague institutions, such as, the Joyce Theater, were also bringing Cuban artists to New York that season, so we all decided to join forces and create a citywide festival, which we called the ¡Sí Cuba! Festival. Ron and I traveled to Havana to prearrange some of the logistics, etcetera, and, lo and behold, Fernando Sáez, was assigned as our host. This was the beginning of a deep and close relationship that has endured beyond Ron's death and the ever-changing political relationship between the United States and Cuba.

Ron was already deeply interested in Cuba, and years earlier we had made one fascinating trip there on our own, accompanied by our old friend, Princess Di gala chair and loyal BAM board member Beth DeWoody, who was an art collector with several excellent works by Cuban artists. For the ¡Sí Cuba! trip, Fernando organized a packed agenda, visiting not only Cutumba in Santiago de Cuba, but also several companies in Havana. Beyond the dance programs, our line producer Nick Schwartz-Hall worked with Joe on the music and with our colleague institutions. These resulted in a wonderful program of both visual and performing arts events were available to New York theatergoers. By then we had learned so much about working with other organizations from the Muslim Voices experience that ¡Sí Cuba! was a piece of cake.

There was one situation, however, that threatened the peaceful atmosphere around the citywide program. The Joyce was presenting Danza Contemporánea de Cuba as their key event in the festival. Contemporánea was a talented company that had a very mercurial director, Miguel Ferrer. He and Fernando, who had been a huge supporter and enabler of this company, had a serious falling out over the way Miguel handled relations with a respected guest choreographer. Following the festival, Fernando split entirely with Contemporánea, but there was a silver lining to the separation. Fernando, along with former Contemporánea dancers, Daileidys Carrazana and Osnel Delgado, decided to form their own brand-new company, which they named Malpaso, the Spanish word for "misstep." Malpaso Dance Company has now been in existence for over five years and they have developed an international following. Linda Shelton, executive director of the Joyce, provides ongoing guidance for the company, which now performs there annually to sold out houses. They have built up an impressive repertory with pieces not only choreographed by Osnel, but also by acclaimed talents such as Ronald K. Brown, Aszure Barton, and Ohad Naharin of Batsheva Dance Company.

In a consummate gesture of respect and love, Fernando and the company dedicated *Dreaming of Lions*, based on Hemingway's novel *The Old Man and the Sea*, to Ron. The piece was choreographed by Osnel and performed with live music composed by Arturo O'Farrill. Of course, I wanted that piece to be onstage at BAM. Joe and Linda agreed and it was a memorable night when we celebrated Ron's life and the Cuban dancers of Malpaso performed at the BAM Harvey Theater.

Opposite:
The Creole Choir of
Cuba, spring 2011.

BROOKLYN CULTURAL DISTRICT

WILLOUGHBY ST

WILLOUGHBY AVE

FLATBUSH AVE EXT

WASHINGTON PK

CARLTON AVE

City Point

Kumble Theater

University Place

Fort Greene Park

ASHLAND PL

LIU Brooklyn

Dime Savings Bank

Paramount Theater

Junior's

DEKALB AVE

FULTON ST

HUDSON AVE

ROCKWELL PL

ST FELIX ST

HANOVER PL

GROVE PL

Fox Square

BRIC House UrbanGlass

BAM Harvey

FT GREENE PL

S ELLIOTT PL

S PORTLAND AVE

S OXFORD ST

CUMBERLAND ST

BAM Strong

BRIC Community Media Incubator

LAFAYETTE AVE

SCHERMERHORN ST

TFANA / Polonsky Shakespeare Ctr

Betty Carter Park

Fowler Square

Irondale Arts Center

Mark Morris Dance Center

The Center for Fiction

STATE ST

Sixteen Sycamores Park

Plaza at 300 Ashland

BAM Peter Jay Sharp Building

FULTON ST

651 ARTS BAM Karen Brooklyn Public Library MoCADA

BAM Fisher

Brooklyn Music School

Cuyler Gore

ATLANTIC AVE

Roulette

One Hanson Place

HANSON PL

80 Arts

A.R.T./NY South Oxford Space

PACIFIC ST

3 AVE

Times Plaza

Atlantic Terminal

Atlantic Center Mall

ATLANTIC COMMONS

DEAN ST

ACADEMY PK PL

South Oxford Park

BERGEN ST

4 AVE

FLATBUSH AVE

ATLANTIC AVE

S PORTLAND AVE

ST MARKS PL

Dancewave

Barclays Center

PACIFIC ST

CHAPTER SIXTEEN:

The Brooklyn Cultural District

As early as 1979, Harvey began to articulate a vision for transforming sections of our Fort Greene neighborhood into a vibrant mixed-use cultural district, which would become a magnet for developers, as well as a home for artists and cultural organizations. He set up a separate nonprofit organization called the BAM Local Development Corporation (LDC), with the goal of initiating this transformation and bringing it to fruition. Harvey didn't exactly understand the full meaning of this undertaking at the time he put this together. He wasn't thinking so much about the needs of other cultural organizations or turning Brooklyn into the world's hippest neighborhood. His orientation was always BAM-centric, and so he was thinking foremost about creating a context for BAM. He believed that the best way to do this was to surround our building with lots of different types of cultural organizations, mostly smaller, so as to establish BAM as the epicenter of diverse culture in Brooklyn.

Though much of the area had fallen on hard times during the 1960s and 70s, it had been solidly and beautifully constructed during the nineteenth century. BAM happens to sit on the third-largest transportation hub in the City of New York at Atlantic Avenue, and fifty-five-thousand cars a day move up and down nearby Flatbush Avenue. The conditions were right for growth and revitalization, even if others didn't share our vision.

Due to urban renewal policies of the past, surface parking lots occupied nearly all of the space between BAM's Main Building on Lafayette Avenue and the BAM Harvey on Fulton. Luckily, our historic buildings were protected, and there was essentially zero displacement as development commenced in the area around BAM.

In fact, the only other large structure on the block was a broken-down single occupancy hotel across the street. This building, known for its history of fires, robberies, and generally poor conditions, had been empty for several years with the exception of one long term resident who was finally given a new apartment by the city. The empty lots created an area of natural opportunity for developers, but at the time most of them didn't think it was worth the effort or the money.

The first big break for the future cultural district came in the late eighties with the renovation and resurrection of the Majestic (now the BAM Harvey Theater).[1] The location of the Majestic organically established the boundaries of a BAM campus/cultural district that spanned several blocks, connecting our Peter Jay Sharp main building at 30 Lafayette

---

1   The Majestic Theater, renamed the BAM Harvey in 1999, is revered by artists of all disciplines. In 2013, with a grant from Joseph and Diane Steinberg, BAM constructed the Steinberg screen, a thirty-five-by-nineteen-foot state-of-the-art screen with forty-two surround-sound speakers, allowing the space to be transformed into a giant cinema and thus increasing the institution's capacity to present movies and shows featuring film and live music.

Avenue to the restored theater on Fulton Street, setting the table for an enhanced cultural presence in the neighborhood.

The next major milestone came when Harvey brought the choreographer Mark Morris to Brooklyn and helped him establish a permanent home across from BAM on Lafayette in an abandoned New York State office building. Mark had been a featured artist at BAM since the beginning of the Next Wave Festival, and he was not against coming to Brooklyn. Harvey, a former dancer who loved Mark's work, was extremely focused on attracting him and his company to the area. Together, they had the drive and the passion to raise enough money to do it. Harvey (with help from board member Dan Klores, who had strong connections to city and state government officials) teed up a million dollars and got the state to donate the building. At the time, many people thought Mark should lease out the first floor of his space, but the company has made the most of every square inch, offering a full range of classes, rehearsal space and public programs 365 days a year. In 2018, Nancy Umanoff, Mark Morris Dance Group's talented executive director, even sold air rights and acquired more studio space in the new Caesura apartment complex next door.

BAM expanded with four new cinemas that opened in 1998 at 30 Lafayette Avenue in the former Helen Owen Carey Playhouse. The flexible Lepercq Space was also reinvented as the BAMcafé offering preshow meals and audience amenities, as well as free live music on the weekends. The film and music programs drove thousands of new audience members to the building, bringing a new vitality to the surrounding blocks and attracting the interest of other culturals, who were now ready to consider a Brooklyn home.

Harvey sensed the growing momentum in the neighborhood and, upon his retirement in 1999, he recreated the LDC as a freestanding, independent entity, which he would lead. Unfortunately, he didn't have the same fundraising firepower that we had established at BAM and, since he was a novice in the real estate field, the LDC struggled for funding and relevance. He did, however, manage to acquire another former state office building at 80 Hanson Place, which became home to subsidized office space for a variety of cultural organizations. This thirty-thousand-square-foot structure, formally known as the James E. Davis Arts Building,[2] or 80 Arts, was in a way a very early version of the co-working spaces now common all over the world. Each group had their own office but shared conference rooms and other public space. As usual, Harvey was way ahead of the curve. Nearby, at 138 South Oxford Street, the service organization, Alliance of Resident Theaters/New York, opened a multi-use rehearsal/office facility and the Irondale Ensemble Project moved into the nearby Lafayette Avenue Presbyterian Church.

By now the tide was turning and many small and mid-sized organizations were interested in Fort Greene. The challenge Harvey faced in this scenario was that many of the companies he wanted to bring to Brooklyn had minimal resources, and therefore did not have the ability to to make the move. This naturally meant that things were moving along more slowly than he had hoped.

2   James E. Davis was a former policeman and a newly elected city council member for the district who was assassinated in the council chamber at city hall in July 2003.

One of the exceptions was Theater for a New Audience (TFANA), a classic-based company with an illustrious and nomadic past that had built an impressive roster of affiliated artists, including directors like Peter Brook, Sir Peter Hall, Bartlett Sher, and Julie Taymor, and actors such as Mark Rylance and F. Murray Abraham. TFANA's founding artistic director, Jeffrey Horowitz, lived in Brooklyn and had a vision for the type of theater he wanted to build in the district, modeled after Shakespeare's Cottesloe Theatre in Stratford-upon-Avon, England. While the company's stellar reputation and excellent track record producing classical plays off Broadway preceded it, TFANA had not raised enough money when the plan for building their Brooklyn home commenced; hence, a project that should have taken two or three years to complete ended up taking a decade. Nevertheless, the company hung in, and after thirty-four years of performing in leased spaces, it raised close to thirty-five million dollars and in 2013 opened the Polonsky Shakespeare Center, a twenty-seven-thousand-square-foot performance space designed by architect Hugh Hardy. This was a triumph for TFANA and their permanent home became an integral centerpiece of the cultural district.

Harvey's dream for the cultural district took decades to materialize, and it evolved in a haphazard, organic, crazy way. Nevertheless, it was mesmerizing to watch, even if it all happened very slowly without any master plan and with city funding being appropriated, then cut, then restored, then cut, and so on, adding chaos along the way. Originally, Harvey had tried to bring in the Dutch architect Rem Koolhaas to develop a comprehensive plan, but again, in spite of all of Koolhaas' incredible ideas, there was no money to support it. Eventually the LDC was subsumed into an organization called the Downtown Brooklyn Partnership (DBP), which was formed to champion not only cultural development of Downtown Brooklyn, but residential and commercial development of the area as well. The DBP was run by a seasoned urban planner and real estate professional named Joe Chan, who engaged BAM's chairman, Alan Fishman, and Bob Catell, the legendary head of National Grid, to serve as his co-chairmen. All of a sudden, with these leaders at the helm, there was a real driving momentum for development and collaboration to take place across many different business lines. Since Harvey was finding it hard to generate the private money he needed to advance his specific vision, it made sense to disband the LDC and move it under the auspices of DBP. But, just as Harvey got settled there and was starting to move his projects forward, he suffered a serious stroke and was no longer able to work. Harvey had taken his ideas as far as they could go under his own, fiery, indefatigable style of leadership. Now it would be up to others to carry the torch and build the district.

During this time, as I served as the president of BAM, we thought endlessly about our own growth possibilities. As the largest institution in the area, we also assumed a leadership role in the district's future.[3] In addition to Alan Fishman's role as board chair, and that of Edgar Lampert, long-time real estate committee chair, I am especially indebted

3   I pushed hard to call the district "the BAM Cultural District," but, naturally, the other organizations felt overshadowed with such a dominant name. Eventually, I gave in, realizing they were right. The eclectic nature of the district and the large and growing number of the other organizations nearby (over fifty in the greater Downtown Brooklyn area) deserved more respect. I withdrew and now believe it was right to give Brooklyn, our home, the pride of place.

to Keith Stubblefield, who joined our staff in 2006 as CFO and whose portfolio included all of BAM's real estate acquisitions and the construction of the new buildings.

The first expansion of BAM under my presidency was the Fisher Building, a wholesale renovation of an historic Salvation Army building built in 1928, located on Ashland Place right around the block from our main building. The construction of Fisher was a very important component related to BAM's growing connection to the local community. Fisher, with its flexible 250-seat Fishman space, the Hillman Studio, and Max Leavitt Theater Workshop allowed BAM to program an intimate venue, that could operate at a much lower and more accessible price point then our other theaters.[4] The original plan was to take down the Salvation Army building and put a high-rise tower in that empty spot, which would house the new, community-focused outgrowth of BAM. We believed that a developer would build the new building, and, as part of the deal, we would acquire a theater space on the bottom floor. The city decided against this plan, because one side of Ashland Place, the street that ran alongside our opera house and the old Salvation Army, was designated as a historic district. The city deemed that the Salvation Army facade was a contributing building in the historic district, so they prohibited us from tearing it down and mandated that we keep the facade. This complicated the project and made it more expensive, slowing down the process, but it also resulted in an elegant architectural solution, which kept the original spirit of the block around BAM, which includes the Williamsburg Savings Bank Tower, now renamed One Hanson Place (erected in 1927), the Salvation Army, and the BAM Peter Jay Sharp Building, which opened in 1908.

As the cultural district grew, and new residential development began, the original owners (aka the Salvation Army) began to see that they had an opportunity to sell their old building with a great financial upside from 1928 when they bought it. They knew that the district was changing and that there were less people in the immediate area who needed their services, so they decided to sell the property on Ashland. A bidding war ensued, and BAM made a serious play to acquire the building. Through our ties to the neighboring Brooklyn Union Gas Company (now known as National Grid), we were acquainted with a former executive, Craig Matthews, who served on the Salvation Army board, so we felt we had a sympathetic ear. However, another developer was also jockeying to buy the building. So we entered a bidding war with them. It was clear if we were going to grow, we needed that site.

Around this time, while attending a cocktail party at MetroTech, I spoke with the successful real estate developer David Walentas about the situation. Walentas's real estate company, Two Trees Management, had transformed DUMBO (another great Brooklyn

4 The Leavitts were donors who resided in San Francisco. They had tragically lost their son, who died by suicide in 2009. Since he had emigrated to Brooklyn as an aspiring artist and actor, they wanted to commemorate his life and memory by naming the workshop, a busy space for students and artistic development, after their son Max. It was a very emotional experience to set up a naming under these sad circumstances, but I believe Max's spirit and energy, which was shared with me by his grieving parents, presides over the vibrant life of that room.

neighborhood—Down Under the Manhattan Bridge Overpass) from a post-industrial no-mans-land into a thriving upscale neighborhood. David had vision for Brooklyn. He also had a checkbook, and we thought he might be interested in doing something ambitious in the BAM area. "If you help us acquire this space," I told him, "then we will go to the city and propose that you be designated the developer of the new tower." David took out his checkbook, on the spot, wrote me a check for five million dollars and told me to go buy the building. With that check, we ended the bidding war, which was a mere skirmish compared to the next several years of negotiations with the city, in partnership with the "Walenti" (as we called David and his son Jed) and with labor unions pushing for jurisdiction. During the years of waiting, we housed the BAM

Hamm Archives in that building, as they were forced to move from their original home in donated space in two dentists' offices at the former Williamsburg Bank, now One Hanson, had been rehabbed as condos! It was like a game of musical chairs set in the aesthetic of the Next Wave Festival. Finally it was determined that BAM would have the entire Fisher site, and that nothing higher would be built there and that Two Trees (the Walenti!) would have sole source access to build a rental apartment tower across the street. This new building, designed by Enrique Norton, is now home to Brooklyn's first Apple store and Whole Foods Market on the ground floor. Soon fifty thousand square feet of

cultural space will also open including an outdoor plaza that is already fully activated. A dynamic mix of culturals will inhabit the building, including the Brooklyn Public Library, 651 Arts, MoCADA (Museum of Contemporary African Diasporan Arts), and BAM.[5]

During the long process of this entire moveable feast coming to fruition, something quite remarkable has happened. The Brooklyn Cultural District has become the quintessential example of a twenty-first-century cultural neighborhood. Historically, the dominant model for constructing large performing arts centers during the twentieth century was to build behemoth fortresses, featuring large marble buildings and fountains which attracted mostly older white audiences to programs dominated by classical music, opera, ballet, etcetera. This model is exemplified by Lincoln Center, which had spent almost one billion dollars in

5   I am particularly proud and grateful that the twenty thousand square feet space BAM will have at 300 Ashland will be called the "BAM Karen" in my honor. BAM will add three new cinemas to this venue, along with along with the Samuel H. Scripps Education Center and a permanent home for the BAM Hamm Archives, named by board member Charlie Hamm and his wife, Irene. It should be noted that the BAM archive began its life housed in a bunch of cardboard boxes stuffed in a utility closet in the basement. We rescued this historical material and began a formal collection process sometime in the late eighties. Compared to the garbage bags, the dentist's office was paradise. The archive has been moved four times and while they have had less sinks to deal with since they departed the dentist's offices, a permanent home will ensure that over 160 years of BAM history will no longer have to be hauled all over Brooklyn.

Above, from top:
The Barclays Center, Brooklyn.

At the BAM Karen groundbreaking with city council member Laurie Cumbo, 2019.

order to be more open and accessible to the audience and their neighbors. This "edifice" concept proliferated across America for decades.

Now a twenty-first-century cultural district, rather than being a large monolith, removed from local street life, thrives as an organic, breathing, ever-changing, and integrated part of its community. It reflects diversity through an eclectic mix of visual, literary, and performing arts organizations, all radically different in focus and size. Everything is next to everything else and the whole thing is pulled together by a common streetscape, lighting plan, and public art.[6] Our district has the advantage of sitting on top of and adjacent to the Atlantic Avenue transportation hub, which integrates it further into larger fabric of New York City. And with the construction of the Barclays Center, we now have a giant commercial entertainment and sports venue at the southern tip of the district. The full impact of this layout means that in a few short blocks there are nine (ten including the arena) cultural venues ranging from 250 seats at BRIC (Brooklyn Information & Culture) on the northern border to nineteen thousand seats at Barclays. This range and diversity of organizations exemplifies the energy of twenty-first-century New York and offers many unique possibilities for collaboration. From BAM to BRIC to Urban Glass (the largest hot glass studio in the country) to the spectacular new Center for Fiction next to the Mark Morris building, thousands of new apartments and public spaces, such as the Betty Carter Park, now complete the "Map" (see illustration on page 266) of the Brooklyn Cultural District.

While all of this development was finally rolling out at a dizzying pace, the issue of gentrification weighed heavily on our minds. We were never going to win the war in the air. The developers have the firepower, and they are going to do what they can do to maximize value. But we committed our energy to waging a serious ground war to keep out as many entities as possible that would render the district bland or uninviting. We, along with the leadership of the Downtown Brooklyn Partnership advocated for affordable and artist-friendly housing and amenities like restaurants and public art that would enhance the integrity of the district.

Of course, it can be argued that there are now too many tall buildings in the district. And the questions of whether a barrage of chain stores (which also have been declining

6   A good example of solving a problem artistically is when a building collapsed on Lafayette directly across the street from BAM. I got sick of looking at the pile of bricks and rubble month after month and finally decided to do something about it. As biking was gaining in popularity, our audience was chaining their bikes to the handrails in front of our building, which rendered them unusable for getting up the steps and caused additional clutter and crowding before the shows. I proposed that we build a bike parking lot on the empty vacant space across the street, and get an artist to design a wall or backing on the side with decorative bike racks and seating in the front. The fantastic artist KAWS accepted the gig and singer-songwriter and avid cyclist David Byrne agreed to design the racks, which we also placed on both sides of 30 Lafayette. The bright KAWS mural and David's amusing bike racks, which consisted of a fractured alphabet, i.e., letters that were flexible and could be taken apart to spell different words, proved to be a fantastic solution. In fact, the lot became a popular spot for bike riders and others to take selfies and pictures with their friends.

along with all retail storefronts) will eventually move in, or whether the neighborhood will become fully gentrified will only be answered in time.[7] Clearly this result is not optimal for the vitality and racial and ethnic diversity of the area. Policymakers, activists, and cultural leaders in these districts must take a strong role to prevent the deadening effects of mass gentrification that destroy the character of the neighborhood. Luckily, in the BAM area, developers did not knock down brownstones. And now there are all these new cultural spaces and approximately 7700 new residents living right in the BAM zone, who will likely become donors, subscribers, and loyal audience members for all of the local cultural organizations. The key to continuing success, I believe, has been and will be to engage each and every developer as a stakeholder in the district (many have joined our board), and not simply to let them achieve personal prosperity without contributing to the neighborhood's vitality. It is my hope that *all* of the developers who have invested in the area will serve on at least one cultural board. This connection will encourage them to maintain an active stake in the neighborhood by making regular and long-term financial and personal contributions to the organizations. And, if necessity dictates that a bank branch or other service business comes into the district, it will be essential for them to also have some type of cultural presence, such as an exhibition space in their lobby. All the commercial tenants should get involved as sponsors of programs too, reinforcing that culture is in the DNA of the district. Beyond philanthropy, other cultural entities and districts, such as the New 42nd Street—which focused on the revitalization of Times Square—actually negotiated fees with developers wherein every tenant in an office tower pays an extra (very minimal) monthly amount, which directly subsidizes the area's not-for-profit cultural anchor, the New Victory Theater. Over 60 percent of the New Vic's budget was covered by these fees, freeing them from much of the annual fundraising burden. For Brooklyn, it would also add value if the public space in the subway terminals at Atlantic Avenue and at Nevins Street included space to announce and promote the cultural events taking place in the district. If everyone—the developers, affordable housing advocates, homeowners, tenants, shop owners and workers, the restaurants, and the staff members of each cultural organization—can work together around these common themes, the Brooklyn Cultural District will be a national model for authentic neighborhood revitalization powered by the arts.

7   As retail presence of all kinds has declined due to COVID-19, Internet buying, and general price sensitivity (i.e., the rent is too high!), it remains to be seen what type of stores or entities will occupy the ground floor space in all the new buildings in the district. I would advocate for a wide variety of creative uses, i.e., maker spaces, community gathering rooms, exhibition space, etcetera, anything that generates street life. Developers should consider offering very low or no rent for these spaces in order to fill them. In this scenario, they could opt to accept lower profits (which is optimal, but perhaps unrealistic), or they could recoup their money by charging more in rentals and sales for the most valuable apartments above. COVID-19 has complicated the issue of ground floor retail usage in New York City. Creative solutions must be discussed at the highest level of city government.

This page, from top:
The corner of St. Felix Street and Lafayette Avenue, Brooklyn.

The Center for Fiction.

Theatre for a New Audience's Polonsky Shakespeare Center.

Opposite, clockwise from top left:
Future home of the BAM Karen.

BRIC and Urban Glass.

The Plaza at 300 Ashland.

The Peter Jay Sharp Building.

The BAM Strong, including the entrance to the BAM Harvey.

Betty Carter Park.

The BAM Richard B. Fisher Building.

Mark Morris Dance Center.

CHAPTER SEVENTEEN:

Beyond BAM

Approximately five months before my retirement from BAM, I got a call from Earl Lewis, president, and Mariët Westermann, the executive vice president of programs and research at the Mellon Foundation. I thought they were calling to talk about making a grant to BAM. My goal at retirement was to leave BAM in the strongest financial position possible, and Mellon had been a loyal and generous donor to us for many years. Instead, they asked me to lunch for another purpose altogether. We set a date, and during the appetizer, they asked me to accept a role as the inaugural Senior Fellow in Residence at Mellon, the first in the foundation's history. From the way they phrased it, the concept had not yet been fully formed, which was fine with me, because I like to originate ideas. They said they wanted to establish a creative presence at the foundation that would energize their staff, expose them to new ideas, and bring thought leaders and practitioners to work alongside the grant makers.

Mellon is a unique foundation with a clear focus. Pre-COVID-19, Mellon historically donated around three hundred million dollars a year to humanities and arts-related programs. Rather than support a wide-range of issues, the foundation concentrates on higher education and scholarships in the humanities, arts and cultural heritage, scholarly communication and international higher education, and strategic projects. After retirement, I had intended to put in part-time hours with an urban planning firm, continuing the type of work I was doing with the cultural district. Immediately, however, I saw the opportunity that Mellon had so graciously offered. I would receive an office, a stipend, a travel budget, and a part-time assistant. They would also support my work on this book and to give me a two-year opportunity to further my research and interests related to the concept of a twenty-first-century cultural district and how the idea might be scaled up.

During my tenure as senior fellow in residence at Mellon, I brought events and people into the foundation that, hopefully, enhanced the culture of Mellon and was consistent with their work. I invited Chuck Davis, the choreographer and founding artistic director of *DanceAfrica*, as well as Dave Isay of StoryCorps and author Jacqueline Woodson, to speak to the staff, because they were all exemplar of Mellon's values and the kind of work they supported. I also organized field trips and site visits for the staff to Brooklyn; bringing them to places such as the Mark Morris Dance Group's studios; Pioneer Works, an exhibition and cultural center in Red Hook; the Weeksville Heritage Center, dedicated to preserving the history of the free Black community in Central Brooklyn, etcetera, so the Mellon staff could gain an appreciation for the breadth of the Brooklyn phenomenon.

Following these events, I decided to focus my energies on two specific projects. The first was a podcast on the "DNA" of creativity. I've always been fascinated by human imagination and ingenuity and wanted to create a show that would explore the conditions that led to creative breakthroughs for great artists, directors, writers, and thinkers. I developed a few pilot segments, with the help of a seasoned NPR producer at WNYC.

The first one was with Matthew Weiner, my new friend who I had met at a BAM event. Matt was the brilliant writer, director, and producer who created the hit show *Mad Men*. For the interview, we focused mainly on the opening sequence of the series and talked about why it had become iconic and resonant for millions of people all over the world. For another segment, I asked Lisa Lucas, then the executive director of the NBF, to interview Jacqueline Woodson about her novel *Another Brooklyn*, which had been short-listed for the National Book Award. After creating these episodes, I developed a report for the foundation about the project, making recommendations on how it could be expanded. But, after hearing my own voice as an interviewer on the radio, I quickly discovered that I am definitely better suited to arts administration than broadcast media; however, I think we found a real star in Lisa Lucas, an African American host whose enthusiasm, knowledge and curiosity in interviews was palpable and engaging. She also has the right voice for radio. Mostly, it was a pleasure to work on this project, something I would have never been afforded the time or luxury to do in my position at BAM, and I was pleased not only to deliver a pilot, but a concept for a potentially exciting new show.

The second project I undertook during my time at Mellon now stands at the center of my work post-BAM. Through it, I set out to answer the following question: How can anchor cultural institutions in low-income communities or communities in transition make maximum economic, artistic, and social impact? In other words, can the BAM Brooklyn experience be applied to other cities and communities in which the conditions have the right energy and voice for transformation and revitalization? We began with the following definitions:

Anchor: Enduring organizations that remain in their geographic places, and play a vital role in their local communities and economies. Anchors generally include colleges, universities, hospitals, libraries, parks/recreation, community foundations, and art organizations.

Anchor Mission: To align core institutional purpose with values and place-based, economic, human, and intellectual resources to better the welfare of the community in which the anchor resides.

We concluded our report with a "blueprint" delineating specific steps that could be relevant for arts organizations of all shapes and sizes seeking to embrace the anchor role. I chose three sites to investigate my thesis. The first was the New Jersey Performing Arts Center (NJPAC) in Newark, New Jersey, an anchor cultural institution in an urban community that over decades has lost a lot of its population, and has a demographic that is more than 80 percent African American. The conditions surrounding NJPAC, are somewhat like the area surrounding BAM in the 1970s. There are many abandoned buildings and empty storefronts. The poverty rate is high and the high school graduation rate is low. Newark faces innumerable, intractable urban issues and yet, NJPAC and its fellow anchors, including Prudential, Rutgers University–Newark, and other leading companies and organizations, endeavor to make the right "anchor" moves; connecting with their community and leveraging their resources to catalyze positive change, I am convinced that Newark will be revived the way Brooklyn was, but with its own character and identity. Positive change is already underway and the future looks very bright. Recently, NJPAC, led by president John Schreiber, launched a project to develop a seven-acre site adjacent to their building which will form the core of a great new cultural district.

The second site I set out to investigate was MASS MoCA, an acclaimed art museum in North Adams, Massachusetts; a storied midtown, now part of the rust belt, which fell apart when manufacturing began to be outsourced to other countries. Mass MoCA occupies 130,000 square feet in the old, local Sprague Electric plant. It's in the eastern most region of the Berkshire Mountains, surrounded by rural poverty, empty buildings, and abandoned factories. The museum itself is a world-class institution, a beautifully converted series of old buildings, showcasing the work of major contemporary and modern artists from all over the world, in enormous, dynamic spaces. It also runs innovative artist residencies—for instance, Laurie Anderson has established her studios there—and has produced a lot of music programming, such as outdoor concerts by Wilco, Stephin Merritt of The Magnetic Fields, and other rock bands that have drawn large audiences from all over the northeast. Their economic model is narrow in focus and mainly sustained by visitors. MASS MoCA, internationally renowned, is now ready to connect even more directly and organically to its North Adams home so that local citizens will reap the full benefit of their presence. Just down the road, less than twenty minutes away, is Williams College, where everything is more prosperous. Other cultural organizations proliferate in Williamstown including the Clark Art Institute, a small, beautiful museum with a focus on fourteenth- to twentieth-century paintings, sculptures, drawings, photographs, and decorative arts, as well as the Williams College Art Museum and the Williamstown Theater Festival. And much like BAM before the revitalization of Brooklyn, MASS MoCA is dealing with additional challenges due to the economic conditions in North Adams, contrasted by the more substantial resources of Williamstown. But, as MASS MoCA finds ways to connect more directly to the surrounding community in North Adams, I believe the situation is perfectly aligned for an organic twenty-first-century "rural" version of a cultural district. Ultimately, the entire Berkshire corridor could lead us to the next iteration of the concept: a full-on regional district incorporating the cultural assets of Williamstown, North Adams, and the rest of the area. These organizations are often promoted jointly by tourist bureaus, but what would happen if they actually created a multi-organizational entity that presented major programs together, supported by a sophisticated collective marketing initiative?

The third site I looked at was AS220, a sprawling, alternative artistic space, featuring galleries, dark rooms, studio spaces, and performance venues in Providence, Rhode Island. Founded by the Italian artist Umberto Crenca in 1985, AS220 started off in a humble, unheated space above the Providence Performing Arts Center. At a particularly low moment of his career as an artist, after receiving some terrible, unforgiving reviews, Crenca decided to create a space that would be un-juried and uncensored, where people could do anything they wanted twenty-four hours a day, so he and other artists like him could create and exhibit their work without being part of the traditional art gallery system. Thirty years later, AS220 has expanded to three buildings (more than a hundred-thousand square feet of space) and runs a massive education program that has trained a lot of youth from underserved communities who have spent time in the criminal justice system. They also house low-income, community-focused artists in a pioneering live-work residency program. Everyone on staff receives the same amount of pay, from the artistic director to the food service staff in the café. And hundreds of volunteers donate their time and energy each year to keeping the artistic collective running and solvent.

AS220 is a strong force in its community. Over more than three decades of its existence, it has spun off more than a dozen nonprofits and has provided service to some of the poorest sections of Providence with educational and vocational programs. It has also ushered in many new businesses—bars, restaurants, barbershops, etcetera—that pay commercial rents. Because of their work and longevity, the city has recognized AS220 as important partner and driver of positive change. The organization has a small budget and functions in a collective, communal way. Aside from the Rhode Island School of Design (RISD), various programs at Brown University and at the Providence Performing Arts Center, which presents short runs of commercial shows, there are no other big cultural institutions in Providence. Nevertheless, the impact of RISD should not be underestimated. It has generated an enduring culture of artists and designers, which permeates the entire town. AS220 taps into and leverages this creative spirit. Everyone knows everyone, and in many ways AS220 bonds the artistic community together. This organization has no shortage of fully realized, strong, organic connections to the community. What AS220 needs is fundraising structure, a large infusion of cash, and a long-term development plan. With my help, I hoped they could create a financial and strategic plan that would empower them to build upon their many successful programs, acting as a linchpin in Providence for decades to come. They are a small organization compared to our other two sites but, as an anchor, they are the cultural bedrock of Providence.

My thought is that, in addition to regular high quality program offerings (which is always the first priority), we can strengthen cultural institutions and enhance their value at the highest level by demonstrating how they serve their communities, welcome visitors and actually achieve positive measurable economic and social results.

It is my core conviction that when arts organizations are financially healthy, programmatically strong, and embrace the anchor role, communities reap the rewards. And now the intensified focus on social justice and racial equity in America rightfully demands that successful institutions of all sizes fully adopt the anchor role and mission in order to be relevant. Each community in our country has its own unique, inherent cultural strengths that are, in essence, natural resources waiting to be tapped. They are not all going to be Brooklyn, nor should they be.

All three of the sites that I chose to investigate possessed unique strengths that I believe can be channeled and leveraged toward lasting, positive change. But to achieve this kind of transformation will require bold, strategic leadership, clear research, and compelling data. I set out to gather this information while simultaneously advising each institution on how it could conceivably make the strongest and most dynamic choices in order to thrive as an anchor at the highest level. Our research team included Bruno Carvalho, a Harvard professor and a humanist and urbanist who specializes in looking at things like history, demographics, segregation patterns, and population trends as connections that inform the future of communities, and Steve Wolff and his team at AMS Consulting, who are leaders in research and consulting on behalf of cultural institutions exploring expansion and undertaking strategic initiatives. The AMS Consulting team gathered key information for each institution, assessing how staff, board, and volunteers spend their time. They plotted the demographics and geographic locations of donors, ticket buyers, and potential audiences that have yet to be engaged. Between AMS' data-driven contributions to the study combined with Bruno's historic, humanistic assessment of the geographic areas surrounding each institution, we generated recommendations with significant long-term implications for NJPAC, MASS MoCA, and AS220. The efforts of the team also benefited from heat maps and other demographic data from SMU/DataArts (formerly the National Center for Arts Research based at Southern Methodist University in Dallas), where I also serve as the Nasher Haemisegger Fellow).[1] Our work on this project culminated at Mellon with a "sounding" or convening for forty people including practitioners, planners, academics, and other leaders in the field. At the end of the two-year fellowship, Mellon provided an honorarium for an additional year to present the research findings at conferences all around the world.

By pursuing the Anchor project through a rigorous and systematic approach, my goal was not only to provide actionable insights and advice for each institution, but also to build respect for the field, which is too-often dismissed as nonessential and hence underfunded and rarely taken seriously by the general public. Sadly, Americans do not value the arts at the level of European governments and people, who believe it is ingrained in their identity. There is room at this table for everyone—small and large institutions with different facilities, programs, and audiences. Ultimately, I hope that programmatic and administrative partnerships will flourish and that organizations will join forces and evolve into cultural districts, enabling the movement to grow and grow until large organically connected partner networks form and serve as a source of both pride and prosperity in their respective neighborhoods and regions and beyond.

Simply put, a robust cultural presence can deliver significant results 365 days a year to individuals and their communities. The arts inspire love of learning, bring people together, house our greatest treasures in our most iconic buildings, and generate tourism and discovery of new and different places. And . . . after all is said and done, art is the only thing that endures from generation to generation to generation.

MASS MoCA,
North Adams,
Massachusetts, 2020.

[1] Ultimately, the arts and culture field must do a better job of gathering data and reporting the numbers and facts regarding topics such as job creation, tourist spending on arts, and other related economic indicators and trends. SMU/DataArts is leading the way in making this information available to the public. If we can demonstrate the impact of culture restabilizing and enhancing the well-being of communities of all sizes, hopefully, serious municipal investment in the arts will occur at a much higher level, supplementing the much-needed funds that are now provided mainly by philanthropy.

When my old life, the life I knew for so long—my Ron life, my BAM life—came to an end, it was traumatic, especially since I had always been a person of "one" (one job, one guy, one son, etcetera). Even though I had wonderful friends, family, and colleagues who were completely there for me, it was challenging to find purpose or commit to a daily routine again. Naturally, after sixteen years of running the place, I missed bossing everyone around. I still craved the company of our staff and board, the nonstop shows, and the creative energy that filled the hallways, dressing rooms and offices of our historic buildings. I missed sitting in the Howard Gilman Opera House alone at the end of a hard day, something I often did on dark nights. It was peaceful, and I was in the spiritual company of the great ones who had graced our stages—Nureyev, Graham, Sarah Bernhardt, Paul Robeson—as well as the ones I helped nurture during my thirty-six years.

My life the year following Ron's death was like a never-ending free fall, filled with indistinguishable months and daily tears. Eventually, though, over time came perspective and renewed purpose. The sense of emptiness remained, but if you are as I am, a generally positive and productive person, you can't help getting involved in things, thereby finding your way back to a more joyous life. The Mellon Foundation fellowship was a lifesaver. It gave me not only a place to work, but also an unprecedented opportunity to think about "big issues" related to the entire cultural field with the support of thoughtful and knowledgeable colleagues. Around the same time as the Mellon fellowship, I was also invited to join the international board of the Alexander S. Onassis Public Benefit Foundation, and, in a moment, I was ensconced in the world of ancient and contemporary Greece. I found myself traveling to Europe regularly for board meetings and enjoyed summer retreats at the most spectacular Mediterranean destinations, hosted by the Onassis Foundation's formidable president, Anthony Papadimitriou, and the talented Afroditi Panagiotakou, the foundation's global head of culture. After three years of serving on the Onassis board, they asked me to increase my participation and also serve as a senior advisor to the foundation. In these dual roles, I am thrilled to be connected to both the Olympic Shipping and Management Company and the Onassis Cultural Centers in New York, Los Angeles, and Athens. Onassis provided the perfect professional next step following the Mellon experience.

Opposite, from top:
With President Lee Bollinger at commencement at Columbia University, 2019.

Crain's Hall of Fame, 2014.

With James Sheldon, 2020.

This page, from left:
South Korea shipyard at the christening of the *Olympic Life* with the Onassis Foundation, 2019.

New York State Board of Regents, 2010.

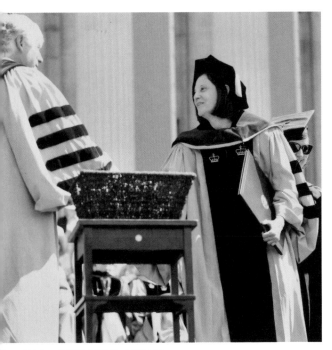

Other projects and boards also take up my time. And, despite my lifelong commitment to fundraising, it is a relief not to face the daily pressure of delivering the thirty million dollars a year needed to run BAM. With my newfound freedom, I also decided to double down on my life in Brooklyn, renovating my house for the first time in over thirty years and hosting regular sleepovers for my three granddaughters. I feel incredibly lucky that the whole gang lives nearby in Brooklyn. Finally, in the midst of it all, my dear friend and fundraising colleague Jane Gullong introduced me to a man named James Sheldon.

I was ambivalent about dating the first year after Ron's death, but because of what I shared with Ron, I understood what it meant to be involved in a heartfelt, intimate relationship, and I deeply missed that connection. So, I pushed myself very, very hard, to stay open to the pos-

sibility of meeting someone new. Jane was a member of The Players, an arts and social club in Gramercy Park, and it was there that she befriended James, who was recently divorced and had returned to live and work in New York. James had formerly been involved in the investment world and then, following his own dream, had become a playwright. When Jane mentioned his name to me, it somehow seemed familiar. I asked her, "Is his mother Eleanor Sheldon?" "Yes," Jane replied, "and she's ninety-six!" "I know her," I said, "she's a donor to BAM. She's been a member of the Producer's Council for decades!"[1] This was a very good sign. Any guy whose mother was a "Bammie" had real potential.

James invited me to dinner (to a Greek restaurant, of course). We were having a nice time on this first date when, during dessert, he reached over and lightly touched my arm. The contact was pretty basic, but it almost took my breath away. I actually thought I might faint right on the table. After our first date, we continued to go out and I learned that he is also obsessed with the beach and the theater, and that he shares the bond of Greece.

So now, once again, I have another great guy in my life, and it has me thinking that, even though I was a person of "one" for most of my years, it's OK to let options two, three and, maybe, even more come through the door. I have learned that life is precious and fleeting, and that happiness is precarious and to be seized whenever it presents itself. Now liberated from the singular focus of my former life, the possibilities seem endless!

---

1   Actually, I think I was even able to recall her specific contributions and the years she donated. Let's face it, when you devote most of your life to fundraising it's hard to stop!

BROOKLYN SANITARY FAIR, 1864.
VIEW OF THE ACADEMY OF MUSIC AS SEEN FROM THE STAGE.

BAM OFFICIAL HISTORY AND FACILITIES

BAM's mission is to be the home for adventurous artists, audiences, and ideas.

The Brooklyn Academy of Music (BAM) is America's oldest performing arts center. Since 1861, it has presented the brightest talents in theater, dance, music, opera, and literature. Today, BAM is a thriving urban arts complex, presenting performing arts, media, film, and visual arts. It's also an integral part of the community, providing a welcoming cultural stage and meeting place for New Yorkers of all backgrounds.

The first BAM facility was located at 176–194 Montague Street in Brooklyn Heights. Originally proposed by the Philharmonic Society of Brooklyn as a home for its concerts, the Montague Street building housed a 2,100-seat theater, a smaller concert hall, dressing and chorus rooms, and a vast "baronial" kitchen. It presented both amateur and professional music and theater productions, and hosted the stars of the day, including such notable performers as Ellen Terry, Edwin Booth, and Fritz Kreisler.

On the morning of November 30, 1903, that first building burned to the ground. The *New York Times* eulogized its achievements: "In short, there has hardly been a great public movement of national import but the old Academy has been at one time or another its principal focus." Ironically, because the value of the Montague Street site was high, BAM's stock price rose on the day of the fire. Plans were quickly made to rebuild at the edge of Brooklyn's business district in the fashionable neighborhood of Fort Greene.

In 1906, the cornerstone for the new building was laid at 30 Lafayette Avenue. A series of opening events were held in the fall of 1908, culminating in a grand gala featuring Geraldine Farrar and Enrico Caruso in a Metropolitan Opera production of Gounod's *Faust*. The Met continued to present annual seasons at the academy through 1921.

After World War II, Brooklyn experienced the same problems plaguing other urban centers throughout America, and BAM's audience and support base declined significantly. Forced to search for income in creative ways, the academy booked language classes and martial arts instruction into performance spaces and rented space to a boys' school that held classes in the partitioned grand ballroom. By the time Harvey Lichtenstein was appointed president in 1967, the programs and facilities needed rethinking.

Lichtenstein ushered in a new and vibrant era at BAM. During the thirty-two years Lichtenstein was at the helm, BAM experienced a renaissance, and it is now recognized internationally as a preeminent, progressive cultural center. In 1999, Lichtenstein's longtime deputies jointly succeeded him: Joseph V. Melillo as executive producer and Karen Brooks Hopkins as president. Karen was succeeded in August 2015 by Katy Clark, who served from August 2015 through January 2021; Joe was succeeded by David Binder in January 2019.

BAM's primary programming consists of the Next Wave Festival—contemporary performance—in the fall and the winter/spring season, typically includes international opera, theater, dance, and music. It also includes a comprehensive slate of education and humanities events, and a variety of community programs.

PETER JAY SHARP BUILDING (30 Lafayette Avenue)

After Brooklyn Academy of Music's first building on Montague Street burned in 1903, Brooklyn Borough President Martin W. Littleton engaged prominent Brooklynites to rehouse Brooklyn's cultural academy and its educational partner, the Brooklyn Institute. Within five years, theater architects Herts & Tallant had built a large, flexible structure on Lafayette Avenue, a multistory building with a main facade in the Beaux-Arts style. Littleton summarized the mission of the new space: "a place where our ever-swelling population might gather to gratify its passion for music, to satisfy its thirst for knowledge, to minister to its love for social communion and to appeal to its patriotism in the great struggles of popular politics."

To promote the goal of social communion, the design included a five-thousand-square-foot grand foyer where audience members circulated before entering various venues. The principle space in the building, the grand opera house, boasted two balconies and approximately 2,100 seats. A concert hall used for both concerts and lectures also had its entrance via the main lobby. That space has now been subdivided into four movie theaters, with much of the original decorative detail preserved. An ornate ballroom on the second floor was redesigned in 1973 as the Lepercq Space, an enormous "black box" theater that was redesigned by Hugh Hardy in 1997 as a multipurpose space housing the BAMcafé. Part of the third floor, above the concert hall and east of the opera house balcony, was reserved for offices, which, in addition to the former classrooms and four-hundred-seat lecture hall, were adapted for administrative use.

Since its opening, BAM's main building has witnessed history-making performances and lectures by a who's who of artists and important figures, including Franklin D. Roosevelt, and the 1962 American debut of Rudolf Nureyev. Named for Peter Jay Sharp in 2004, it has far exceeded its original turn-of-the century mission, and now prides itself on being the largest venue at "the home for adventurous artists, audiences, and ideas."

FACILITIES INCLUDE:

BAM Howard Gilman Opera House
2,104 seats

Lepercq Space
home of BAMcafé

BAM Rose Cinemas
cinema 1 has 110 seats
cinema 2, Ellen Hermanson, has 155
cinema 3, Peter Jay Sharp, has 272 seats
cinema 4, Donovan-Fisher, has 225 seats

Dorothy W. Levitt Lobby

Richard Alan Hillman Attic Studio

**Richard Alan Hillman
Penthouse Studio**

**Aashish & Dinyar Devitre
Patron Lounge**

**Diker Gallery
(Charles and Valerie Diker)**

BAM STRONG (651 Fulton Street)

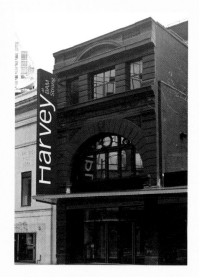

The venue we now know as the "Harvey" first opened in 1904 as the Majestic Theater, one of many theaters in the then-bustling entertainment district in downtown Brooklyn. The Majestic presented a variety of dramas, light opera, musicals, and vaudeville, featuring brand-name stars such as Katharine Cornell, and it became an important trial theater for productions headed to Broadway, including Noel Coward's *Home Chat*.

In 1942, the Majestic was transformed into a first-run movie house in elegant European style by a Parisian and his two sons, wealthy showmen who had fled the Nazis. By the 1960s, however, the advent of television and a shift in the population forced the closure and repurposing of theaters in the district.

The Majestic sat abandoned for nearly two decades. In 1986, Harvey Lichtenstein was looking for a location to stage the acclaimed British theater director Peter Brook's nine-hour production of *The Mahabharata*, and decided to investigate the derelict building he passed on his way to BAM. It was just what he was looking for, similar to alternate spaces being repurposed in Europe, such as Brook's Parisian venue, the Bouffes du Nord.

Lichtenstein raised funds for an award-winning renovation of the theater, completed in 1987. Retaining original architectural elements, the theater's designers maintained an aged, distressed look that creates a visceral bridge between the past and the future. In 1999, the BAM Majestic was renamed in honor of Harvey Lichtenstein, who was retiring.

FACILITIES INCLUDE:

BAM Harvey Lichtenstein Theater
837 seats

Steinberg Screen at the Harvey Theater

Robert W. Wilson Sculpture Terrace

The Rudin Family Gallery

Jessica E. Smith Patron Lounge

In 2019, a facilities expansion took place that included a renaming of the entire building—the BAM Strong—named for the family of BAM trustee Brigitte Vosse.

BAM FISHER (321 Ashland Place)

I n 2012, BAM expanded its campus to include the forty-thousand-square-foot, seven-story BAM Richard B. Fisher Building, named in honor of longtime friend and BAM Endowment Trust chairman Richard B. Fisher (1936–2004). The BAM Fisher features an intimate and flexible new performance space, adding a third stage for BAM's world-renowned Next Wave Festival.

The new facility was designed for LEED Gold certification as a green building, and is located at 321 Ashland Place, around the corner from BAM's Peter Jay Sharp Building. Following a new, twenty-first-century model for an arts center, the BAM Fisher offers affordable ticket prices, subsidized rehearsal and performance spaces, and an expanded roster of talks and education and family programs. The BAM Fisher is a place where artists and community come together, and where the audience is an active participant.

The 2012 inauguration of the BAM Fisher was a cornerstone of BAM's 150th anniversary celebration, and its design and programming signaled a commitment to the future.

FACILITIES INCLUDE:

Judith and Alan Fishman Space
250-flexible-seat theater

Rita K. Hillman Studio
rehearsal and performance space

Max Leavitt Theater Workshop
classroom and artistic development space

Samuel H. Scripps Stage
in the Fishman Space

Geraldine Stutz Gardens
on the BAM Fisher Rooftop Terrace

Peter Jay Sharp Lobby
exhibition space

BAM KAREN (300 Ashland Place)

The newest addition to BAM is cultural space that will be located in a new thirty-two-story tower at 300 Ashland Place, across the street from the Peter Jay Sharp Building and BAM Fisher. The building includes residential, retail, and cultural uses. More than forty-five-thousand square feet will be dedicated to cultural space for several organizations, including BAM.

At the April 28, 2015, gala celebrating Karen Brooks Hopkins's retirement after her thirty-six-year career at BAM, it was announced that the cultural space designated for BAM's use would be named the "BAM Karen" in her honor.

FACILITIES INCLUDE:

BAM Rose Cinemas
3 screens

Samuel H. Scripps Education Center

BAM Hamm Archives

Selection of renderings for the interiors of the BAM Karen, 2019.

Following spread:
The BAM Staff assembled on the steps of the Peter Jay Sharp Building, 2012.

ACKNOWLEDGMENTS

had a wonderful time writing this book! It was so invigorating to walk down memory lane, revisiting stories of the incredible people and events that marked my thirty-six-year career at BAM. I cannot begin to express my gratitude to all who shared the BAM "crusade" with me. What a great run we had.

First, I would like to thank my family, who were so patient and supportive of my work. My son, Matt, is the joy of my life, along with his wonderful wife, Annie, and my cherished granddaughters, Adrienne, Natalie, and Caroline. Ron Feiner, with whom I spent twenty-two remarkable years, was my loving partner, trusted advisor, and soul mate. Ron's children—his son Daniel, along with his wonderful wife, Meri and their sons Chase and Dylan, and his daughter Anna—are extended family and close to my heart. James Sheldon, who entered my life at a dark time, brought back joy, companionship, and romance. My parents, Paula and Howard Brooks, and brother, Ronnie, believed in my abilities and never discouraged me from a life in the arts.

At BAM, I was surrounded by the most talented and passionate colleagues, including Harvey Lichtenstein, my mentor and boss for twenty years; Joseph Melillo, executive producer during my tenure and my professional partner in life; our indefatigable CFO, Keith Stubblefield, who always got the job done; Alice Bernstein, our executive vice president, who never missed a budget task; and all of the great "Bammies" on our staff who worked so hard and embraced our cause. Ultimately, BAM's success was only possible because of the astonishing creations of the thousands of world-class artists who graced our stages and screens, and the thousands of world-class donors who made it all possible. The work of the elected officials over many administrations, who supported our quest to move our part of Fort Greene, Brooklyn (now unquestionably the coolest neighborhood on the planet) from desolation to destination cannot be underestimated. I am also appreciative of the efforts of the members of our board of trustees for their guidance, generosity, and dedication. I am particularly proud of my work with BAM chairmen Alan Fishman, Bruce Ratner, Franklin Weisberg, Asher Edelman, and Neil Chrisman, as well as vice chairmen Adam Max[1] and William Campbell.

My dear friends, who tolerated my "BAM obsession" and loved me anyway, also deserve recognition. Thank you to Tina Silverman, Carla Perlo, Jane Gullong, Susan Feldman, Jan Winarsky, and Carol Polakoff. You girls are the best! And, thank you, Ellen Hollander, for your guidance and wisdom over many decades.

Following my retirement from BAM, I have been so fortunate to have had many opportunities to continue to work in the field. I am grateful to Mariët Westermann and Earl Lewis for the fellowship at the Andrew W. Mellon Foundation; to Dean Sam Holland,

Above:
Button made from *Wall Street Journal* photo, 2015.

Right:
On the stage of the BAM Howard Gilman Opera House during the Karen gala, 2015.

---

1 Adam Max succeeded Alan Fishman as Chairman in 2016. Sadly, he passed away at the age of 62 in 2020 and was succeeded by Nora Ann Wallace, BAM's first woman to be elected as Chair.

Zannie Voss, and Nancy Nasher for the fellowship at SMU/DataArts; and to Christina McInerney for inviting me to serve as a trustee of the Jerome L. Greene Foundation. And, I would be remiss if I did not acknowledge the outstanding president of the Onassis Foundation, Anthony Papadimitriou, where I serve as board member and senior adviser.

I profoundly appreciate the excellent team who brought this book to life, including Violane Huisman, who introduced me to my agent, Zoë Pagnamenta; our excellent creative director Francesca Richer, production director Robert Avellan, and publisher Daniel Power at powerHouse Books; the persistent and dedicated Louie Fleck, who both navigated and fact-checked volumes of material in the BAM Hamm Archive on my behalf; rights usage researcher Julia Redden; image retoucher Alina Patrick; additional graphic design by Rafael Weil; copy editor Anne McPeak, proofreader Gail McRae, and patient and talented copy editor, proofreader, and indexer Laurie Prendergast; publicist Sally Fischer; photographer Bob Klein; the amazing Mary Reilly and Susanne König for book tour and event support; Mark Jackson for legal guidance; and Tamara McCaw for advice on content.

I will close by acknowledging two particularly special individuals who made this publication a reality. First, thank you, Clare Nelson, who helped prepare the manuscript, valiantly tolerating my incessant rewriting; and finally, major credit goes to the brilliant and inspiring Bryan Doerries, who gave the book structure and focus and helped me find its voice.

The afterwords of most books tend to be written by one supremely accomplished individual who has a close relationship with the author. However, since my career at BAM spanned so many decades and included connections with leaders from so many different sectors, ranging from elected officials, community leaders, and donors to colleagues and artists, I decided that the most interesting afterword would be one that featured statements from exemplary representatives from all of these different professions. I am placing this "Afterword" at the end of the book to serve as a "coda" to the entire text. I am deeply grateful to these collaborators for their contributions to this book and for the opportunity I have had to know and work with each and every one of them.

I was so lucky to be part of an era when Harvey and Karen were creating the center of the New York performing arts world—BAM. The world they brought into being made it possible for me and so many other artists to make work that didn't fit in the traditional institutions yet was treated with respect and celebration. The New York art world would not be the same without these two wild visionaries.

—*LAURIE ANDERSON*, Artist, Performer, and Musician

The Brooklyn Academy of Music has emerged as an iconic arts venue that reflects the energy, the audacity, and the genius of the city it calls home.

—*LEE BOLLINGER*, President, Columbia University

Just one word—Harvey—and countless memories flicker and shine in the mind. Much has been written of this exceptional loving devoted inventive timeless friend. Today I only wish to add one precious aspect—Karen Brooks Hopkins. I am so happy that Karen has taken the task upon herself to bring back to life the incredible and amazing story of BAM.

—*PETER BROOK*, Director

As a novice to both opera and originating major works for the stage, my burning desire to create The Mile-Long Opera was like a leap out of an airplane without a parachute. In 2011, fueled by equal parts conviction and naïveté, I decided to pitch my project directly to institutional heads.

Joe Melillo liked the project but it was geographically problematic—if only it could have been sited in Brooklyn. Joe had one piece of advice: call Karen Brooks Hopkins.

I met with Karen in October 2015, who was just several months into retirement from BAM, hoping she would somehow take on the project. She patiently listened to the premise and her emphatic response was "No." Karen was shutting the door, however, she continued to probe deeper and deeper into the piece. She left a crack in the door and agreed to take my occasional calls for informal advice on fundraising.

Clockwise from top left:

With Sufjan Stevens.

With Caroline Kennedy, James Davis.

With Dr. John.

With Patrick Stewart, Sunny Ozell, and Joe Melillo.

With Joe Melillo and Fred Ho.

With Joe Melillo and John Hurt.

With Jeffrey Wright and Rufus Wainwright.

With Ron Stanton, Joe Melillo, and Maestro William Christie.

Over the course of three years, crossing the hundreds of hurdles to realize the performance, Karen became my mentor. She counseled me on some of the thorniest of issues—from the composition of the team, to sharpening the vision, to the tough logistical challenges ahead.

The Mile-Long Opera was the most challenging project I have ever done. Karen Brooks Hopkins is thanked in the playbill but her contribution should rightly have been acknowledged among the collaborators.

—*LIZ DILLER, Architect*

Karen Brooks Hopkins is one of the most talented and innovative minds in fundraising, culture, and arts administration. During her tenure at BAM, she revolutionized all three fields by seeing them as one and by building a community that spoke with a forceful, unified voice about the value not just of the arts, but of radical experimentation.

—*BRYAN DOERRIES, Artistic Director, Theater of War*

Karen Brooks Hopkins helped turn BAM into a personal and essential part of New York's cultural landscape, but her influence goes far beyond the already expansive walls of BAM. She has been a mentor, a guide, an advocate for all of us. Nobody combines her savvy about running a large nonprofit, her experience in navigating the complicated New York political environment, and her absolute clarity about the necessary role of the arts in the life of a nation. When I first arrived in New York, bewildered by the challenges of turning the Public Theater around, Karen was always there with advice, warnings, examples, and heart. Like so many others, I owe her more than I can say. New York wouldn't be the same without her."

—*OSKAR EUSTIS, Artistic Director, The Public Theater*

The renaissance of the Brooklyn Academy of Music mirrors and sparked in many ways the renaissance of urban communities across America. Unarguably, BAM had that impact on Brooklyn. My daily interaction with Karen was generally a high point of my day. It did not matter if it was a crisis or a triumph; the spirit, ingenuity, devotion, and determination displayed by Karen and our coconspirators always brought this unique and wonderful institution to a better place.

—*ALAN FISHMAN, BAM Chairman (2002–2016)*

Clockwise from top left:

With Kate Winslet.

With Joe Melillo and Princess Caroline of Monaco.

With Steve Buscemi and Bob Balaban.

With Joe Melillo, Ruth Bader Ginsburg, Alan Fishman.

With Bruce Ratner, Philip Glass, and Laurie Anderson.

First produced in 1977, DanceAfrica is BAM's longest-running program and America's largest celebration of African and African American dance, music, and culture. Under the guidance of Karen Brooks Hopkins, for the past twenty-two years, BAM and Bedford Stuyvesant Restoration Corporation's Youth Arts Academy, now known as RestorationART, have partnered on DanceAfrica. The RestorationART/BAM DanceAfrica partnership teaches Brooklyn youth dances from across the African diaspora as well as local African music, visual arts, and history. Under Karen's leadership, our partnership has thrived by educating thousands of young people. We at Restoration are fortunate she has embraced us as a partner, advisor, and friend.

—*COLVIN W. GRANNUM, President and CEO, Bedford Stuyvesant Restoration Corporation*

As a lifelong New Yorker who grew up having access to so many different forms of art and culture—music, dance, visual arts, theater—I know that having institutions like BAM be able to grow their programming, strengthen their financial position, and deepen their roots in their community, is key to assuring that all New Yorkers have the same opportunities I had.

I couldn't have had a better partner in that work than Karen. She was relentless in her advocacy and commitment to making sure that the Brooklyn Cultural District was firmly established, that BAM was able to increase its real estate portfolio to assure its ability to grow its offerings, and to figuring out how to best leverage the public sector's commitment to arts and culture in order to increase private investment. Karen is a true force of nature, someone who sees the whole playing field and will bring all her passion and skills to challenges most people would shy away from. We are lucky to have her as one of our city's great builders and leaders.

—*ALICIA GLEN*, Deputy Mayor of New York City (2014–2019)

We love Grandma Karen. When we come to her house, she always has art projects and fun activities for us. She takes us to lots of shows too. And her stories are way better than her cooking![1]

—Granddaughters *ADRIENNE (9), NATALIE (9), & CAROLINE HOPKINS (7)*

I learned long ago that a theater is not a building, it is the people who fill it; or, to be more specific, the people who run it.

I was first introduced to BAM through the Harvey, with its stripped-down interior reminding me that the true glory of theater is what comes across the footlights into our minds. I was educated and mesmerized by their program, never disappointed, always invigorated. And then my wife played there as a member of the Bridge Project with The Winter's Tale and The Cherry Orchard, and I began to know Joe and Karen and her team. I saw how they treated people, audience, cast, and staff. And I really liked what I saw. I decided that if I was ever to return to New York to play theater, it has to be at BAM. And so, it turned out, that is what I did; a show about Ingrid Bergman with her daughter Isabella, a goodbye gala for Joe Melillo, and Richard Eyre's production of one of the world's greatest plays, Long Day's Journey into Night. The play was an especially happy time, and although we arrived just after Karen stepped down, her and Joe's spirit held us in the palm of their hands.

—*JEREMY IRONS*, Actor and Director

1   The granddaughters have a lot of opinions about cooking—not my greatest talent. The worst night was when I decided to roast a duck for guests. After several hours, people loudly proclaimed they were starving—"Where is the duck?" I ran into the kitchen and checked the cooking time on the plastic wrapper that held the bird, only to find that I was cooking it for the price instead of the weight! Chinese was ordered in immediately.

Clockwise from top left:
With Hillary Clinton, Melba Moore, Dr. Edison O. Jackson (former President, Medgar Evers College).
With Kevin Kline and Liam Neeson.
With Matt Weiner.
With Bibi Anderson.
With Tim Robbins.
With Donald R. Mullen Jr., Sinéad Cusack and Jeremy Irons.

For those of us who can remember the first seasons of the Next Wave Festival, we might recall the limousines pulling up in front of BAM's historic façade, disgorging the hip and glamorous who sometimes had to weather a hail of invectives hurled by the folk who lived in the 'hotel' across the street. It was a seismic era, the echoes of which are still felt today. Inside the building, everything was cool and hot! I've always attributed that to a canny strategy of Harvey Lichtenstein, Joe Melillo, and Karen Brooks Hopkins, who had their hands firmly on the levers of the New Cool Brooklyn that was beginning to form.

—**BILL T. JONES**, *Choreographer and Director*

BAM is now one of the most respected, influential performing arts organizations in the world. The vision, leadership, and sheer guts it took to transform the oldest continuously functioning performance center in the United States into the most innovative and exciting one is also a story of community building, marketing, money, and—above all—passionate belief in creativity, in taking risks, and in serving artists and audiences by bringing them together. Karen has been at the heart of it all.

—**KATE D. LEVIN**, *Commissioner of the New York City Department of Cultural Affairs (2002–2013)*

Thanks to Karen Brooks Hopkins and BAM . . . Brooklyn defines innovative performing arts in America! Karen at BAM . . . how sweet it was!

—**MARTY MARKOWITZ**, *Brooklyn Borough President (2001–2013)*

Karen's contribution to the entire field of the arts has been an inspiration to so many and specifically helped me build the foundation's program. I will be forever grateful.

—**CHRISTINA MCINERNEY**, *President of the Jerome L. Greene Foundation*

With Karen Brooks Hopkins as president, BAM became the best theater on planet Earth.

—**CHARLES MEE**, *Playwright*

In 1999, Karen and I were given the privilege to be respectively president and executive producer of BAM in a joint professional relationship. We very soon learned that we enjoyed a shared vision for the cultural institution we would jointly helm. It was an exceptional professional journey, redolent with many institutional challenges over the years together, but we jumped into the problem-solving united to find answers or solutions to those problems. It was always a "we," never an "I." The success of this partnership was the foundation of trust and respect that we authentically shared, which happily endures today in our post-BAM lives.

—**JOSEPH V. MELILLO**, *BAM Executive Producer Emeritus*

I was born into the world of BAM in 1984, when my neonatal company, the Mark Morris Dance Group, was presented at the Lepercq Space. For me, at that early time, Karen was an eminence . . . rarely seen and slightly feared. Over the years, I grew to respect her, to know her, and inevitably, to adore her.

—**MARK MORRIS**, *Founder, Artistic Director, and Choreographer, Mark Morris Dance Group*

Clockwise from top left:
With Hugh Jackman.
With Letitia James.
With John Turturro.
With NYC Mayor Bill de Blasio.
With Nathan Lane.
With Peter Brook.
With Anthony S. Papadimitriou.
With NYC Mayor Michael Bloomberg.

Karen Brooks Hopkins is the leading expert in the field of fundraising. This book is an absolute must read for anyone in the industry looking to step up their donor support and fundraising initiatives. Her practical yet critical advice for museums, performing arts entities, and cultural organizations could make the difference in their future success.

—*NANCY A. NASHER*, Coowner, NorthPark Center, and Board Member, Nasher Sculpture Center, Dallas

Getting involved in composing a deeply personal work based on a miraculous book by Hemingway for one of the finest dance companies on earth was an effort commissioned by Karen for the Harvey Theater at BAM. Karen garnered the best out of all of us, not just technically, but she taught us to bring our innermost selves to the surface and fearlessly exhibit them. This is the example set by this brilliant woman: bring forth from the center of your soul, bare it without shame or judgment, and fight for it with all that you have, and you will change the world. Because of Karen, institutions exist, crazy projects are brought to life, and chances are taken that sometimes would get lost in the world of metrics and deliverables.

—*ARTURO O'FARRILL*, Founder and Artistic Director of Afro Latin Jazz Alliance, Composer and Performer

I met Karen Brooks Hopkins through BAM and vice versa, BAM through Karen. We adopted BAM's idea of delocalizing and expanding to various sites within the community. From the outset she selflessly and enthusiastically offered ideas and suggestions, arranged meetings with the people we needed to meet, and provided general and specific support. Her experience and know-how were important in our decision making for our cultural center in New York as well as in Athens. We stand in her debt and appreciate our continuing work together.

—*ANTHONY S. PAPADIMITRIOU*, President, Onassis Foundation

Working with Karen and BAM in 2012 and creating the mural Gesture Performing Dance, Dance Performing Gesture at the BAM Fisher building allowed me to explore a gestural mark-making process influenced by a performative line painted directly inside the theater lobby. The painting led me to think on a large architectural collaborative scale and the project led me to other opportunities.

—*JOSÉ PARLÁ*, Visual Artist

I liked working with Karen more than just about anybody in the for-profit and nonprofit world. Karen is smart, competent, and funny. I never had to worry about the institution. I got more out of my experience as chairman from her and Harvey than she got from me, really! Harvey was the creative genius and Karen, the "co-CEO." Harvey would always say, after he had a big idea or thought, Let's ask Karen.

I miss Karen as I write this.

—*BRUCE RATNER*, BAM Chairman (1992–2001)

At BAM, to put it simply, Harvey Lichtenstein, our Diaghilev, decided what should happen but Karen Hopkins actually made it possible. In my case, The Desert Music, a huge piece for orchestra and chorus conducted by Michael Tilson Thomas, was scheduled for performance at BAM in 1984. To cover the cost of those performances, Karen had her hands full. On top of this, Nonesuch Records wanted to make a studio recording of the piece but could only afford part of the costs, so Karen stepped in to complete the task. Throughout the whole process she maintained her special positive/ironic attitude. Karen has the gift of making you laugh at her complaints. Her comment about all this fundraising was, "BAM is my job. Steve is my hobby."

—STEVE REICH, *Composer and Performer*

Karen created at BAM a feeling of a "family," of belonging to a community of artists. Belonging is important because, like many other artists, I am also prone to discouragement and insecurity. Karen's support was the perfect antidote to that awful inner voice that I hear in my head: "Isabella, enough with wanting to be an artist, go get a real job." My real job had been to be a "beauty;" in fact for many years I was a fashion model, and executed the mandate "Be Beautiful and Shut Up" to perfection. But life is not over at 35, and I wanted to do more. As a member of the audience at BAM, I was inspired by the many different performances, the variety of voices, the originality of productions. Karen is not like a critic saying, "This is good, this is bad," but rather is interested in the search, in the attempt, in the experiment. She gives artists their voices. When I started to write for theater (on the subject of insects mating, of all things), I called Karen. Without hesitation, she said, "Let's see what we can do for you," and she opened a new chapter in my life.

—ISABELLA ROSSELLINI, *Actor and Author*

Karen brings the experience and wisdom of a lifetime to every conversation. What she knows is prelude to the next big thing she's about to invent. She is thrilling, exhausting, fearless, and devoted. Ignore her advice at your peril!

—JOHN SCHREIBER, *President, New Jersey Performing Arts Center*

Working at BAM has been a highlight of my theater career, performing for an audience that is representative of our diverse city, mixing young and old, the curious and adventurous. Karen Brooks Hopkins and Joe Melillo have built upon Harvey Lichtenstein's legacy to create a special environment for a unique audience. I have been an avid BAM theatergoer since 1983. Doing Endgame and The Master Builder with Karen and Joe in the Harvey Theater were creative experiences I treasure. Karen is one of those people who generously give of their energy, humanity, enthusiasm, and intelligence, always encouraging you to think big.

—JOHN TURTURRO, *Actor and Director*

From grand theatrical stages to cozy folk clubs, in every venue worldwide there's a distinct hierarchy. Karen Hopkins completely eviscerates this whole concept. Each and every time I had the wonderful opportunity to work with her at BAM I was instantly

amazed by how fluid her relationship was with every level of the organization. Karen seemed to be always roaming the theater, actively engaged in the artistic atmosphere. Yes, she was everywhere, truly ubiquitous, a woman for all seasons who thankfully never lost her head!

——*RUFUS WAINWRIGHT, Composer and Performer*

The Ford Foundation has supported BAM for decades, working with Karen since 1979 and Harvey Lichtenstein since he arrived in Brooklyn in the late sixties. It has been so rewarding for the foundation to be involved in every major BAM initiative. Leaders like Karen and Harvey, who stay the course, working on behalf of their institution during good times and bad, demonstrate the enduring power of the arts as a force in building vibrant, inclusive communities.

——*DARREN WALKER, President, Ford Foundation*

Karen Brooks Hopkins is one of the more visionary cultural leaders of our times. In her decades-long career at BAM, she was instrumental in taking an historic and respected but "backwater" institution and making it one the most paradigm-shifting cultural institutions of the late twentieth and early twenty-first centuries. What started as a single facility is now a hub for the arts, that has been central to the revival of Brooklyn as an international artistic mecca.

——*ADAM D. WEINBERG, Director, Whitney Museum of American Art*

As a New Yorker, I had been aware of BAM's upward trajectory as an arts presenter and driver of Brooklyn's renaissance, and I had heard of Karen Brooks Hopkins as BAM's motivating force. In philanthropy there can be resistance to Karen's kind of focused ambition, but I found it refreshing once I saw how deeply she grounded her work in love and knowledge of the arts and artists.

As our first Senior Fellow in Residence, Karen formally reported to me, but I, in fact, worked for Karen. I learned from her, and she brought her vision, her networks, her questions, and her utter humanity to all we did. She livened up our quiet Mellon offices with public interviews, readings, panels, and even a great call and response dance performance. She took our staff over the bridge to her beloved Brooklyn, on field trips that exposed us to new thought partners, new ways of thinking about what we could do.

Karen exceeded our expectations of what a fellow could do for and with the Mellon community.

——*MARIËT WESTERMANN, Vice Chancellor Professor of Arts and Humanities, NYU Abu Dhabi and former Executive Vice President for Programs and Research of The Andrew W. Mellon Foundation*

When I think of Karen, I am reminded of Yeats's immortal question, "How can we know the dancer from the dance?," because the sum of whatever she touches, manages, and pulls together is always greater than its parts.

——*DUSTIN YELLIN, Visual Artist and Founder and President, Pioneer Works*

Clockwise from top left:

With Ian McKellen.

With NYC Mayor Rudolph Giuliani and Brooklyn Borough President Howard Golden.

With Isabella Rossellini.

With Joe Melillo and Julianne Moore.

With Joe Melillo, Fiona Shaw and Mathew Byam Shaw.

With Mark Morris.

With Alan Rickman.

With Joe and John Kani and Winston Ntshona from the 2003 production of Athol Fugard's The Island.

Following spread, clockwise from top left:

Rabbi Schmuley Boteach, Michael Jackson and Ron Feiner.

With Lin Hwai-Min.

With Joe Melillo, Cate Blanchett and Liv Ullmann.

With Brooklyn Borough President Eric Adams and New York City Councilman Mathieu Eugene.

With Ohad Naharin.

With Susan Sarandon.

With Philip Glass, Joe Melillo and Steve Reich.

With Willem Dafoe.

Karen HOPKINS UndeRST
AND BUSINESS IS ART. duRin
oF BAM sHE changed Fc
SOCíAL and CULTURaL sceM
SHe set an example .S
robe

Nds ART is BUSINeSS
HeR TiME as PResidenT
eVer the FACE OF the
iN NYC and the entire country
led THE WAY.
wilson bERLin 3.31.20

Orchestra seating
and stage of the
BAM Harvey, 2016.

IMAGE CREDITS

David Byrne's remarkable alphabet bike racks in front of 30 Lafayette Avenue. The staff had fun reassembling them regularly to spell out different messages. Another example of embedding art in every aspect of the organization's work.

BAM. . .And Then it Hit Me

© 2021 Karen Brooks Hopkins
Image credits and permissions are listed on pages 312–313.

Published in the United States by powerHouse Books,
a division of powerHouse Cultural Entertainment, Inc.
32 Adams Street, Brooklyn, NY 11201-1021

www.powerHouseBooks.com

First edition, 2021

Library of Congress Control Number: 2021936190

ISBN 978-1-57687-838-5
eBook ISBN 978-1-57687-800-2

Book and jacket design by Francesca Richer

Printed by Pimlico Book International, Hong Kong

10 9 8 7 6 5 4 3 2 1

Printed and bound in China

KAREN BROOKS HOPKINS is the president emerita of the Brooklyn Academy of Music, where she worked for thirty-six years, serving sixteen as its president. As president, Hopkins supervised the institution's 230 full-time employees and its multiple theaters and cinemas, ranging from the 2,100 seat BAM Howard Gilman Opera House to the flexible 250-seat Fishman Space.

Hopkins has served as the chair of the Cultural Institutions Group, has been a member of the mayor's Cultural Affairs Advisory Commission and the New York State Board of Regents, and has served on the Boards of NYC & Company, the Downtown Brooklyn Partnership, and currently sits on the Trust for Governors Island.

Hopkins was appointed Commander of the Royal Order of the Polar Star by the government of Sweden, named Chevalier de L'Ordre des Arts et des Lettres by the Republic of France, and awarded the King Olav's Medal by Norway. She was designated a "Woman of Achievement" by the professional association, Women in Development, in 2013 and in the same year was named one of the "50 Most Powerful Women in New York" by *Crain's New York Business*. In 2015, Hopkins was one of ten esteemed business leaders appointed to the inaugural Crain's Hall of Fame. Her widely read book, *Successful Fundraising for Arts & Cultural Organizations*, is currently in its second edition.

Among the many honors BAM has received during her tenure is the National Medal of Arts, the highest award given to artists and arts organizations by the US government. President Obama presented the medal to Hopkins at a White House ceremony in 2014.

Following her retirement from BAM in June 2015, Hopkins served as the Inaugural Senior Fellow in Residence at the Andrew W. Mellon Foundation, as senior adviser to and board member of the Alexander S. Onassis Public Benefit Foundation, advisor to the New Jersey Performing Arts Center, board member of the Jerome L. Greene Foundation, and for five years ending in June 2021, served as the Nasher Haemisegger Fellow at SMU/DataArts.

A graduate of the University of Maryland, Hopkins received her MFA from George Washington University in Washington, DC. She has received honorary degrees from St. Frances College, Pratt Institute, and Long Island University, and a prestigious honorary Doctor of Laws from Columbia University.

Archival research and fact-checking: Louie Fleck
Image editor: Francesca Richer
Image retoucher: Alina Patrick
Manuscript preparation: Clare Nelson
Copy editors: Anne McPeak and Laurie Prendergast
Proofreaders: Gail McRae and Laurie Prendergast
Indexer: Laurie Prendergast
Representation: The Zoë Pagnamenta Agency

for Karen
in celeb
25 year

clap 1

clap 2

How can I ever thank
given me over these yea
the Cave, Three Tales and
friend to count on.